I0605474

MAKE ME COMMISSIONER

Also by Jane Leavy

Squeeze Play: A Novel

Sandy Koufax: A Lefty's Legacy

The Last Boy: Mickey Mantle and the End of America's Childhood

The Big Fella: Babe Ruth and the World He Created

MAKE ME COMMISSIONER

I KNOW WHAT'S WRONG WITH BASEBALL AND HOW TO FIX IT

JANE LEAVY

GRAND CENTRAL

NEW YORK BOSTON

Grand Central Publishing
Hachette Book Group
1290 Avenue of the Americas, New York, NY 10104
grandcentralpublishing.com
@grandcentralpub

First Edition: September 2025

Grand Central Publishing is a division of Hachette Book Group, Inc. The Grand Central Publishing name and logo is a registered trademark of Hachette Book Group, Inc.

Library of Congress Control Number: 2025937244
ISBNs: 978-0-306-83466-0 (hardcover), 978-0-306-83468-4 (ebook)

Printed in the United States of America

LSC-C

Printing 1, 2025

For
Emma and Nick
Sid and Di

CONTENTS

IN THE BEGINNING

On the night that Cal Ripken broke Lou Gehrig's record for consecutive games played, something else happened. I was sitting behind and just to the left of home plate in a small section of seats tucked beneath the upper deck at Camden Yards in Baltimore when Orioles leadoff hitter and leading man Brady Anderson came to the plate.

I was on the aisle with my commemorative game program and my "I Was There" T-shirt tucked between me and the Camden green Baltimore Baseball Club insignia that marks the end of every row. "Wee Willie" Keeler standing tall between two crossed bats.

Never in all the games I saw as a kid—at *the* Yankee Stadium, one long, loud foul ball from my grandmother's parlor; or at Shea, a half hour from home on the Long Island Rail Road; and as a reporter at old Memorial Stadium in Baltimore and Municipal Stadium in Cleveland; at Fenway, Wrigley, and The Stick, not to mention Tiger Stadium, the Big A, and Chavez Ravine—had I so much as sniffed a foul ball. Though I always brought my glove just in case. Until now.

I do not remember the count, the inning, or the name of the pitcher whose offering Brady Anderson fouled back on Cal's magical night. The ball traveled on a fierce diagonal, like a knife cutting a Passover brisket, whistled over the protective netting behind home plate, and headed my way. Whatever the pitch, he was late on it.

The ball got bigger and bigger as it spun closer and closer. Hard to say how fast it was traveling, but fast, because I can get out of the way when motivated. Once I leaped out of a moving car, over my father's ample belly, when a misguided bird plummeted through the moonroof and landed in my lap. My family calls it "the day the bird flew in and mommo flew out."

Anderson's foul ball adopted a downward trajectory by the time it got to our section, heading straight for my *pupik*, the Yiddish word for belly button, which my grandmother had transposed to further south of the equator. And so, it landed, smack-dab between my thighs, and I squeezed it tight. It was the best catch I ever made.

While admiring my trophy and my dexterity, I felt a hand reaching for the ball. Some guy across the aisle had vaulted over the black railing dividing the concrete steps in an attempt to snatch the ball from my, well, you get the idea.

My shriek marred Cal's otherwise perfect day.

"Get out, you fuck!"

Loud enough that Brady could have heard me. Loud enough to scare the interloper away.

I know I have that ball somewhere.

I feel about that ball, about that game, about that place, about Cal's 2,131-game curtain call, the big number one unfurling on the wall of the B&O warehouse behind right field, the way that I feel about baseball. It's mine. Baseball is mine the way my lungs are mine. It animates me. And it will animate you, too, if you let it.

I don't mean to be proprietary, but I did write Cal's Rookie of the Year story for *The Washington Post* in 1982 when the streak began, and roasted him at some chichi dinner in Washington, DC, when it was over. I remember presenting him an Orioles cap with Hebrew letters neither of us could read.

When beautiful Camden Yards was in the planning stages, my neighbor Larry Lucchino—then right-hand man to owner Edward Bennett Williams—spotted a book on my shelf about America's ballyards. A gift from my ex-husband, it had photos neither Larry nor I had ever seen, and more importantly it had blueprints. Larry asked to borrow it from me.

I never got it back and never found another copy.

On the other hand, he was the only one of us building a ballpark. One day maybe two decades later in Cooperstown, I was introduced to Janet Marie Smith, the goddess of ballpark design, who got her start with Lucchino at Camden Yards, and said, instead of hello or nice to meet you, *Where's my book?*

She said, "Oh, yeah, I think we cut that up."

So, yeah, I feel a little bit like the place belongs to me.

I don't remember my first big-league ball game. I do remember the first game I *wasn't* allowed to attend. I was three years old when my father inexplicably took my older sister, who hates sports, to see the Dodgers at Ebbets Field in their last year as Brooklyn residents. They brought me a souvenir as a peace offering, an insulting girlie hat, definitely not a ballcap, with a wide brim and alternating panels of Dodgers blue and white, which I stomped into the grass of our Long Island backyard. It was my opinion, then and now, that you're never too young for baseball.

When I was five, my grandmother, Celia Zelda Fellenbaum, and I boarded the CC local train at 161st Street and River Avenue to buy a baseball glove. She was no feminist, my grandmother, and no baseball fan either. She was never tempted to set foot in the ballpark that cast a shadow over her Bronx parlor, but she knew where to go for "only the best," which is what she wanted for me.

I dressed for the occasion in black patent leather Mary Janes and white tights, which caught on a shard of subway wicker and tore. I always got tangled up when I tried to be a proper girl.

Stunningly, Saks Fifth Avenue had a Sam Esposito model glove, stuck on the left hand of a mannequin in the window facing Fifth Avenue, for an Opening Day display: Spalding "form pocket" model 1161. It was an ungainly thing, padded like a wistful teenager's bra—so wadded up in the thumb and pinky that the glove could not close around a ball.

"I'll have that for my granddaughter," Celia Zelda Fellenbaum said. The flummoxed salesman in the fragrance department knew better than to argue.

Baseball made me different from all the other girls at East Hills Elementary School, which, by junior high school, did not exactly thrill me. Pretty Gwen Morris explained why I wasn't getting Bar Mitzvah invites: *The boys think you like baseball more than boys.* Which was probably true.

Baseball accompanied me to synagogue at the Concourse Plaza Hotel up the hill from the ballpark where, with the aid of my grandmother's too-big mink coat, I celebrated the High Holidays with Sammy and a spiffy red plastic Motorola transistor radio with a daisy speaker that had taken up residence beneath my pillow.

Baseball forged an alliance between me and my father, who as a boy watched Giants games from an outcropping of Manhattan schist known as Coogan's Bluff high above the Polo Grounds. At age ten, in 1927, he descended the heights to the vast greenness below, where he was anointed water boy for the New York *Football* Giants. The coveted post was a perk of my grandfather's career as a bookie and rumrunner who supplied stadium denizens with prohibition booze.

Baseball found me on a deeply wooded road in the Ardennes Forest one spring night in 1970 when I was eighteen, a senior in high school, living in a Belgian convent. (My parents were worried about sex, drugs, and rock 'n' roll.)

In a clearing at the top of a hill, I heard the crackle of static on the driver's radio tuned, I presume, to Armed Forces Radio and then...

Holy cow!

It was the Scooter, Phil Rizzuto, calling the game from the big ballpark in the Bronx.

The sounds and rhythms of the game made themselves at home in my dreams and never left.

Baseball gave me a career and a subject. Baseball got me through my divorce and through the COVID-19 pandemic, when I was actually jealous of the cardboard cutout fans lounging behind home plate in $2,500 seats.

When friends began giving up their season tickets; when *The Wall Street Journal* estimated that there are only seventeen minutes and fifty-eight seconds of action in a three-hour game (more than an average NFL game); when my buddy Dave Smith, who created a digital repository of two hundred thousand major-league games called Retrosheet, said, "I think I've given enough of my life to baseball"; when *The New York Times* celebrated opening day of the 2022 season with a guest essay headlined "Baseball Is Dying; The Government Should Take It Over"; when DraftKings, the official daily fantasy partner and an authorized gaming operator of MLB, began selling "Baseball Is Dead" T-shirts on its website, I scoffed.

Scoffing did not suffice when MLB began selling off parts of itself like organ brokers, from biceps to batting-helmet flaps, and turning pitching mounds and base lines into billboards. "Roman," an online purveyor of Viagra and other necessities of modern male life, debuted behind the pitching rubber.

* * *

There's no scoffing in Cooperstown, especially on induction weekend, when every baseball myth, including baseball's preposterous origin story featuring Civil War hero Abner Doubleday, passes for truth. Imagine my surprise, then, at a prepandemic breakfast with Sandy

Koufax and Joe Torre on the veranda of the Otesaga Hotel, the holiest of baseball's holies where only Hall of Famers have right of passage, when they began to talk about today's game. Torre was there to celebrate the induction of Mariano Rivera, the first unanimous selection to the Hall of Fame, who helped him win four world championships with the Yankees. Koufax was there because he is Koufax.

Today's game is not the game they played. Inevitably, the subject turned to how hard pitchers are throwing and how little they are pitching. "Half the time, the pitchers don't know even where the ball is going," Sandy said.

"Hard to watch," Joe replied.

"I don't watch," Sandy said.

I thought: How is it possible that I watch the MLB Network by day, and some ball game—any ball game—by night, and follow computer-simulated Yankees games on my iPhone under the table during dinner parties (even ones that I host), and they don't?

I wrote my first baseball story when I was ten years old. It was a homework assignment from my sixth-grade teacher: "A Day Planned by Me." Dated May 11, 1961, a week after Alan Shepard vaulted into space, it begins, "We would take a rocket ride around New York City and go to Coney Island. Then we would go to a Yankee Dodger baseball game at the Yankee Stadium. It will have 1,000,000 innings. It would end at 5:00 o'clock in the morning. We would ride home in our Jet Rocket. When we got home, I'd get my gang together and we would go back to the Yankee Stadium and play a 1,000,000-inning game of baseball. But! The Yankees would split up on both teams. That's my idea of a busy and Happy day."

Baseball is still my lullaby, my wingman, my alter ego. I am the person who never fell out of love with the game. There was a brief crisis of faith when George M. Steinbrenner III told me about his plan to turn Monument Park into a waterpark. I quit wearing the ultimate regift, a

Yankees warm-up jacket Steinbrenner had given to Supreme Court Justice John Paul Stevens, who had given it to me. For this unconscionable wobble I was remonstrated by Gail Mazur, poet, friend, and Red Sox partisan, who told me I was unworthy of calling myself a fan if I let The Boss dictate my relationship with the game. I started wearing the jacket again.

In this way, and only in this way, baseball reminds me of my grandmother, who had the gift of elastic love and made each of her seven grandchildren feel most cherished. Like baseball, Celia Zelda Fellenbaum always showed up for me.

This was not the book I wanted to write. After spending more nights alone with Babe Ruth than either of his wives or both of them put together, I fully expected to find another baseball life story begging to be told. The fact that I couldn't think of one told me everything I needed to know about modern baseball. There was no longer any way I could ignore the evidence—it bombarded me on every data-sodden game broadcast—analytics had become the story of the game, not the people who play it.

That breakfast at the Otesaga provided the germ of an idea that became a full-time inquest. On January 14, 2021, the day MLB charged ghost-busting boy genius Theo Epstein with the task of making baseball fun again, I resolved to resume the journey that began on the CC local to go in search of the soul of *my* game.

Maskless, I hit the road in Waldorf, Maryland, home to the Southern Maryland Blue Crabs of the Independent Atlantic League, literally the "avant-garde" in baseball's quest to reinvent itself. The robo-ump was fired up and ready to adjudicate balls and strikes for a weekend series between the Crabs and the Long Island Ducks, their first home games at Regency Furniture Stadium since before the pandemic.

Seven games into the season, people were already bitching about the automated strike zone, Manager Stan Cliburn told me in the home dugout. But the subject of the day was Spider Tack.

That's the sticky stuff big-league pitchers were using to increase their purchase on the ball and the RPM on their heaves. No wonder there were six no-hitters by the end of June. When MLB peremptorily banned the goop, I applied a glob to the crown of my head figuring it was like pomade. It was a reportorial move. The bald spot lasted two years.

Daryl Thompson, the Crabs' pitching ace and pitching coach—who had a cup of coffee with Dusty Baker's Cincinnati Reds—saw another apocalypse on the horizon. On the first day of the second half of the season, Atlantic League pitchers would begin pitching from sixty-one feet, six inches—one of Theo's goofier ideas for how to save the game—without so much as a day of practice from the longer distance.

He didn't much like his guys being used as guinea pigs, but that was the job. So when push came to start he took the ball himself, pitching seven scoreless innings, and told me later his ribs hurt. Little wonder he was a favorite in Crustacean Nation, where he mowed lawns for a living.

I called Mike Rizzo, the Washington Nationals general manager, from the grandstand. He told me not to worry. "Never going to happen," he said. "They're not that fucking stupid."

He was right. They aren't. Also, the one-foot change did not produce the desired improvement in offense.

Steve Lombardozzi, a former big leaguer who had spent his winter digging potatoes from frozen fields in hopes of one more shot at The Show, led off the game with a measly grounder in the hole between first and second base. I marked my scorecard reflexively, 4–3. When I looked up it was as if all the bedroom sets in stock at the Regency Furniture showroom had shifted in feng shui balance.

The hateful shift, first essayed in the Atlantic League, was gone.

My equilibrium was upended repeatedly during four seasons of reporting and rereporting, writing and rewriting, as baseball evolved and convulsed in anticipation of Theo's new rules, rules he said were intended to make baseball feel old.

Baseball was on the clock and so was I. I made it my mission to see the game in all its iterations in 2023, to gauge the impact of Theo's engineering and gather intelligence on what more needed to be done. I started in West Palm Beach, before the regulars reported, at the shared home of the Washington Nationals and the world-champion Houston Astros. I visited big-league ballparks in Washington, Baltimore, Philadelphia, Cleveland, Atlanta, Pittsburgh, Kansas City, Los Angeles, the Bronx, and Queens. I went to minor-league games in Eastlake, Ohio, and Worcester, Massachusetts; watched pick-up games on the Mall in Washington, DC, where I once played for *The Washington Post*; and stopped by the side of the road to watch Little League and T-ball games.

I went into locker rooms I was way too old to want to visit; to Driveline, the data-driven training center in Kent, Washington, and to MIT, host of the biggest annual sports analytics conference; to spring training in Florida; to Savannah Banana games in KC, West Palm, and Cooperstown; to the USA Baseball National Training Complex in Cary, North Carolina; to Tornado Alley in Stillwater, Oklahoma, home of the Oklahoma State University Cowboys; and to the Jackie Robinson Training Complex in Vero Beach, which used to be Dodgertown.

Zigzagging this way and that, I did my best to avoid the usual suspects and the received wisdom. I went in search of smart guys, funny guys, honest guys—answers. I asked everyone the same questions. What happened? How did baseball lose America? Why doesn't it move people the way it once did, the way only it can, the way it still moves me? Who now speaks for the game? And what can I do to help?

When, in early 2024, Baseball Commissioner Rob Manfred announced he would give up the gig at the end of his term in 2029, I knew what I had to do.

Make me commissioner. I know what's wrong and how to fix it.

CAPE COD PART I

Eldredge Park, Orleans, Massachusetts

Eldredge Park, home of the Orleans Firebirds of the Cape Cod Baseball League, is my field of dreams. It is not at all like the one Hollywood built for the set of the 1989 movie, which looked lush and green when Shoeless Joe stepped out of an Iowa cornfield augmented by plastic stalks of corn.

Nor is it like the pop-up ballparks built by Major League Baseball in an adjacent cornfield for Field of Dreams games, that featured photogenic faux-wood adhesive padding on the outfield walls.

Eldredge Park has bona fides. The rickety two-story press box behind home plate is a leaning tower of authentically sea air–laminated pine. The splinters are for real.

People have been playing baseball at Eldredge Park since 1913, when local businessman Lewis Winslow "Win" Eldredge donated the land in the natural hollow where the Firebirds make their home. The field, manicured and maintained to big-league perfection, supported by an annual $100,000 MLB contribution, is still swaddled by a natural grass bowl where babies crawl and puppies frolic. My dog Bette, a part-time mascot, takes infield practice with the home team here under the watchful eye of manager Kelly Nicholson—Coach Nick—who tosses her grounders and pop-ups and marvels that nothing gets past her.

Here the best seats in the house are beach chairs and beach blankets splayed on the hill along the first base line behind the home dugout. Hot dogs sear on charcoal grills hauled to the park by uncomplaining volunteers. The price of admission is the cost of a 50/50 raffle ticket, and that's voluntary.

Here the sun sets over the band shell in deep center field that doubles as a clubhouse and a winter refuge for mice huddling inside forgotten jock straps. Every spring, General Manager Sue Horton extracts said mice from said jocks. She saved one future major leaguer from self-harm when he came looking for a safety pin for his torn jock. "Oh, I don't think we want a safety pin, darling," said Miss Sue.

Here is where baseball cognoscenti come to see "the stars of tomorrow shine tonight." Where the best college players come every summer to show what they can do with wooden bats in their hands, a last chance to impress major-league scouts gathered behind home plate before the annual Major League Baseball Amateur Draft.

The history of baseball is suffused with Cape Leaguers, 1,700 of them at last count. Big names: Aaron Judge and Pete Alonso; Adley Rutschman and Jason Varitek; Pie Traynor and Red Rolfe. A third of all 2024 draft picks were Cape Leaguers, including the sixth number-one pick in seven years.

My Birds are well represented in this esteemed flock: Hall of Famers Frank Thomas, Todd Helton, and Carlton Fisk; Yankees Manager Aaron "Fuckin'" Boone; number-one pick in the 1989 draft Ben McDonald; and Cy Young Award–winner Corbin Burnes. Thirty-one of Coach Nick's players have been drafted in the first round since he became manager in 2005; 130 of his former Firebirds have played in the major leagues.

They stay with host families, as required by the league. Buck Showalter, the 1976 League MVP and batting champion, lived with a family that ran a car-rental agency and sported a set of hot wheels during that hot Cape Cod summer: a Chrysler Cordoba with Corinthian leather. Players make a little money on the side, twenty-five dollars an hour, by coaching in team-sponsored baseball clinics for kids. When Nomar Garciaparra was here in 1993, he tutored his charges in the big-league art of spitting. Years later, when he was inducted into the Cape Cod League Hall of Fame, he was confronted by the grandfather of two expectorators. Nomar explained:

"Ya gotta know that."

Here is where once upon a time, my children chased fireflies on the outfield grass between innings in knee-long Cardinals T-shirts they wore to bed after falling asleep in the car. Baseball at Eldredge Park made it easy to believe that nothing had or would change.

But there were signs and portents. One summer evening in 2009, I arrived in Cardinals gear to find they had become birds of another feather. During the offseason, MLB had presented each of the Cape League franchises boasting a big-league nickname with a big-league ultimatum: Buy MLB-licensed merch or get a new moniker. Three teams refused. The Chatham Athletics became Anglers; the Hyannis Mets became Harbor Hawks; and the Cardinals became Firebirds, a mythical bird that takes on myriad forms in fable, ballet, and automotive showrooms, with plumage so bright a single feather could light up an entire ballpark.

For Miss Sue, it was a no-brainer. She wasn't about to betray the local merchants that have supported the team since the dawn of the modern era when the league was sanctioned by the NCAA in 1963. She gave away $60,000 in Cardinals merchandise, which was just about her budget then, mostly T-shirts and onesies, but not team jerseys. "Those are earned," she said firmly.

In recent years, strategies became major-league too. Coach Nick employed infield shifts liberally and mused aloud about seven-inning games. "Never," I said.

I went back to Eldredge Park in 2021 after a season lost to COVID-19. One sweet evening as I camped on the hillside, fortuity allowed me to introduce two of baseball's most original thinkers: bon vivant and author Daniel Okrent, creator of Rotisserie League Baseball and the first metric of the analytic age, and Bill "Spaceman" Lee, the lefty legend of Fenway Park, who was there to throw out the first pitch.

The conversation proved short. Turning his back on us and the diamond, the Spaceman bent over to stretch his Achilles tendons against the slope, watching the game between splayed legs. It didn't occur to him that he was mooning the field. "It wasn't intentional," he said later, "but that's the consequence of genius."

He wasn't impressed with what he saw from this unique vantage point. "The pitchers are too scared to throw the ball over the plate," he declared. "The outfielders double-tap before making a throw, and the hitters are as fidgety as deer ticks in Lyme, Connecticut."

The problem with modern baseball, he decided finally, is "anal retention."

A few days later, I met Spencer Pugach.

He was sitting in the dugout leafing through a large black binder ominously bulging with stat sheets. He introduced himself as the Firebirds' director of baseball operations, head of a three-man crew of volunteer college stat geeks in the Birds' first-ever analytics department. As there was no money in Miss Sue's budget for Spencer's services, he did the team's laundry in order to get paid.

I haven't been the same since.

In my thrall to long-extinguished fireflies, I had managed not to notice the TrackMan box tethered to the press box behind home plate; or the pizza box–sized Rapsodo device on the grass between the mound and the plate during BP; or the Blast Motion donuts squeezing the knobs of every batting practice bat—each a new and improved high-tech device to measure the location, trajectory, spin, and speed of batted balls and max-effort pitches. Except for the ones Coach Nick threw to Bette.

"MLB wants the data," he said glumly.

Everybody wants the data.

Some things haven't changed. The atonal Orleans Chorus, a motley crew of barefoot kids from diverse zip codes, still gathers under leafy elms to croak "Take Me Out to the Ball Game" at the seventh-inning stretch. Scouts armed with stopwatches congregate behind home plate and like what they see.

The Spaceman still pitches in senior-league games in Vermont, Florida, and California as he once did at Eldredge Park. I still camp on the hillside with Dan Okrent, who dutifully arrives six hours before the first pitch to stake out a prime spot on the hill.

Coach Nick's pal Al Leiter, the all-star lefty and philosopher manqué, was there that night too.

When Leiter quit pitching after nineteen years, two World Series rings, and one no-hitter, he began bringing his family to the Cape every summer—same as me. He regards it as a pilgrimage, same as me. "It's Americana," Leiter said. "It's so baseball."

He met Coach Nick in 2010 when he brought his ten-year-old son, Jack, to Orleans to enroll him in the Firebirds Clinic. Leiter is a broadcaster now for the MLB Network, which is perfect for him. He was born camera-ready, and he knows how to yak.

These days, with his family grown, he travels solo on the Cape and always makes time to talk with Coach Nick's players. Perched briefly on the lip of the dugout, in preppy pink, and bouncing a Top-Sider against poured concrete, he faced the pitchers, some sitting across from him on the bench, some on the ledge above it, all wishing to be as blessed by the baseball gods as Jack appeared to be, having been picked second overall in the 2021 draft.

He talked and talked right through team lunch describing the spin on pitches he threw twenty years ago with Bugs Bunny sound effects—*berrrrttt, berrrrtttt, berrrrrtttt*—before coming up for air.

He told them about being a goofy Yankees rookie in 1988, sitting beside Don Mattingly in the visiting dugout in Milwaukee. Donnie Baseball was having a rough go. Leiter was too young to know what a rough go a life in baseball can be. "For as good as the good is, the bad's not far behind," Mattingly said. "And it sucks."

"This was Don Mattingly, MVP, perennial All-Star, *fucking bad ass*," Leiter told the Birds. "And it's kind of fucked up because you're trying to enjoy this shit, but you always know that failure's looming. Shit's *gonna* happen."

It wasn't until after Leiter's second shoulder surgery, which limited him to pitching a total of 8.3 innings over three seasons and left him contemplating a new life as a stockbroker, that he fully understood what Mattingly had been trying to tell him. And it wasn't until he met Harvey Dorfman, the mental-skills coach and author of *The Mental ABC's of Pitching* that he understood how to do his job: a mantra he repeated several times in the Firebirds dugout until Coach Nick's players could repeat after him. "The job of a pitcher is to be mentally and physically prepared to execute quality pitches consecutively without distractions getting in the way until the game is over or the manager takes the ball."

Under the best of circumstances, Leiter is twitchy. Twitching led to pacing, which led to stalking back and forth from one end of the dugout to the other, waving a scroll of stat sheets like a fungo bat and demanding to know whether their college programs used all the analytic-generating equipment that Jack's coaches had employed at Vanderbilt. Because he was getting concerned, he said, and pretty soon worked up, about what he had seen in Jack's first year in pro ball. "You guys can get frozen in what you're trying to do, which is play a baseball game like when you were little boys, of just having fun and allowing your body to do whatever it does. And if you get caught in the information, you start thinking about the metrics of things."

He waved the wad of printed numbers. "Whoever's playing tonight, don't look at this shit. Unless you think these numbers define you. If you think this defines you, you are a shallow, uninteresting person. This doesn't define you. The work behind this defines you. It's not a number. *Noooo.* Refuse that. And even if it's a good number, guess what? You've had a lotta success? Don't be a douche."

* * *

More than any sport and perhaps any industry, baseball has preserved, protected, and defined itself through numbers. Numbers stamped on the back of baseball cards. Numbers allocated to positions on the field and in the batting order. Numbers inscribed in perfectly aligned rectangles on game-day scorecards. Numbers tabulated in batting averages printed in the Sunday newspaper. Numbers preserved in prized annual editions of *The Baseball Encyclopedia.* Numbers stitched on wool and now on polyester double-knits. Numbers engraved on plaques in the Hall of Fame. Numbers that allowed for debate and comparison, making history and character come alive in digits and percentages. Numbers engraved in memory—2,131, .406, 755 home runs, 130 bags, twenty Ks.

The raw data collected by nineteenth-century baseball statisticians attested to the game's seriousness of purpose and laid the groundwork for the analytic revolution. The collection and collation of baseball's numerical present and past made it different from other sports.

These are the numbers Dan Okrent used to create Rotisserie League Baseball, cited by today's analytic elite as the model for general managers building real-life rosters in the present day. They are the numbers that made baseball the perfect incubator for the data-driven present and the envy of American industry, according to Harvard Professor Emeritus James Heskett, author of *Corporate Culture and Performance.* "General Motors still doesn't know as much about analytics as the Oakland A's or the Rays because they don't know that much about their competition."

Baseball didn't originate doing better business through Big Data. But the publication of Michael Lewis's *Moneyball* in 2003 and Brad Pitt's movie eight years later popularized an efficiency-driven approach to business. Baseball's always been a business—in which players always got fucked—but this felt different.

The gospel of analytics, which argues that there are better, more efficient ways to build a club, score a run, and win a pennant, spread throughout the league and to a cadre of nerdy-smart, tech-savvy boys who all wanted to be Billy Beane and look like Brad Pitt.

These numbers—what analytic folk call "a clean data set"—drew math-and-science whiz Anette "Peko" Hosoi to baseball. I cold-called her one day at her office at MIT where she is, among other things, the Pappalardo Professor of Mechanical Engineering with appointments in the Institute for Data, Systems, and Society (IDSS) and Mathematics. She is also cofounder of the MIT Sports Analytics Lab, an academic enterprise that produces real-world solutions for the NBA, MLB, and FIFA. I call her a humanist with math skills.

"Baseball comes from a beautiful and rich history of collecting data," she said instead of hanging up. "It naturally drew in people who are analytically minded, who find that part of the game beautiful."

Numbers and equations made me nauseous like when I was supposed to pith a frog in high school biology. I refused as a conscientious objector. It was the sixties.

"Analytics fucked baseball," I told her. "Don't you think it's your responsibility to unfuck baseball?"

Thank God, Peko laughed.

I invited her to join me at Eldredge Park for Firebirds baseball, lobster rolls, the best onion rings on Cape Cod, and a conversation about the proliferation of data in the modern world.

Peko goes by Peko because her grandmother thought she looked like the red-cheeked, pigtailed six-year-old girl on the wrapper of a popular Japanese candy bar. She arrived at Eldredge Park with a good appetite and a colleague from MIT. They were waiting for me on the bottom row of Miss Sue's bench, the only actual seats in the yard—a stack of aluminum bleachers parked beside the home dugout.

Peko's interest in sports analytics grew out of competitive zeal. She wanted to improve her times on the downhill mountain bike trail her husband carved for her out of New Hampshire countryside. She says she does her best thinking on the bike.

I wanted to talk to her about "noise," a word that had begun to insinuate itself into baseball conversation along with "efficiency." I'm not talking about the joyful cacophony of pregame thunks, thwacks, and thuds filling the hollow along with the jangle of Bette's dog tags and the sweet high-pitched voices of children calling her name, but something new and discordant. "The noise is this massive ocean of analytics," said catcher-turned-scout Scott Hatteberg, whose career was extended by numbers that now threaten to engulf him in an undertow.

In data science, noise is a metaphor used to describe the surfeit of extraneous and erroneous information. The signal is useful information. And the signal-to-noise ratio is the ratio of useful or true information to false information, also known as "horseshit" in baseball vernacular. When horseshit interferes with the "signal" in the data, errors become inevitable. "It becomes very easy to get things wrong," Peko said.

Baseball has a great signal-to-noise ratio because it has the cleanest data set, the cherished numbers the industry has been collecting and collating since Henry Chadwick's day. Between onion rings, Peko's colleague Ali Jadbabaie, head of MIT's Department of Civil and Environmental Engineering, explained a few real-world perils of data glut. "Cognitive overload," Ali said.

Imagine a dugout decision. The computer-driven blitzkrieg of data, delivered in real time to iPads populating dugouts throughout the country, produces a kind of paralyzing brain-suckage, defying the mind's ability to separate the numerical wheat from Big Data chaff. "You get so much that you take in nothing," Ali said.

"There's way too much information coming at all times," Peko said.

"You mean in the modern world or always?" I asked.

"Always," they replied in unison.

The ballpark lights had come on, and a breeze rippled through a copse of trees under a funky tent where locally sourced Firebird merch was for sale. Bette the Dog, in her fire-engine red Firebirds jersey, was playing catch with barefoot children. The on-deck circle was no more than five feet away.

"If you look at this field, that leaf over there is moving," Peko said, pointing to a tree behind the third base line. "There's a whisp of cloud over there, and there's something crawling over there. There's too much for your brain to process.

"That's true for every sports team right now, which doesn't mean you cannot pull out useful information. But it is a nontrivial exercise to pull useful information out of a giant pile of data."

She advocates hiring data coaches.

The data deluge is not just a baseball problem. Ninety percent of the world's data has been created since 2023. With the global datasphere reaching 181 zettabytes this year, *Forbes* magazine offered perspective for literary folk like me. "If an average novel is two megabytes, 181 zettabytes would be 90 quadrillion books—enough to fill the Library of Congress . . . 2.3 trillion times." Then compare the 402.74 quintillion bytes created every day with the ten quintillion bugs that call earth home, one of which was parading across Peko's field of vision.

"You know who else has the same information problem?" Ali said. "Modern soldiers."

He had won a five-year grant from the US Department of Defense to develop "a unified theory of rational decision-making with behavioral and computational constraints." A fancy way of saying he was trying to figure out a way for soldiers to make life-and-death decisions when bombarded with a plethora of information provided by modern weaponry. "There's so much, they turn it off."

That's nontrivial, as Peko likes to say. What does that mean for a hitter assaulted by noise, metaphorical and otherwise, who must identify, swing at, and barrel up a 100-mph pitch in less than .41 of a second?

She gazed at the field saturated with artificial light, at the still-empty on-deck circle awaiting a late-inning pinch-hitter, at the umpire's brush whisking dirt from the plate, and one tenacious bug meandering across Peko's big toe, only a few of the distractions that a brain might be diverted by while trying not to get hit in the head by a rising fastball.

"That could really mess up your brain," Peko said. I think she meant the data, not the fastball. "The problem is not *having* information; it's deciding what's important.

"There's a warning built into the data right now, we're in an era where we're collecting data on everything. If you have a phone, the amount of data your phone is collecting about you is unprecedented, and subsets of that data are going to different entities, and those different entities are using the same kind of algorithms that baseball does to make decisions that have a global impact. We're going to face a crisis about what we're going to do with this deluge of data. So, baseball may be a canary in a coal mine."

The late summer air, heavy with humidity, occluded the final numbers on the scoreboard in deep left field. Still, they glowed, backlit by stanchions of ballpark lights, as baseball numbers are wont to do.

CHAPTER 1

JANIE GETS SCHOOLED

Meeting the analytic enemy in its corporate lair

I went to the seventeenth annual MIT Sloan Sports Analytics Conference in Boston to find out why baseball reminds me of the worst brownie I ever ate. It was the diabolical creation of my ex-husband's long-dead grandmother, universally acclaimed a terrible cook, who got worse with age because with age came concern about her husband's robust waistline.

So, she set about improving her recipe for brownies. First, she cut a third of the sugar. (At least you could still taste the chocolate, which wasn't so good to begin with.) Then, she got rid of a third of the butter. (You can only imagine.) Finally, she cut back on the unsweetened Hershey's cocoa, leaving just enough as food coloring.

Her chubby husband, whom I adored, employed a ruler to measure perfectly formed squares, which she arranged on a bed of white paper doilies on her finest china and draped with a veil of confectioner's sugar. So armed, she pressed the brown sludge squares upon us. And we ate, and ate some more, wishing to please her, because she was someone you wished to please, hoping with each gag-inducing bite to taste something, anything, resembling a brownie—which, of course, encouraged her to pass the plate again (what could it hurt?) and promise to make more.

Baseball, in February 2023, was like that. It *looked* like baseball; it *sounded* like baseball; but despite the imaginative reinvention of ballpark food enticements such as the Pitcher's Mound served at Truist Park in Atlanta—"A pile of waffle fries topped nacho-style with smoked brisket, spicy cheese sauce, pico de gallo, salsa roja, and lime crema"—baseball just didn't go down the same.

And so, I headed for Boston to hang with the analytic glitterati for the twentieth-anniversary celebration of *Moneyball* and a panel discussion of the new rules made necessary by *Moneyball* to find out why the game I love was leaving such a bad taste in my mouth.

Stepping brightly and briskly off the escalator to level three of Boston's John B. Hynes Veterans Memorial Convention Center at 8:00 a.m., a time at which I do nothing brightly or briskly, I was catapulted into a maelstrom of cheap blue blazers. I hadn't noticed "business attire required" in the press packet, which explained the blazers draping the bony shoulders of 2,500 analytic groupies and wannabes, undergrads seeking internships, matriculated students hawking resumes, and postgraduates seeking corporate funding, each of whom had paid $1,000 to attend this Davos for Big Data.

Was I the only idiot trapped in the navy mosh pit otherwise known as the Boylston Hallway who failed to grasp the significance of "Sloan," as in the Sloan School of Management—MIT's business school—before "Sports Analytics Conference"?

"Aha," I thought, "it's a job fair."

The blazers had come to schmooze with sponsors (ESPN, Ticketmaster, FanDuel, Caesar's Sportsbook and Casino, DraftKings, Microsoft); moderators, marketers, coders, analysts, chic on-air talent, and team execs from five of LA's professional sports teams, seven NBA franchises, including the Celtics who brought their lead owner; six NFL franchises; two national pickleball associations; NASCAR, FIFA, MLS, NWSL, a new lacrosse league, and god knows how many occupants of named academic chairs.

Deus ex machina, my smart friend MIT professor Peko Hosoi appeared in the crowd: "Come to Room 311. That's where the real action is."

Also on hand: four chess grandmasters, one of whom self-identified also as a professional poker player and author; three retired MLB players; two basketball champions (Sue Bird and Shane Battier), one soccer throw-in coach; the managing director of FC Bayern Munich in the Americas; one retired astronaut/Navy Seal; one bioethicist; one female psychologist, one congressman, one Norwegian triathlon performance coach, and three supernovas of the baseball analytic firmament: Michael Lewis, Nate Silver, and Bill James.

It was a regular clusterfuck for the Analytic Industrial Complex. The press of eager maleness in the mosh pit was suffocating.

Morgan Sword, MLB's executive vice president in charge of everything that matters, was the headliner in the Sue Bird room, leading a panel discussion on "Revamping the Nation's Pastime: The Effect of Rule Changes in Baseball." Amy Howe, CEO of FanDuel, MLB's newest gaming partner, would hold court in the much larger Bill James Room.

But the doors weren't open yet. So I took a closer look at the agenda. Shoe-horned between the tenth annual Hackathon, a pickleball demonstration for which I brought the wrong shoes, panel discussions featuring 162 speakers, an impressive number of whom were women, many in fuck-me shoes, presentations by the seven finalists in the Student Research Competition, and twenty-seven Competitive Advantage spielers ("How Bobsleighing, the Roman Army, and Throw-in Coaching Innovated the World of Soccer"), I saw exactly three time slots devoted to baseball.

Michael Lewis broke it to me gently: "I think from the conference's point of view baseball has been deforested."

* * *

Baseball was on the precipice of the Great Leap forward: new rules intended to make baseball look like baseball again. A pitch clock to prohibit laggardly pitchers from being laggardly and dallying batters from dallying; bigger bases to encourage speed on those bigger bases; a ban on defensive shifts, requiring infielders to play the infield; a limit on the number of times a pitcher can step off the pitching rubber per at bat (two) and how many times a batter can call time to scratch what itches and adjust his cup (one); and a ten-second limit on walk-up music.

They were the first consequential changes in on-the-field play since the designated hitter came to the American League in 1973 and so traumatized Major League Baseball that it took the National League forty-nine years to do the same.

Decades of dithering ensued. Meanwhile, the cyber world juiced up, training brains, like thoroughbreds chomping at the bit in the starting gate, to demand more of everything quicker.

In 2004, when Gloria Mark, professor emeritus of informatics at the University of California, Irvine, put a stopwatch on computer-dependent workers, they averaged two and a half minutes on a given task before turning away from the screen. In 2012, they lasted seventy-five seconds. By 2023, when she published her book *Attention Span*, they could manage just forty-seven seconds of undivided attention.

Little wonder that Gen Z had no patience for baseball. Except maybe for a clip on TikTok. Hard to blame them. The average time between balls put in play in 2021 was three minutes and fifty-two seconds. "You have twelve minutes to sell the game to a six-year-old and you're going to get two or three balls in play in that time?" said MLB tempo czar Theo Epstein. "It's impossible."

The decades-long impasse between the forces of old and new devolved into a standoff between spikes-high baseball libertarians and good government reformers. Libertarians, such as the Nationals' Mike Rizzo, believed that because baseball is a game of adjustments, players would adjust and quit hitting ground balls into defensive shifts, as Willie Mays said he would have done: "I woulda bunted four or five times. I hit the ball a lot to right field using an inside-out swing. I can't explain how. I just did it."

But they didn't bunt or go the other way. "They don't know how to hit with two strikes," moaned Mr. October, Reggie Jackson, at an annual national coaching convention. Next thing he was crying. "Like literal tears," said modernist hitting coach Jason Ochart.

They didn't do it, either, because they didn't know how, because no one had taught them; because it's hard to bunt a spheroid coming at you at 2,700 RPM, or because some coach said "It will mess up your swing." Or because analytics documented the inefficiency of the approach.

Hitters got bigger and fitter and tighter in pursuit of power because power paid. Pitching elbows tore like tissue paper on badly wrapped Christmas presents because power paid. More traffic commuted to and from the injured list than between first and third. A veritable conga line of overly buff bodies shuffled back and forth between major-league rosters and minor-league rehab assignments. As former Braves third baseman Terry Pendleton said, "We were better off fat."

You can't pull fat.

Baseball's unique patois, a lingua franca nurtured over decades in dugouts, locker rooms, and newspaper print, became a dead language. *Hit 'em where they ain't. Toolsy. Fungo. Duck Fart.* The language of baseball became computer code.

Whither pepper?

Add to the equation the new-age managerial imperative to get your shit together between every pitch. "Part of this problem we've created with all the sports psychology stuff that we've done over the years," said former Manager Joe Maddon. "Don't step into that box until you're absolutely ready. Don't get on the mound until you're absolutely ready. Don't get too quick, clear your mind."

To which I can only reply: *om.*

"You can't really rush thoughts," third baseman Alex Bregman said.

Somehow Babe Ruth managed to hit 714 home runs without thinking or overthinking. And as Bill James pointed out that morning, The Babe played in an era when games began at 3:00 p.m.—three o'clock lightning. Sunset was the pitch clock, a deterrent to the dilatory.

Commercial breaks got longer over the years too. And relief pitchers marched across impeccable green lawns with every new batter. (Thank you, Tony La Russa.) Moneyballers imposed new winning strategies, ganging up on left-handed hitters with defensive shifts and demonstrating the stupidity of batting flappy bat-control guys second in the lineup. And, sacrilege of sacrilege, they called into question the existence of clutch hitting. Baseball was a lot more fun when you could believe in clutch hitting.

Analytics placed a premium on "working the count," "taking your walks," and "grinding out at bats," "making the pitcher work," exhausting him—and fans—to get rid of him early. That became moot once algorithms definitively demonstrated that no starting pitcher should face the lineup three times; max-heave pitching meant he wouldn't last that long anyway.

Put it all together, and you had yourself an aesthetic problem. As Miami Marlins Vice President of Player Personnel Sam Mondry-Cohen put it, "The game's smarter, stronger and uglier."

"I hate modern baseball," Roger Angell said the last time we spoke, before his death at age 101 in 2022. "They've taken away the power alleys. It's all strikeouts and home runs. Half of offensive baseball is gone. Nobody's moving up runners. The whole nature of the game has changed."

Mystics and nihilists may aspire to nothingness, but it was hard to call that kind of baseball entertainment. Harder still to argue the game's merits with my "never-baseball" pals whose long-standing complaint—nothing happens!—turned out to be not only true but also a goal of analytically driven play. Red Sox pitching coach Brian Bannister let the cat out of the bag in a 2018 interview with *The Boston Globe* explaining that the way to win in the analytic age is to prevent the chaos of the ball in play.

I think I broke Roger's elegant baseball-loving heart for good when I told him about that. "The chaos of the ball in play is what baseball is all about!" came his anguished reply.

Out of that chaos comes choreography.

* * *

When the doors to the Sue Bird Room opened, ESPN host Kevin Negandhi introduced the panel, which included Bill James and Raúl Ibañez, then working in the commissioner's office. Morgan Sword got right to the point. "We've played ninety-five games so far. Spring training games are down about twenty-four minutes relative to spring training last year. Run scoring's up a little bit; batting averages up; stolen base activity is up and we're starting to see the number of [pitch clock] violations tail off a little bit as players, coaches, and umpires get adjusted."

Faster is better. Nobody misses guys consulting their inner life coaches between pitches. But the game that promises you might see something that's never happened before devolved into one lacking variety, nuance, subtlety, and strategy. "It's so fucking boring," the great Bill "Spaceman" Lee said. "You know why it's so fucking boring? Because everyone knows what's going to happen. Somebody is gonna hit a home run and the closer is going to strike out the side in the ninth."

In a game subsumed by numbers, it's sometimes hard to know which matter. These matter: In each of the last seven seasons, including

2024, strikeouts outnumbered hits. In each of those seasons, more balls were fouled off than put in play.

More than a third of at bats resulted in one of the dreaded Three True Outcomes: a walk, a K, or a home run. Just shy of 5 percent of all pitches hit in 2024 were home runs.

"Bill, your thoughts," the moderator said, turning to Bill James.

"On the way over here, a gentleman said to me, 'They're moving too fast,'" Bill said. "I said, 'Well, yes, we're rushing to get stuff done that should have been done thirty years ago.' I know a lot of people don't know that there was a rule in the books, when I first became a baseball fan, that restricted the amount of time between pitches. You were supposed to deliver the ball within twenty-five seconds. No one ever enforced the rule so I guess it eventually went away, but there always should have been some sort of manner to keep the game moving along and it's great that they finally have it."

Letters Sword had sent to players pleading "please play faster" were ignored, as were the fines attached to follow-up correspondence. And so, they introduced an element of time into a game that reveled in its timelessness, in the poetry of timelessness, an analog game trying to be cool in an AI world.

The boys at MLB batted around plenty of other ideas, Sword said: "Any rule that we have, we've talked about changing: change the bats, change the balls, change the bases, change the geometry of the field, change the number of players on the field, change the batting order, change the number of innings, the number of balls and strikes. We talked about regulating the height of grass on the infield to speed up ground balls and create more hits. I personally like the drop-third-strike rule where if it gets away from the catcher you can just bolt to first base and see if you can get there. Nobody likes that except for me." And the Savannah Bananas.

Bill James suggested a constellation of small changes that could "return baseball to a more normal form." Move the batter's box back one inch. Do it again in three years to counteract the effect of increased velo.

"An inch does make a difference," Ibañez said. "Charlie Manuel, our manager in Philly, used to say a little means a lot when it comes to hitting and I totally agree with that."

James predicted (correctly) an increased batting average of four to six points in 2023. It went up from .243 to .248.

It didn't take long for Morgan to invoke MLB's "aesthetics of the game" trope, which I first heard from Theo when explaining why defensive shifts had to go. "Silly as it sounds, there is something to having infielders play where they've played for 150 years and move them back to where they used to be," Morgan said.

It didn't sound silly to me.

It wasn't silly to Morgan's father either. "It would make my dad legitimately angry to see a line drive to right field that was a ground out all of a sudden, angry to the point where he would stop watching the game," he told me later.

What's more, early returns from the players were encouraging. "Putting them at their traditional positions, they feel, allows them to range to make great defensive plays and puts the game back in the players' hands and allows them to dictate outcomes rather than who has the best algorithm for positioning the infield."

Sword wears so many crowns it's hard to imagine how he puts his head down at night. As executive vice president of baseball operations, he oversees MLB's competitive system, including free agency, salary arbitration, the minor leagues, the draft, and international player acquisitions, as well as on-field issues such as umpiring, rule changes, and the balls home plate umpires stuff in their pockets.

He's also the guy who disenfranchised forty-three affiliated minor-league teams, severing baseball from a large swath of grassroots

America while depriving small-market teams of the larger pool of talent they need to compete with the big boys.

"They're cutting off their supply chain of new fans who are ten years old now," said former Oakland A's President Roy Eisenhardt. "But when they are twenty-five, they're going to want them to be part of their demographic. Learning to appreciate baseball is like learning a language. You can do it well when you're young. Later on, it gets harder."

The first time we met I asked Morgan to define his job in one sentence. He did not mention any of the above. "My job is to make the major-league game entertaining, fair, emotional—"

"Exciting?"

"Exciting as in the years when I fell in love in the late '90s and early 2000s with the New York Mets. I was completely invested in the game and its outcome."

He began to enumerate the "emotional notes" of baseball's many versions—college, the Cape Cod League, softball in Central Park, the Dominican League where there's a dance party throughout the game—that together "hint at what the major-league game should be."

He sounded more like a sommelier than a baseball executive with an MBA. "A summer softball game in Central Park, there's a visceral serenity to that and it's paced appropriately to what you're doing."

I'm not sure I ever experienced visceral serenity in Central Park's Sheep Meadow—I hope he has—but I still have my blue T-shirt with the name "Chicken Wing" on the back from my days playing for G. P. Putnam's Sons in a publishing-house league.

Sword's playing days ended with high school in Lawrenceville, New Jersey, where he was a catcher and an outfielder with an unruly shank of red hair. Upon admission to the University of Virginia, he emailed the new baseball coach to offer his help and was named team manager. He did the laundry, fetched takeout, and hatched analytics projects, a fascination spurred by reading *Moneyball* in high school.

His lowest moment in baseball and the strongest emotion it elicited was watching "Carlos Beltran striking out on a Wainwright curveball."

That's when Beltran faced St. Louis rookie reliever Adam Wainwright and looked at strike three with two outs and the bases loaded in the bottom of the ninth inning of Game Seven of the 2006 National League Championship Series.

"I remember being physically sick," he said.

I was happy to hear him declare his heart. Many in and around the game believe the people running it don't love it as they should. Not the way Yalie Commissioner Bart Giamatti did. True, I saw Commissioner Rob Manfred consult his watch after two innings of a Cactus League game. True, he was booed after every selection in the 2023 MLB draft. True, he felt compelled to declare, "I don't hate baseball."

One major-league manager, who wisely withheld his name lest he get shitcanned, said, "The people that run the game are not fans of the sport. Yes, they like baseball. I mean of course they're fans now, but I'm talking about, 'I will go right now and watch a high school game and just sit there at 3:15 p.m. and watch kids play baseball.'"

That's a tough standard. I wouldn't qualify for commissioner on that basis either.

"It's like they don't care about the fan," my manager friend said. "Like all they're thinking about is gaming systems and finding loopholes and not what's best for the game. They're gaming the game."

I got an intimation of where Sword's heart lies when he was asked during the Q&A about the specter of the robo-ump. Norman Rockwell's square-jawed arbiters at Ebbets Field—Larry Goetz, Beans Reardon, and Lou Jorda—trying to decide about a rain delay with the Bums behind 1–0 are some of the last vestiges of unassailed American authority. (Even they couldn't have stopped *Saturday Evening Post* editors from brightening the dark skies over Brooklyn, much to Rockwell's dismay.)

Former ump Jim Joyce knows better than most everyone in baseball the power of being wrong. He's the guy who made the wrong call on the last out of Armando Galarraga's otherwise perfect game. Much as he rues the day, much as he appreciates Galarraga's gracious acceptance of the outcome, he laments the passing of improvisational foot-stomping, plate-tossing, dirt-kicking theatrics killed by replay. "That was the fun part of the game," he said.

You can't even have a good bar fight anymore. I don't know about you, but I'd rather risk getting my ass kicked in said bar than know all the answers.

Sword attested to the wonders of the tracking system, which, he told the conference attendees, could reliably put the ball or strike call in the umpire's ear. "Then he or she would make the call," he said, which was nice, though my sports orthopedist immediately put the kibosh on the idea of umpire school.

"Interestingly, we got a really loud negative reaction from players and coaches about that system," he said.

What followed gave me hope. "As we've made the game more clinical, we're no longer presenting a game like it was originally presented," Morgan said. "It was a human game of failures and successes. We live in the era of the glorification of 'we can explain everything.'"

Just because you can—or think you can—doesn't mean you should. Don't they know control is an illusion?

* * *

The conversation about baseball's future continued through the weekend in hallways, at dinners, and on subsequent panels: Has baseball changed enough to keep up in a universe of hyperspeed entertainment delivery systems feeding constant stimulation and updates to doomscrolling sports fans? Should it even try?

"It would take putting a lion on the field to get baseball moving again," Michael Lewis told me. "A hungry lion. I'm gonna have to make a special trip to Africa because there's no lion in the country that's sufficiently ferocious. I need one that is used to the taste of fresh meat and that really wants to hunt."

Nate Silver, creator of the foundational metric PECOTA that projects player performance based on historical comparisons, and Daryl Morey, who brought analytics to the NBA, piled on Bill James during the last panel discussion. "Is baseball's structure in trouble no matter what they do?" Morey demanded. "If baseball was invented five years ago, would it have any chance of breaking through?"

Fair question because no matter how much quicker baseball gets, no matter how many seconds they shave off the pitch clock, baseball is still a nineteenth-century construct, born at a time when pocket watches were in vogue.

"Yes," Bill said cheerfully, "because if it had been invented five years ago, it would not yet have developed all these bad habits."

"But it has all these structural things that you said are bad," Morey said. "Like the right fielder stands there forever and doesn't touch anything."

"Hah," said aging techno wunderkind Nate. "Like if you simulated the world a thousand times, I don't think you'd end up with a sport like baseball."

"Yep," Daryl agreed. "That's exactly what I mean. 'Whaddya trying to do? Throw it? Hit it with a stick?' It would be like no."

My beloved Red Smith, late bard of the press box, woulda told 'em what's what: "Ninety feet between home plate and first base may be the closest man has ever come to perfection."

Red would have dropped dead had he lived long enough to see the sacred geometry compromised by these newer, bigger bases.

CHAPTER 2

ROOM 311

The reporter asks: Is all this really necessary?

Windowless, airless, coffeeless Room 311, where the seven students left standing in the smarty-pants research competition were about to make their presentations, was at the far end of the 268-foot-long Boylston Hallway. In other words, a schlep.

Its 3,244 square feet of fungible event space had been configured for a crowd with a small stage up front, armed with what we used to call AV equipment, a white board, a judge's table, and rows and rows of seats from which peers and profs could take your measure. This was "the real action" Peko had put me on to.

Presenting is always a challenge, made harder in this instance by the thwocks of pickle balls being thwocked in the auditorium below and the pings of golf shots landing on simulated greens next door.

Peko was seated up front with the other three judges. I plunked myself down at her shoulder and turned on my tape recorder. I knew I was going to have to listen to these guys more than once. Connor Heaton, a PhD candidate in informatics at Pennsylvania State University, was on the stage, introducing an updated version of the paper he had presented the year before, "Learning Contextual Event Embeddings to Predict Player Performance in the MLB."

I dinged him right off for "in the MLB." It's not *the* MLB. How many times had I heard Billie Jean King correct tennis illiterates: "It's Wimbledon—not Wimble*ton*."

You may think I'm being picky but I'm not. Nor was the *New York Times* sports editor who returned my letter begging for a job with a scribbled note in the margin saying, "Next time spell the editor's name right."

This is what is known in analytics as *domain knowledge*.

"Counting stats have their shortcomings," Connor began.

So far, so good. I understood the first sentence, or so I thought. But no. That's because I foolishly assumed that "counting stats" was something you did, not a noun used to describe old-fashioned Black-Ink baseball numbers.

"Almost all sabermetrics is based upon counting statistics," Connor said. "For some more rudimentary statistics like batting average, that's aggressively obvious. You're just counting a number of hits, counting the number of at bats and dividing one by the other. Different metrics have to employ more pointed math."

I must have missed that class.

"In the early days of computational linguistics," he continued, "language was described by counting the number of times different words appeared—an approach known as the 'bag-of-words' method.

"Modern state-of-the-art techniques derive contextual representations of language, analyzing the context in which words appear, a much more faithful description of the language. That is, instead of having a static understanding of the word *single*, models will contextualize the representation of *single* based on the words in the surrounding context."

You see the problem.

"We view the sports analytics community as currently in the

bag-of-events era and offer a stepping stone for advancing to the era of contextual embeddings."

I started scribbling. *Bag-of-events era. Bag-of-words vector. Bag-of-words events. Word token.*

As Connor appropriated context from context with cheerful abandon, I began to dissociate.

It wasn't my own incompetence that unmoored me. I'm used to that. Later, Peko would say, generously, that data science is a muscle that has to be exercised, like all the others I'm currently ignoring. I've made peace with the fact that I was born without this one.

But to feel not of the world at a conference serving up what I realized was a mere amuse-bouche in the all-you-can-eat buffet of sports analytics, it was enough to make me mix my metaphors.

And pity the poor coaches, whose mental musculature is stuck in the era of *Hmmm, babe!* Their job really isn't so different from mine: trying to translate the work of the Connor Heatons of the world into actionable intelligence for baseball men whose eons of experience count less than a computer model "trained on only ten games worth of play-by-play data. We can make single-game pitcher strikeout and binary batter has-hit predictions that are competitive with major sportsbooks in the US for the 2021 MLB season."

That I understood. The whole shebang was about laying odds on the future.

Charts, tables, and equations floated across the whiteboard: $RunsCreatedi = \alpha event1 \cdot Cevent1,i + \alpha event2 \cdot Cevent2,i + \cdots + \alpha eventN \cdot CeventN,i$ and "Single Embedding Visualizations" that reminded me of slices of fried NFL brains preserved on glass slides by CTE researchers. My brain felt like tau clusters were assaulting my neurons.

Sealed in my own ignorance, I was an idiot interloper gone undercover in the name of journalism to penetrate an altered reality. A reality where word tokens had replaced words and Large Language Models had replaced language.

Personally, I prefer my words whole and my realities unadulterated. You won't find me shelling out $3,000 to log into Apple's augmented reality (MR) headset. I think it has something to do with having spent the first three months of my life in an incubator.

"You can't really recover the secrets of events as they actually happened," Connor said. "What actually happened on the field that these statistics are describing."

Whaddya mean you can't recover the secrets of events? That's my job. That's what I do. Go read the sports section where some writer has told you that the single is, in fact, a duck fart that fell between three infielders because it was hit off the handle of a bat, not a line drive off the left field wall.

And furthermore, why, other than looking for an edge, do you want to predict what's going to happen? The joy of baseball is in not knowing.

I remembered something Joe Torre once told me about the inherent tension between baseball and analytics. "Our game is unpredictable in a good way," he said. "The unexpected happens. Rajai Davis—no way he's gonna hit a home run against the Chicago Cubs off Chapman in the seventh game of the World Series. But he did. That's the unpredictability that makes our game exciting."

He referred to the game-tying home run in the bottom of the eighth inning of Game Seven of the 2016 World Series launched by Cleveland's reserve outfielder, Rajai Davis, off young fireballing reliever Aroldis Chapman.

"You're pretty much only going to use that guy if you're forced to," Torre said. "You're not going to use him because he can't do it until he does it. That's why you have to stay tuned. You can't run the clock out. You've got to get twenty-seven outs."

Boing. It hit me. A whole damn industry of data scientists, and baseball operations guys, and layers of management had conspired to remake baseball into a world where the improbable has been rendered moot or not worth the trouble. Where the most likely outcome has been given sole dominion, and the zeal for finding fractional advantages has compromised originality, precluding the forever plays that run on a loop in baseball's collective memory. "They're trying to make an imperfect game perfect," Torre said. "I resent that."

Connor said he was happy to take questions. Where to begin? I didn't understand the judges' questions any better than I understood Connor until Judge Nate Silver, former baseball-stat geek turned electoral-stat geek, started his inquisition.

"Let's say I'm at a game," Nate said. "I go get a hot dog. I come back. There's one out and runners on first base and third base, and your model can kind of tell me what's the chance that they got there by different sequences? By two walks and then a wild pitch versus a walk and a single that advanced the runner to third."

Connor nodded tentatively. "Don't we already have that information?" Nate said. "I mean, we can look at the game log and see what the sequence was."

Connor braved a reply that had something to do with a bottleneck. Nate grew impatient. "Why do you need a machine model? I'm just trying to figure out the problem you're trying to solve."

"Good question," Connor replied.

Finally, I got the point. There wasn't any.

"Welcome to academia," Peko said.

* * *

Nothing about Connor's presentation or the ones that followed was obvious to me, aggressively or otherwise.

"So, the numbers can tell us what the probability is that Rajai Davis might hit a home run over ten games, to use this model," Peko said.

"But it cannot tell us what the probability is that he will hit a home run in this particular moment against this particular pitcher on this particular day with the rain starting to come down in a World Series Game Seven because he's never faced that situation before.

"No matter how granular the information is, it can't predict accurately a specific occasion that's never happened before. That is baseball's specialty, producing that which has never been seen before. That's why you go to the ballpark to see something that's never happened."

She paused, eyeing me sideways. "Have you actually tried ChatGPT?"

"Why would I do that? I'm a writer."

"Oh, my God. Okay. The first thing I asked was: 'Please write a poem about the second law of thermodynamics in the style of Dr. Seuss.' I have to say the poetry was not great, but it did a pretty good job of capturing the second law of thermodynamics.

"It's not that the machine learning algorithm won't give you a probability," Peko said. "It will happily give you a probability, which is why it's dangerous. If you ask ChatGPT your question, it will happily give you an answer that looks good, which is probably completely wrong. What you need to ask is: 'What is the uncertainty around that answer?'"

And you can't know the right question to ask if you have no idea why the answer makes no sense. Data isn't the problem. Analytics aren't the problem. "The problem is arrogance in the community of people who are very good at writing these algorithms," Peko said, mounting her rhetorical soap box. "They are not experts in the domain and they don't think it matters, and that's a big problem because it matters a lot."

Domain knowledge is in the logbooks. It's also in knowing you never say "the" MLB.

"I guarantee you there are people using these analytics extremely well and who are making great decisions because they are not using them to replace the human decision-makers who know the game; what they are using them for is to give the human decision-makers more tools so that they can factor those in to the decisions they're making."

The way I was using Peko to make me sound smart.

"What we should be using them for is to push what we can do orthogonal to what people are already doing well, right?"

* * *

I couldn't stay for the second session of presentations, which conflicted with a panel on how to create fans. I had already missed a presentation that featured a lively discussion on using AI to generate personalities for Fox hosts.

The panel on "The Future of the Fan: Innovation, Data, and 'Always On' Engagement"—presented by Ticketmaster—featured five prominent female sports executives representing the NFL, Amazon, Spectacor Sports in Philadelphia, and two of the most powerful industry analytics corporations, including the Kraft Analytics Group (KAGR) and its CEO, Jessica Gelman. Of all things, they were talking about storytelling.

"Data without story is useless," Valerie Camillo was saying. She was a big cheese at Spectacor Sports & Entertainment, the business arm of the Philadelphia Flyers and their arena.

You won't be surprised that my heart fluttered just a bit. The validation of storytelling was a big relief because I was starting to feel really useless. Then, Val began to tell her story. "I'm on this stage because as a little girl I used to collect baseball cards, free content. When I started, I used to look at the pictures and I would look at all the different guys, and then at some point I liked math, and I turned the cards over and I started to think about the data."

She was hooked. Growing up in Washington, DC, during baseball's absence from the nation's capital, the game itself remained distant. But the cardboard men became inseparable from the beating heart of data. "My parents took me up to Baltimore to see a game at

Memorial Stadium, and we were late. My parents were often late and it's far, so we were rushing in, and the game was already underway. I believe it was Memorial Day weekend. We came out of the 'vom'—the vomitorium—into the stadium and at that moment, I swear, Reggie Jackson had hit a home run, and the ball was going over the fence. I'm this little kid and I'm watching it and in my head I was like, 'This is it. This is what I want to do for the rest of my life.'"

Bill James must have been thinking of Val when he wrote: "A chart of numbers that would put an actuary to sleep can be made to dance if you put it on one side of a card and Bombo Rivera's picture on the other."

This is how fans used to be created, before the COVID-19 pandemic, before tickets got so expensive, before streaming, virtual, and esports, before AI, before studies had to be commissioned to explain that fandom was dependent on going to a live event or going to said event with someone important in your life. Val was the perfect fan, the fan you want to nurture and create—except maybe for the word "vom."

* * *

By the time I got back to Room 311, Dubem Mbeledogu, a hip Black data scientist turned out in an impeccable white turtleneck and a natty blue suit with pegged trousers and thin lapels, had been named winner of the research-paper competition for his how-to on gambling: "Robust Daily Fantasy Sports: Maximizing Reward via the Robust Optimization Paradigm." He accepted kudos from the judges on his look as well as his presentation, after which he acknowledged a certain lack of domain knowledge.

In the cab on my way home, I asked ChatGPT to use "orthogonal" in a sentence Dr. Seuss might have written.

CHAPTER 3

ACTIVATING J. P.'S BACKSIDE

Going inside the man cave where it happens

Briefly the hops capital of the world—until aphids did in the crop—the tiny town of Titusville, Washington, reinvented itself as "The Lettuce Capital of the World" in the midst of the great depression. The welcoming soil of the White River Valley and the growing population of Issei farmers combined to produce a crop so prodigious it demanded celebration.

To that end, publicity-minded city fathers organized an annual Lettuce Festival with lettuce floats that floated in a lettuce parade presided over by a lettuce queen, who waded into the World's Largest Salad Bowl in a bathing suit and rubber boots to dress the World's Largest Salad with one hundred gallons of ready-mix mayonnaise. With the help of two stalwart ladies-in-waiting, she served ten thousand portions to two thousand townsfolk via pitchfork.

Kent's arable past, coincident with the rise of baseball in rural America, long ago ceded right of way to a swath of high-tech start-ups, industrial parks, and warehouses, each identical to the next, like those suburban medical complexes that make it impossible to find your doctor: 23211 66th Avenue in South Kent is one of those.

Nothing about the low-slung, postindustrial metal canopy above the door or the unimposing reception area with a tacky dropped ceiling prepared me for the chilled vastness of the interior space, airplane hangar–esque in dimension. The color scheme—*black* black, storm gray, and nacho yellow—testifies to the seriousness of its purpose.

This is Driveline, the data-driven performance center that turned pitching into an extreme sport and major-league hitters into eunuchs. Forty thousand square feet of tricked-out training space divided into rectangles by sheaths of black netting dangling from a three-story ceiling. Shiny black hulks of the latest "don't fuck with me" exercise equipment marked with the whooshy Driveline logo line the gray concrete walls. Even old-school weight benches, dusted with a patina of chalky effort, have a modern purpose, having been retrofitted with Tendo Power Analyzers with Bluetooth sending units that measure bar speed and power output while lifting.

Natural light is a no-no; nothing can distract from the solipsistic pursuit of spin and barrels. In lieu of windows there are monitors and computer screens bulging with numbers arranged in arcane equations, percentages, miles per hour, and revolutions per minute.

Numbers on framed jerseys ring the perimeter. Clayton Kershaw, Kenley Jansen, Tony Gonsolin, Daniel Bard, Tim Lincecum, Alex Cobb, Michael Fulmer, and Shohei Ohtani, who wintered in Kent in 2020, working with pitching guru Bill Hezel, who was hired away by the Los Angeles Angels to work with him.

Numbers on a whiteboard listing the leaders of a "best new ideas" competition. Founder Kyle Boddy was in last place with minus one. Numbers on medicine balls, some weighing twenty pounds, sometimes used in volleyball games.

Numbers on weighted balls. Numbers scrawled in chalk on paper-lined walls at which otherwise sane human beings launch those weighted balls in kamikaze heaves called “Pull Downs,” “Crow Hops,” and “Run ’n’ Guns,” pausing between throws to inhale smelling salts.

If you want to understand what’s happening in baseball, what needs to happen in baseball, you must come here.

And come they do: two hundred MLB draft picks, one hundred MLB players, forty all-stars, five MVPs, and four Cy Young Award–winners and counting as of spring 2025, all lured by the American promise of self-improvement. Among the recent pilgrims: pitchers Joe Ryan, Sean Manaea, Logan Gilbert, and Luis Severino; and hitters Paul Goldschmidt, Nolan Arenado, Richie Palacios, and Amed Rosario.

I was there to meet Jason Ochart, creator of Driveline’s antidote to Driveline, a speed training program using weighted bats to even the playing field between the two ends of the pitcher–hitter continuum. Pitch tracking, which arrived in 2006, gave Kyle Boddy and his quant disciples a head start in mining data for advantages in how to throw a baseball.

Hunched in a folding chair, a Red Sox watch cap pulled low on his brow, Ochart watched J. P. Crawford, shortstop for the Seattle Mariners, use Ochart-designed bats and Ochart-designed drills to reshape his swing under the supervision of Ochart-trained hitting coach Maxx Garrett.

Most big leaguers who’d wintered at Driveline, including Mookie Betts and most of the Dodgers’ starting lineup, had departed in advance of spring training. Crawford, who’d been working out three times a week since early December, was standing like a flamingo at home plate in one of Driveline’s tech-heavy batting cages.

The Flamingo drill is also known as the Kershaw drill, named after Dodgers pitcher and future Hall of Famer Clayton, whose idiosyncratic left-handed delivery is distinguished by his stork-like balancing act on the pitching rubber before his body begins to move forward in space.

"It's designed to help players load correctly," Jason explained. "So, for J. P. we wanted him to really get his weight on his back side and into his back hip so that he could fire his hips more explosively. Flamingo forces you to be centered and find your balance point before you start your swing."

Seems that J. P. needed to activate his backside, the inactivity of which had made him a "Punch and Judy hitter," not that anybody knows who they are. Back in the day he was content to "filet a ball over into left field." But now baseball has become a do-some-damage game.

He was swinging one of three speed-training bats. A set includes two overload bats that are each 20 percent heavier than a game bat, one with extra weight in the barrel and one with added weight in the handle, and an underload bat that is 20 percent lighter than a game bat.

There's also a long bat, thirty-seven inches long and thirty-seven ounces in weight, which is seventeen ounces lighter than the hunk of hickory Babe Ruth used early in his career; and a short bat, twenty-eight inches and thirty-one ounces.

Watching Crawford were three trainers and a HitTrax machine armed with two beady-eyed cameras set in a small, red, rectangular box perched on a black pedestal opposite the batter's box. It looked like a bedside table the Flintstones might have coveted.

J. P. was trying to hit heavy, sand-filled balls called Plyos with the game bat–length underload bat. "The heavier they are, the harder they are to hit," Jason said. "You have to hit them absolutely square, otherwise they'll spin off your bat. You really have to accelerate your bat through contact. And the whole idea is to make the training harder than the actual game so that when they get to the game, it's easier."

One camera tracked the incoming ball and the other tracked the ball leaving the bat. Together they predict the on-field result, projected on a HitTrax monitor mounted behind the cage. It glowed with a cheerful yellow likeness of Pittsburgh's PNC Park with the Roberto Clemente Bridge in the distance. The numbers from Crawford's last swing flashed on the screen, and they weren't good.

Launch angle: 29 degrees. Exit velocity: 81 mph, which together produced a tepid fly ball that traveled 292 feet before being caught by a virtual center fielder.

Swings like that are the reason Seattle Mariners President of Baseball Operations Jerry Dipoto and Manager Scott Servais took Crawford to dinner after the 2022 season and, midway through dessert, told him they wanted him to winter at Driveline. Crawford was at first dubious for all the throwback reasons a throwback player such as himself would find compelling. "I thought they're a little too much with technology. They've taken the beauty of the game away from baseball."

Of all the ways baseball is out of whack, nothing is more whacked than the current imbalance between pitching and hitting. The last time it was this skewed, in 1968, the mound was lowered five inches to its current ten-inch perch. Thanks to Driveline and its ilk, and in-house pitching labs like the Yankees' Gas Station, fastballs are faster than ever and thrown higher than ever, up under the hands where no one can reach them, but less often than ever. Fastball usage is down, from 60 percent of all pitches to 48 percent in the last seventeen years.

That's partly because hitters can adjust to "high heat," which gets straighter as it gets faster. But, also, because "stuff"—power changeups and sweepers—has gone from filthy to disgusting to gross.

"*Sucio*," Ochart said. "That's gross in Spanish. I've seen pitchers that throw sliders that are breaking twenty-plus inches. And they're *hard*."

Jason shook his head. That's why, he said, "I've made it my life's mission to make baseball fair to hitters."

* * *

As with other notable West Coast upstarts—Amazon, Mattel, grunge rock—Driveline was birthed in a garage. This garage belonged to college dropout, Olive Garden server, Microsoft systems analyst, weight lifter, professional gambler, and high school baseball coach turned pitching guru Kyle Boddy. Like pretty much everyone else with a passing interest in baseball, Boddy read *Moneyball.* Unlike everyone else, Boddy wasn't impressed. Big deal. So, Billy Beane found an undervalued asset in a dead-armed catcher named Scott Hatteberg with an all-star on-base percentage. Boddy thought, *Yeah, sure, but shouldn't we be developing Scott Hattebergs?*

PITCHf/x pitch-tracking technology was installed in major-league ballparks in 2008, unleashing streams of pitching data for geeks like Boddy to play with and giving pitchers a decade-long head start in the analytic reformation.

PITCHf/x was diabolical in its ability to demonstrate new ways to blow hitters away—as long as you didn't care about your appendages. And it was primitive compared to the Statcast system of cameras and radar that revolutionized the revolution in 2015, and its Hawk-Eye successor, optical technology installed in every ballpark in 2020 that uses twelve cameras, including five that record motion at three thousand frames per second.

That's also when the deluge of new hitting metrics arrived, changing the vocabulary and the conversation about hitting: exit velo and batted ball distance; barrels, launch angle, and launch angle sweet-spot percentage; EV50, whatever that is; and the newest stat released to the public in May 2024, bat speed. No more "his bat looks slow" or "his swing looks long."

Thanks to all the data, Jason said, "We have a very objective understanding of what good is. And in the hitting world, that hasn't really existed. But with Driveline over the years, we've collected so much data and we have so many swings in our database, full kinematics of MVPs, big leaguers, I mean thousands of swings. I'm literally just looking at what the best hitters we have are doing. And it so happens that Ted Williams is right, he's completely right, when it came to bat path matching the plane of the pitch."

For a dead guy in a cryogenic vault, Ted Williams gets a lot of love here. It was the third psalm to the Splendid Splinter I'd heard in my first ten minutes on the training floor. "They're pandering to you," said Jason, who still keeps his copy of *The Science of Hitting* on his desk.

Ochart isn't one of those broadcloth, East Coast Ivy League types, reviled on sight and on principle by baseball old-timers. He's more scruffy-one-day-growth California—Glendale, California, to be specific, where he was the Most Valuable Player in high school and a two-way player at each of the three colleges he attended. He graduated from Vanguard University in Southern California with a bachelor of applied science in kinesiology. For his senior project, he developed a data-driven speed training program for hitters, employing teaching principles he gleaned from classes in motor learning. He got an A+.

He first put his theories into practice as hitting coach at Menlo College in 2014. Three years later he was hired to create a speed training program for Driveline. Two years after that, he was hired away by the Philadelphia Phillies. Skepticism greeted him in print, online, and in the dugout. "How the Phillies Plan to Reboot Their Minors Hitting Program with a 28-year-old Who's Never Played or Coached Pro Ball" is the way his hiring was described by *The Athletic*.

Former Philadelphia manager and all-time oldster Charlie Manuel, affectionately known throughout baseball as Uncle Cholley because he likes everyone and everyone likes him, chimed in: "I like Jason—I really do. But he doesn't know how to throw soft toss!"

It's nothing Och hasn't heard before. "I'm aware I didn't play in the big leagues. I don't need to be reminded of that, although it was my life's dream."

"Mine too," I pointed out.

Och is a lovely guy, so lovely that I asked him to marry my daughter, whom he's never met. "There's time," he replied gallantly.

But that's not what I like best about him. What I like best is he doesn't doubt that I love baseball as much as he does.

I gazed longingly and stupidly at one of the empty pitching cages, hoping to throw a few. But Jason had checked out video of me throwing a ceremonial first pitch at Yankee Stadium. It's true: Driveline has film on everyone.

"I've seen you throw," Jason said.

My peripherals suck.

Pesky philosophical differences—old school, new school—ended his tenure in Philadelphia just as the Fightin' Phils marauded their way into the 2022 World Series. Two months later, the Red Sox swooped in and claimed him.

His task wasn't small given the apparent disinterest of Red Sox ownership in winning after finishing last in the American League East in 2022. Fenway Park had become the main attraction. Trying to be helpful, I put forward an idea that figured to be a big hit at the Fens. "Dig up Ted's head, plant it under glass beneath home plate, and let all comers slide in over Ted's head. For good juju. Or attendance."

Jason offered a considered reply. "I don't think Ted Williams fans are capable of sliding."

* * *

Not that long ago, in the home dugout at Nationals Park in Washington, DC, when Bryce Harper was failing to live up to *Sports Illustrated*'s expectations of him, a Nationals batting coach grumped, *He's listening to too many people.*

Now teams like the Dodgers and the Mariners *want* players to listen to other people. This is as radical a transformation as the equipment and training that Driveline used to reshape J. P. Crawford's swing.

Jerry Dipoto, once a major-league pitcher and president of player development for the Mariners since 2015, recalled the moment that the team resolved to change its ways. It was during spring training in either 2015 or 2016, he wasn't sure which. "We had a guest come in and visit our spring training camp from one of these third-party facilities," he said. "We're sitting with our entire organization's worth of hitting coaches from our major-league group to our coordinators, each of our affiliate hitting coaches.

"We're talking about modern technologies and how to implement them day-to-day. At one point, a hitting coach, a former major-league player, raised his hand and said, 'You don't understand what it's like to go into our hitting tunnels and walk up to Nelson Cruz or Robinson Canó and say, this is what we want you to do. You can't do that with hitters of that quality.'

"Our guest paused for a moment and said, 'You don't understand. I'm already doing that.'

"That was an aha moment for us. The best hitters in the game are paying tens of thousands, hundreds of thousands of dollars, to coaches to teach them the thing that we are unwilling or unprepared to teach them. So, we determined we are going to engage in this world and modernize our programs rather than trying to force players to stay in a game the way we remembered it."

The Mariners had invested heavily in Crawford, bringing in infield guru Perry Hill to work with him at shortstop and awarding him a five-year $51 million contract extension prior to the 2022 season. "The team flows through him," Dipoto said.

He's the guy who got up in front of the whole team in spring training and did a reggae song that he made a game-day ritual, reprising it exactly thirty minutes before game time to get his crew ready. The guy who procured a nine-pound, seventy-two-inch-long "highly collectible and officially licensed replica of Aquaman's Trident" from Amazon with which to celebrate every Mariners home run. The guy who burned sage in every corner of the clubhouse and the batting cage when the bats went cold.

"This is my squad," Crawford said. "This is my team. I got to go out there and meet 'em every day. Some days you're not going to be your best, and sometimes you're going to be banged up. But you got to fake it and get the guys energized and keep them ready."

He started out well enough in 2022 before injuries and wear and tear set in, and his numbers plummeted. For the year, he slashed .223/.320/.296. "Slashed," used as a space-saving verb to convey accomplishment or the lack thereof, is an ugly numerical haiku that says more than it intends about the encroachment of analytics on storytelling and language. For which reason, this is the first and last time I will use it.

Anyway, that was not a good slash line. "As the season wore on J. P. wore down," Servais said. "He didn't hold his weight. He wasn't as strong as he could be. Nutrition wasn't the greatest. The weight training throughout the season wasn't great. He's just kind of an old-school throwback player. '*I'll be okay.*' But by the end of the year, he was gassed."

They chose Driveline because it was close to home and because of the company he was likely to keep. "He's the most competitive guy on our team," Servais said. "A lot of these guys, they go to their little boutique trainer, and they just train one-on-one. I wanted him to work around other ballplayers and everybody in the place knows, 'Hey, that's J. P. Crawford.'

"So now he's got to show up and give a great effort every day. Knowing his competitiveness, he would do that. Like, 'I'm J. P., man. I'm the fucking guy. I'll show you guys how to work.'"

Crawford had planned on working out in Seattle at T-Mobile Park during the offseason. "I knew something was wrong, but I had gotten away with it," he said. "When things got tough, I'd go back to what felt comfortable—hitting down."

It's what he'd done since he was kid, what his high school coaches taught him, what they preached at MLB's Compton Youth Academy. "Swinging down—hitting low line drives, hitting the top half of the ball, not the bottom."

"You'll beat it out," his daddy said.

But then baseball turned itself inside out—the way my mother taught me to do my laundry. No more pitching to contact. No more making your infielders work. Pitching became all about swing and miss. "Pitchers began throwing up, and I'm not on the same plane," J. P. said. "I have to be perfect to match my plane to the plane of the pitch."

I asked Servais, who learned the same outdated 1990s swing, for a slo-mo demonstration. An old catcher with knobby catcher knees, he lifted a bat high over his head, cocked as if to cleave left brain from right brain. "His elbow was really high," he said. "For this to go all the way around and get on plane is a *looong* swing. They had to teach him to get his elbow down and keep the barrel closer to his head. This would allow him to be much shorter to the ball. That's in layman's terms. That's old man talk. That's not high-tech Driveline hitting coach talk."

* * *

Ochart never wanted to coach. He never thought there would be a place for him in Major League Baseball. He lacked the bona fides of a prospect and the big-bark persona of a stereotypical American coach. I doubt he's ever worn a whistle around his neck. He wouldn't want to interrupt. But then he ruined his younger brother's swing and had to make it right.

They are a year, an inch, and ten pounds apart. "He's a good 200," Jason said. "I'm a bad 190. That's what coaching will do to you."

When Adam decided to go out for the baseball team at Glendale Community College, where Jason had been a first-team all-conference player, he took it upon himself to make his baby brother into a ballplayer. He deconstructed Adam's swing using all the conventional wisdom he had at his disposal. All the same advice J. P. Crawford had followed from his old-school coaches. Adam was cut from the team.

"I had ruined him," Jason said. "The coach called me saying, 'Hey, your brother was hitting balls 450 feet when he tried out a year ago. Now he can't get it out of the infield.'"

Manny Ramirez was his favorite player. So, he analyzed what made Manny Manny, a joint-by-joint exegesis, and saw that he moved the way Adam had moved until big brother got a hold of him.

"I realized that Manny had all the alleged 'swing flaws' that my brother had. He was swinging slightly uphill, his shoulders were rotating, his back foot was coming off the ground. All these things that I coached out of my brother were why he was good."

When Jason came home for Christmas vacation, he brought new tools of the trade: weighted balls, a janky weighted bat, and a Hula-Hoop he hung from a batting cage to give Adam a target. He told him to hit inside the bottom of the ball to the top right corner of the batting cage, over the second baseman's head, as high as he could, violating every batting precept in the coaching manual.

He threw so many pitches, he tore the ulnar collateral ligament in his elbow. He continued his research on Google Scholar, finding among other things 1980s studies by University of Hawaii Professor Coop DeRenne about how weighted bats helped increase bat speed.

When Adam transferred to Menlo College, Jason accepted a job as an unpaid volunteer coach so he could continue making amends. He earned $5,000 a year as assistant hitting coach—"and that was after a raise"—and spent a year sleeping on the floor of Head Coach Jake McKinley's office because he couldn't afford anything that wasn't free. He had to get up at 5:00 a.m. to make sure the cleaning staff didn't catch on.

He implemented his speed training program using heavy sand-filled balls. He jerry-rigged a prototype overload bat using an old wooden bat with pennies taped to the barrel. "A few times when I was flipping underhand toss, I got pennies in the forehead right between the eyes—an inch away from blindness."

One of the Menlo pitchers, who had trained at Driveline, loaned him Kyle Boddy's tome on pitching, *Hacking the Kinetic Chain*. It might as well have been the Book of Revelation.

Ochart wrote to Boddy to tell him he had changed his life. They followed each other on Twitter. A bromance bloomed.

When Boddy invited him to apply for a job building "a data-driven hitting program," Jason sent him the hitting manual he had written in college and the data he had meticulously collected on his Menlo hitters, measuring their exit velocity every two weeks.

"It was a program which as far as I could find didn't exist," Jason said. "This was Kyle's vision—the next step of *Moneyball* was using information not only to make decisions around optimizing your roster, your lineup, and strategy, but how do we actually use this information to get baseball players better?"

* * *

First you go to the Launchpad. "That's where they dress you up like you're in a video game," J. P. said.

It's basically a souped-up batting cage with force plates embedded beneath the batter's box and high-speed Edgertronic cameras that measure the twitch of every muscle and the bend of every joint.

By the winter of 2023, measuring had gotten so sophisticated that Jason's phone pinged every time there was a change in the stride of one of his Red Sox hitters. "They could probably measure scratching," said Max Dutto, Driveline's director of player development.

J. P. found the whole thing a bit weird, not to mention awkward, stripping down to his skivvies as trainers pasted motion capture sensors to every relevant part of his person, giving him the look of a bad case of blackpox. He took twenty swings or so, from which eight were culled to generate a biometric study that showed more angles than he knew he had. "It's your whole-body swing, what's good and what's bad."

Some of the toys on the training floor—their word not mine—are now ubiquitous. Rapsodo, TrackMan, HitTrax, KinaTrax, Blast Sensor, Edgertronic. Everybody has those. Among the "Other Toys" listed on their website: a Keiser Infinity Series functional trainer to measure rotational power, which was how they knew J. P. wasn't working out with a Hula-Hoop.

Emotiv Flex electroencephalography headsets that analyze brain wave patterning in vision-related tasks. Pupil Labs' Pupil Core gaze tracking, a pair of big nerdy glasses without lenses, like the ones I wore after my nose job, equipped with cameras that track whether a batter is actually keeping his eye on the ball. "Tons of hitters aren't even close to looking at the release point," Jason said.

Somaxis Cricket Wireless electromyography measures the voltage of flexed biceps. Omegawave heart rate variability and DC potential sensors calculate neuromuscular fatigue and readiness. "If a player is really wasted from a hard day in the weight room or a hard night out, the machine will know it," Jason said.

Pulse, an early entry in the hot wearables market, monitors workload and fatigue in pitchers using a sensor hidden inside a sleeve, especially valuable during rehab. "When Shohei Ohtani came to Driveline in 2020 before his big year, he was wearing it out in the field," Jason said.

When coaching became a science, it also became an industry that gets techier by the day, the result being that by the time you read this there will be a whole new generation of sci-fi lab tools, wearables generating measurables and newer, faster computer programs concocting new metrics and more data.

Driveline replaced the irritating sticky sensors in 2024 with a proprietary version of the *au courant* technology called Markerless Tracking. I first heard about it in 2021 from Glenn Fleisig, director of biomechanics research at the American Sports Medicine Institute in Birmingham, Alabama. "This is the next *Moneyball* in terms of analyzing what a person's body is doing," he told me.

Now every team has it. "Now baseball fields are laboratories. They can track how movement changes during the season and also how it changes from inning to inning. You can even track other teams. You can analyze good or bad mechanics—does he bend his arm too much or his knee too much?"

So, the only thing that can be said with confidence in 2025 that will still be true in 2026 is what Scott Servais had to say on the subject: "It's fucking crazy what has happened."

J. P.'s sticky biometrics report documented what was bad about his swing—and it was really bad. His attack angle, the angle at which his bat was moving relative to the ground at the point of contact, was subterranean at minus 2.9. The rotational speed of his pelvis was in the forty-fourth percentile. Not rotating is not good. At contact, the barrel of his bat was facing the opposite field. Kind of like a lazy Susan that turns only as far as the dreaded stuffed pimentos.

* * *

When I'm in need of biomechanical straight talk, I call Rob Gray, professor of human systems engineering at Arizona State University. He explained to me years ago why Mickey Mantle couldn't verbalize how he did what he did with a bat in his hands. Not that Mick was great with verbalizing altogether. It has to do with "expertise-induced amnesia," Rob said, which means the better you get at something the stupider you sound trying to explain it.

I can't begin to fathom The Mick in the age of analytic verbalization.

"Have you heard of constraints-led coaching?" Rob asked. "Sometimes it's known as the 'ecological dynamic approach to coaching.'"

Rob is coauthor of the 2023 textbook *A Constraints-Led Approach to Baseball Coaching*, based on studies he conducted with college players. "You don't want to use all the analytics to get a batter or a pitcher thinking about everything," he said with something approaching distaste. "That's not good for performance."

Half the hitters received verbal instruction—or attentional cues, which made them "very conscious of the instruction of how to get the ball in the air," he said.

The other half of the group participated in a constraint-led study in which Gray moved the outfield fence in and out, forcing hitters to teach themselves how to get the ball in the air and over the fence. "They had to figure out how to change their mechanics to clear it," he said. "The Dodgers had their guys working with weighted bats to improve bat speed, which is better than telling them, 'You need to swing faster by bending your knees more.'"

"Yes," I said, "they were at Driveline just before I got there. Mookie didn't like it much."

"The question is now: 'How do we take all that analytic information and get people to use it?'" Rob said. "That's my job."

He became a skills acquisition specialist working for the Red Sox along with Jason.

"So, Jason's a revolutionary?" I asked.

"I think so," he replied.

* * *

Driveline doesn't sound like baseball. White noise emanating from God knows how many computer servers forms the back track to a belligerent playlist, punctuated by the odd thwocks of Max Composite and Armor Alloy Ultra bats colliding with sand- and foam-filled balls.

Only the coaching exhortations sounded familiar. "That's good, dude," Maxx called from the far end of the cage. "It's good."

It's quiet coaching. Jason doesn't chew and he doesn't spit and the veins in his neck don't bulge. He says he has a terrible case of impostor syndrome.

"Imagine the opposite of Mickey Mantle," he said. "That was me. Mantle had no idea what he was doing with his swing. I knew *everything* I was supposed to do and was thinking about one hundred different things. None of my brain power was on 'see the ball, hit the ball, and be on time.'"

No surprise, then, that his best season as a player was the summer before he joined Driveline when he was player/coach for the Leksand Lumberjacks in the Swedish Elite League. "Which was professional in the sense that I got paid," he said.

Nobody told him what to do. No one told him he couldn't pitch and hit or how to hit. He won the Swedish Cy Young Award, and the Lumberjacks won the World Series. "It was the most fun I've ever had in baseball," he said.

* * *

Right off, Kyle Boddy gave Jason a Driveline company credit card and an anxiety attack, telling him he had two years to produce enough data to justify a data-driven hitting program. "I thought I was a good coach, but Kyle was like, 'We're going to find out. We're going to have really smart people looking at everything and trying to understand if you're actually getting players better.'"

He recruited a test group that thrived. He devised a ball that could withstand twenty thousand swing-from-your-ass swings, hitting ball after ball into the concrete walls of an unlit, unheated closet in the warehouse until he found one that didn't explode. He developed constraint-led drills that forced bodies to do things differently.

Sometimes the constraints are built into the implements like the weighted bats produced by the Axe company located in a nearby warehouse. Sometimes, the constraints are imposed on the environment like Rob Gray's movable fence. Either way, they moot the problem of explaining all the analytic mumbo jumbo to hitters unfamiliar with, impatient with, or intimidated by the numbers and the vocabulary. No one gives them the answers, only a challenge. It's a whole lot like being a kid in the way kids used to be kids when they taught themselves how to hit by playing Wiffle ball in the backyard.

Jason uses the HitTrax machine to create drills that mask as friendly competition. "Players get points based on hitting a ball over a certain mph at a certain launch angle," he said. "So, they get five points if they hit it over 100 mph on a line and ten points if it's over 105 mph. We create a game that way. All they're thinking about is 'hit the ball hard at a good angle' and nothing else."

J. P.'s personalized program included standard Driveline drills, constraint-led challenges, and lots of time with "long implements," otherwise known as the long bat that forced his lazy-Susan six pack to rotate faster and more efficiently. Alternating between the barrel-loaded overload bat and the handle-loaded overload bat helped him to develop proprioception. "Which is just a big word for where things are at in space and where you are in space," Maxx said.

Two staple Driveline drills are "the Babe Ruth" and the "Happy Gilmore," the latter being a PhD version of the former. "It's from a movie," Jason said, helpfully.

I thought, "Does he really think I'm that old?"

Jason introduced me to the Babe Ruth drill when I contacted him in 2017 for help analyzing the Babe's swing. I shared with him a sliver of film in which The Babe "walks into a pitch"—no doubt because he was trying to time his swing to early twentieth-century pitching slop. "We do a drill like that," Jason said. "Happy Gilmore is similar, but it's a little more intense. They're not walking through; they're shuffling through and moving really fast.

"We do that with guys who are lacking rhythm. Often, young players are coached out of rhythm, out of fluid movement, unfortunately, and into more and more robotic movement. So, we have to have them do Happy Gilmore to become more athletic and generate more momentum."

The Babe also inspired a drill called "Hook 'Ems." He would stand in the batter's box with his right front foot crossed over his back foot, coiled in anticipation of the pitch. "Babe Ruth did it to generate momentum, inward coil," Jason said, looking at the ancient footage. "It's dancing. It's art, really."

J. P. did a lot of "Hook 'Ems" and for the same reason: to give a zetz to his otherwise laggardly torso.

J. P. hit a lot of malleable, sand-filled PlyoCare Balls, ranging in weight from 200 to 350 grams. "The heavier they are, the harder they are to hit," Jason said. "You have to hit them absolutely square, otherwise they'll spin off your bat. If you catch the bottom or the top, they don't go anywhere. Guys adjust to that very quickly because obviously they don't like seeing that poor ball flight."

A mis-hit on the next pitch produced an unhappy *arrrrgh* from J. P. He repositioned his feet into a 45 degree angle from the top right corner of the plate, with his mid-section toward shortstop for a drill called "offset closed," which made it really hard for him to turn his pelvis as much as he needed it to if he was ever going to pull the ball in the air.

"Regular swings here," Garrett shouted from the far end of the cage. "I want you to keep an eye on your back, and your attack angle."

J. P. grabbed a skinny Smash Factor bat, one-and-a-half inches wide at the barrel, while Maxx fired up the iPitch machine, which can be programmed to throw any pitch at any speed randomly from 54 feet, which in the real world is how far from home plate the average major league pitcher releases the ball. The leering, lurking pitching bug began spitting out three-ounce foam balls the size of a regular baseball.

"When you're hitting off a pitching machine at high velocity, especially if you're getting 80 to 100 swings a day, the last thing you wanna' do is take a full swing on a 95 mph fastball and hit it off the end of the bat," Jason said. "It's extremely painful. Because of that hitters will tend to throttle themselves back. The Smash Factor Ball takes away that pain, that fear of pain."

It was almost quitting time. Maxx fixed a Blast Motion Baseball Swing Analyzer below the knob of J. P.'s bat, which generated a whole other data set of numbers, some of which actually matter. The digital "97" that flashed on an iPad screen measured "early connection," the angle of the bat relative to his spine when his hands start going toward the baseball.

"And the old-school version of this?"

"A batting tee, soft toss, or BP with lots of mechanical cues," Maxx said.

He had shown extraordinary forbearance with my kinetic myopia, answering repeated questions and phone calls, until finally he said, "He's trying to turn his barrel more, sooner, and deeper in the zone."

When J. P. emerged from the cage, I confessed my confusion. "Honestly, I really didn't understand what they were saying at first either," he said, which made me feel lots better.

"The training bats make you uncomfortable in your swing. They work different body parts. One bat, it has all the weight in the barrel, which causes you to control the barrel through the zone. The other bat, all the weight is in the hands, that causes you to control the hands through the zone. One keeps your barrel in check; one keeps your hands in check. And once you get the feel of both of those going at the same time—that's why you switch them off, to get that feel—and you go to the normal bat, it's just a flick of the wrist. It's really easy and the ball's coming off harder with less energy."

"What does it feel like when you square it up?" I asked, knowing it wasn't something he'd experienced often.

"That's when you say, 'Let it eat.'"

That's baseball player for "ready to do some damage."

* * *

In retesting, J. P.'s attack angle vaulted into positive numbers: from -2.9 to 4.7. His bat speed had increased from 65.6 mph to 71.1 mph. His exit velocity had improved from 92 mph to 101 mph. The rotational speed of his pelvis had jumped from the forty-fourth percentile of everyone tested at Driveline to the sixty-ninth percentile. He didn't need to see the numbers. "I just knew," he said.

Then, he got to spring training. "He looked bigger, he looked stronger," Servais said, and he looked terrible at the plate. "I don't know if J. P. hit a single ball hard in spring training. I was very worried. I did not think it was going to work. His mechanics did not look good."

He conferred with Mariners Hitting Coach Jarret DeHart, who counseled patience. "What Driveline does for some players, it gives them an understanding of how their body is supposed to work," he told Servais. "Who knows when it's gonna click?"

Garrett checked in regularly, especially when J. P. got off to a slow start. "Some of your expected numbers look better," Garrett told him. "And you're moving faster, but your attack angle is still really low."

"He was like, 'No way. Wow. All right. Thanks for letting me know.'"

Then, in the second week of April, the Mariners went to Cleveland, and something clicked. It was just one at bat. One swing, really.

CHAPTER 4

YU TOO

It's the elbow, stupid...

Driveline was loudly empty when I arrived the next day. Then I saw Yu Darvish, the elegant but aging San Diego Padres pitcher, skipping merrily across the AstroTurf floor, followed by a waddle of handlers—agent, personal catcher, and assorted others in a row—to the insistent rhythm of Showtek: "This is my life, this is my music... so fuck you!"

Even guys with the moolah to have the place to themselves don't get to pick the music.

He was a vision in Padres brown—except for the white shoes and socks. He looked smaller and trimmer than six feet, five inches and 220 pounds, maybe because he is in such perfect proportion. "If I could build an ideal pitcher, it would probably be somebody like him," said Brandon Mann, the pitching trainer with whom Yu was spending the day.

"To die for," my mother would have said.

High-stepping across the gym, he reminded me of dragonflies skimming the surface of my favorite Cape Cod pond, alighting for only the briefest instant before continuing on their way. He was that graceful, that light on his feet.

Agent and catcher did not skip.

Yu came to rest on a mat to begin warming up. Sitting cross-legged, he began flinging balls at the wall behind him, only backward.

"Ouch," I said to Jason, who was waiting for me in the same cold corner, in the same folding chair, by the same batting cage, where we had met the day before. "It's called a pivot pick," he said. "It constrains the lower half. It isolates the arm path and clears up arm action."

Pitchers come to Driveline chasing velo and RPM, which is what everybody is chasing except maybe me and Yu Darvish. Nearing age thirty-seven, Yu was chasing the fountain of youth.

Mann stood off to the side of the tricked-out cage reviewing data prepared by Driveline analysts. He had arrived at 4:30 a.m. after staying until 11 p.m. the night before. He said he wasn't nervous—the Mets' Kodai Senga had put in a good word—but Darvish was by far his most accomplished pupil. "He's Yu *Freaking* Darvish!" he exclaimed, more than once.

"Baseball's forgotten how to be fun," I moped, surveying the array of bleeping, blinking electronics surrounding the cage, each generating its own particular set of data to be swallowed and parsed upon command.

"One hundred percent," Mann said.

He is a one hundred percent guy.

It's hard to improve someone who is as good as Darvish has been since he left Japan to pitch in America in 2012 and who has as many pitches in his repertoire as anyone in baseball. The analysts had found only a couple areas of potential improvement. "The late movement profile on his split was second-lowest in MLB," Mann said. "There's maybe two that can scale up."

Scaling up became a thing when everything became measurable.

"He's the only pitcher in the major leagues that uses seven different pitches at least 5 percent of the time but his usages on some of those pitches are a little low," Mann said.

Which is like having too many white foods on your plate.

He's always experimenting, constantly on the lookout for something newer and cooler. "If *you* had a grip he'd try it," catcher Peter Summerville told me. I wasn't sure I liked his implication.

As Yu pushed aside the black netting, Springsteen's "Glory Days" boomeranged around the gym, which seemed a bit unkind. Then Pat Benatar commanded: "Hit Me With Your Best Shot," and Yu complied. Climbing atop the plywood and Astroturf pitching mound, he launched his body forward.

I had no idea what he was throwing, but even from twenty feet away, even through three skeins of overlapping netting, it was mesmerizing. Balanced for an instant on his back right leg, hovering above a pretend pitching mound, Yu stopped time.

And it wasn't even the real deal. Mann had imposed a speed limit (84–87 mph) and a pitch limit (sixty) to minimize the stress on his arm.

An Edgertronic camera mounted on the wall behind his head tracked the ball from his release point to its intended destination, taking super-slow-motion video that allowed him to see how the ball came out of his hand, how his grip related to the desired spin of the pitch. He paused after every delivery to check the screen while Mann demonstrated the optimal seam orientation to achieve more arm-side run. Holding a ball aloft, Mann turned his wrist this way and that like a kid making shadow puppets on a wall.

"They're talking about angles at release," Jason said, hunched intently in his chair.

A look of wonder followed by despair came over his face. "Oh, my God, we're watching Yu Darvish develop a splitter," he whispered.

* * *

Unlike Yu Darvish, I never had a splitter with or without unique characteristics. What I had was a Long Island driveway clotted with bluestone pebbles, because my mother liked the way the color contrasted with the truly shocking pink she had painted the house. The only vaguely normal part of the tableau was the black garage door.

It was divided into nine squares, like a heat map, though nobody knew what that was when I dug my P. F. Flyers sneakers into the stones and went into my windup, thinking not about command or control but, "How could she do this to me?"

I pretended I was Ryne Duren, the myopic Yankees reliever who had trouble locating the plate and scared the shit out of every batter he faced. I'd like to imagine this is how Yu started—alone with a ball, a target, and determination.

Darvish is as exceptional as he is typical. Exceptional in his craft, he is typical of the way baseball elbows are shredding like cabbage in a Sunday slaw. He had Tommy John surgery in 2015, and arthroscopic surgery three years later due to an inflammatory reaction in his elbow, which is what you get before the elbow tears again.

Pitching is an unnatural act, one of the few missing from the Bible. Probably that's because back in the day, chucking rocks and hurling spears at max heave was a matter of survival and not something you were likely to do one hundred times in a day. "Unlike today's hurlers, those cavemen were heaving their projectiles upward," said Dr. Jeffrey R. Dugas, orthopedist at the Andrews Sports Medicine and Orthopaedic Center Clinic in Birmingham, named for his mentor, Dr. James Andrews. "They weren't throwing 'em down. They weren't throwing from a mound and weren't winding up to make it more emphatic."

The change in trajectory and today's max heave imperative to throw every pitch as hard as humanly possible can turn big-league arms into roadkill, candidates for one of the three surgeries now available to repair or replace the ulnar collateral ligament. "It's an epidemic we have grotesquely failed to control or to even make a dent in," said Dugas, a member of an elite group of sports orthopedists for whom the elbow is a cause and a career. "By we, I mean we in baseball and we in health care. Despite multiple decades of knowledge and experience, it's not going in the right direction."

On the fiftieth anniversary of the original Tommy John surgery performed by Dodgers team doctor Frank Jobe on September 25, 1974, independent baseball analyst Jon Roegele posted a list on social media of all the Tommy John pitchers he'd been able to document since that inaugural procedure. Darvish was one of the 2,547 baseball professionals to bear a telltale UCL scar—that included major and minor leaguers, as well as signed draftees and seven veterans of the Little League World Series. Among them were 151 pitchers to have had "revisions," a nice medical word that obviates the pain of a second surgery and the reality that only 72 percent of revisionists are able to return to play at any level, MLB says, and only 59 percent return to the same level of play.

Roegele calculated that 38.8 percent of pitchers active in 2024 or on the Injured List had had elbow surgery. And that's bupkis compared to the 240 minor leaguers who fell into the same category. What MLB benignly calls "elbow-induced Injured List placements" have tripled since 2005 when it was still the Disabled List and the number of days spent on that list has soared from about 12,000 to 32,000, according to an MLB chart. Two thirds of the one billion dollars that teams paid injured players not to play were the result of arm injuries. No wonder manager Ron Washington says, "I'm tired of money sitting on the bench."

But the cost cannot be measured in dollars or personal travail alone. This self-inflicted, industrywide wound bolloxes the wiring of fandom. You can't root for guys who aren't there.

* * *

So, what precisely is killing all the elbows?

I consulted Jim Palmer, the Hall of Famer, who was twenty years old when he beat Sandy Koufax in Game Two of the 1966 World

Series, the last game of Koufax's career, cut short at age thirty by traumatic arthritis in his left elbow that couldn't have been repaired by Tommy John surgery had it even been available.

Those guys threw more often, more innings and more pitches. Not that a lot of pitchers back in the day of four-man rotations weren't abused and discarded. "Sure seems like the less they throw, the more they get hurt," I said.

Kind of like certain private schools in Washington, DC, where the more you pay, the less your kids go to class.

"They're throwing less and they're babied more," Jim said. "They have physical wellness and mental wellness. They have hygiene and diet. They have their quiet time. I've been told that they need their two and a half hours of quiet time."

Koufax had a tub of ice, a sleeve made from an inner tube, and three cans of beer chilling beside his elbow. Ice was newly recognized as a treatment for inflammation. He timed the polar plunge by how long it took him to drink the beer.

"Is it the velo, Jim?" I asked.

Palmer answered with a story about a visit to the Diamondbacks where he watched a hot, young phenom throw to former Orioles catcher Caleb Joseph. "He threw thirty pitches and when he finishes, he goes right over to the iPad and asked the young pitching instructor, 'What do you think?' And the guy goes, 'God, your spin rates were great, the shape of your pitches was fabulous.'

"And then he turned to Caleb and said, 'What do you think?' Caleb said, 'I thought you really sucked. You hit my glove twice in thirty-five pitches.'"

"Is it the RPM, Jim?"

"Like we didn't know what spin rate was?"

"What about the pitch clock?"

Palmer replied, as is his wont, with a winding tale about a winding drive through Tom Seaver's vineyard in Calistoga, California, the town where I was once held hostage in a mud bath. Pitcher Steve Trachsel went along for the ride with Palmer. "When we get to the top, Seaver is standing at the front door screaming, 'Trachsel, throw the fucking ball!' Because Trachsel was *really* slow. If you're any good, you throw in fifteen seconds."

"Is it because they took away their Spider Tack?"

That's the foul-smelling gunk created to give the strong men who chuck 353-pound Atlas Stones for fun in Strongmen competitions a way to hold 'em until they chuck 'em.

"I have a friend who's a cardiologist," Jim said. "I said to him, 'If you used something to hold onto the scalpel during a valve replacement surgery, and all of a sudden they told you, 'You can't use it.' How would that go?'

"He says, 'It wouldn't end well.'"

"Is it the ball?" I asked.

Jim demurred. "I've never thrown it."

Neither has Dugas but he treats major league pitchers who have. "All the pitchers that I've talked to this year—and I've had a slew of them—are saying the balls are like pearls, they're too smooth," he said. "They decreased the height of the seams a while back. They'll tell you they're having to put a lot more finger pressure on the ball to get spin rate. As you decrease the tack on the ball, the pitchers are going to have to find a way to compete. They're not just going to sit there and say, 'Oh, well.' So that's where the development of the sweepers came from."

"Is it the designer pitches, the sweeper and the power change?"

Ben McDonald, Palmer's partner on Orioles telecasts, and the number one pick in the 1989 draft, noticed one day that Dean Kremer's sweeper had gone missing. "After the game, I was like, 'Dude, you didn't throw any sweepers today.' He said, 'I'm not throwing it anymore. I'm doing some things to try to create this spin and to create some shapes that are not natural to what my arm typically does. It bothers my elbow when I try to create the right to left in it."

Keith Meister, team doctor of the Texas Rangers, gave team podcasters an explanation. "The power change demands a tremendous amount of down vertical movement. Guys are dramatically and forcefully turning over the ball into what we call pronated position and trying to create arm-side run. And it does that in an incredibly efficient way, but it also does that with creating a huge amount of stress on the inner side of the elbow. I can look at an MRI scan and almost predict the way they're throwing a baseball because of the pattern of injury."

The result, Dugas said, "We're seeing more extensively injured UCLs."

It's a risk lots of aspiring pitchers are willing to take. It's a risk Brandon Mann would have taken. Sixteen years after he was drafted, after pitching in 342 minor league, independent league, and Japanese league games, he had a demitasse in The Show in 2018. He made his big league debut in a pink uniform on Mother's Day and was done seven games later. "They have a short time to make money in this game," he said. "They're going to take that chance, one hundred percent."

No doubt, the multiplicity of surgical options now available factors into their thinking. In traditional Tommy John surgery, the severed ligament is replaced with a tendon woven into a bone tunnel. That was the standard of care until 2013 when Dugas, then medical director at ASMI, pioneered an internal brace using plastic anchors, tape, and a suture to repair what remains of the UCL, a procedure that can halve the 12–14 month recovery time from traditional TJ. Five years later, Keith Meister pioneered a hybrid surgery marrying the two techniques, which he performed on Shohei Ohtani in 2023. "That's the game changer," said Glenn Fleisig, director of biomechanics research at the American Sports Medicine Institute in Birmingham, Alabama.

"If there were no surgery to correct the problems, then you'd have people approaching it differently," Buck Showalter said. "But they can go in there, supposedly fix it, get paid while they're on the IL, then come back and pitch until it blows again."

Palmer and Koufax pitched in four-man rotations compared to today's five-, sometimes six-man staffs in which the standard of care is a one hundred pitch limit, first advocated by James Andrews. Palmer threw the first of his 211 complete games at Fenway Park in April 1966. He threw 177 pitches that day and hit a home run too. After the game, someone said to Orioles Pitching Coach Harry Brecheen, "'Harry, that's a lot of pitches,'" Palmer recalled. "Harry says, 'Yeah, we wanna get that pitch count down into the 140s.'"

He missed most of the 1967 season and all of 1968 because of shoulder surgery. The Orioles left him unprotected in the 1968 expansion draft. The Kansas City Royals and Seattle Pilots passed on him.

But here's the thing, Jim says. "These guys will never ever experience what the great pitchers of the past experienced. Try getting Rice, Yastrzemski, and Fisk out in Fenway Park when you're throwing 140, 150, 160, 180 pitches with a one-run lead.

"You wanna learn how smart you are? You wanna learn how big your heart is? You wanna learn how well-conditioned you are? These guys never ever have to do that. It was what you got paid for: Dig down or mix stuff up. Keep people off balance. Use all your wits."

That baseball is gone.

Jim said, "My question is: What is the effect on fans?"

* * *

Nothing much surprises Dave Wallace, pitching coach emeritus for the Red Sox, Dodgers, Mets, Orioles, and Braves (twice). It's quite the resume, but it's not the best thing about him. The best thing about him is he's a guy who brings a ball and a glove to dinner at a beach bar just in case. (I didn't bring mine.) On this occasion, he also brought a good dose of old-fashioned outrage. "Do you know we don't play catch anymore?" he demanded. "We 'catch play'! I gotta go out and 'catch play.'"

This was in February 2023. He said without prompting that he'd heard from five pitchers who'd signed contracts with the Tampa Bay Rays that they were told up front: "Here's what's gonna happen. You're gonna come in. You're gonna throw every fucking ball as hard as you can. And when you break, we'll get someone else."

Rays Manager Kevin Cash didn't blanch when I repeated the story. "Kyle Snyder, our pitching coach, he really says it best. 'It's like they're doing a full deadlift every time they release a ball.' They're trying to maximize every ounce, every pound, every muscle in their body to get to 98 instead of 97, and you're asking 'em to recover quicker and get rid of the ball quicker."

As an advisor to Major League Baseball, USA Baseball, and Little League, Glenn Fleisig, otherwise known as the "Biomechanics Man," has tested 5,000 pitching arms in his lab in Birmingham. Every time an elite pitcher throws the ball, the shoulder rotates seven thousand degrees per second. "That's like a wheel turning at over 65 miles an hour," he said.

Every time a pitcher squares to face home plate his arm cocked in a layback position with his body moving in opposite directions is a moment of extremis, when opposing forces create peak torque in the elbow. The painter R.B. Kitaj captured its brutality in an oil painting of Koufax in the collection of the Los Angeles County Museum of Art—squinched, lips pursed, his features distorted by the force of the effort, he looks like an old person who's lost all the fat beneath the flesh.

"The force on the shoulder and elbow required to stop your arm from going back farther and get it going forward is equivalent to holding five–twelve-pound bowling balls in the palm of your hand," Glenn said. "And then after you let go of the ball, it's as if someone is trying to pull your arm out of your shoulder socket with 200 pounds of force."

Just listening to him made my shoulder ache, which is part of the problem. "If you can't dissipate the force through the shoulder, the next stop on the train is the elbow," Dugas said.

"So, how come they're not all hurt?" I asked Dave Wallace.

He had just returned from visiting Bob Keyes, owner of Bio-Kinetics Research and Development in Utah, and author of the aptly named *Pitching Biomechanics* with Nolan Ryan's skeleton on the cover. Ryan worked with Keyes and his UCL somehow lasted 27 big league seasons. Bob says the problem is that current training methods have broken the kinetic chain, that stream of elastic energy that travels upward from your pins through the large muscles of the core and gets dispersed through the shoulder to the elbow, the hand, and off the fingertips. It requires a solid foundation—big legs and a big butt. Dave and Bob and Buck are old enough to remember when pitchers ran "poles" on the warning track—in spikes!—with coaches tossing balls in front of them to urge them on.

"Now people are out there creating the most ridiculous unimaginable ways to throw," Bob said, "which is anatomically impossible for the body to work. Throwing from one knee. Throwing a shot put into a trampoline or into a wall thinking, 'More is better.'

"When you practice against the kinematic chain enough, thinking you make your arm real strong, then add your body back in, you've trained the body to work out of its natural sequence. What ends up happening is the joint stress outputs are increased and the force outputs are decreased."

That's because pitching has become more science than art. "Hopefully we can get back to being an art," Dave said. "The science-based information is great but it's become the sole measuring stick of how we evaluate players. And my question is, from a pitching standpoint, how do you teach it?"

* * *

I was watching Brandon Mann teach it.

"What's that?" I asked Jason, pointing to a large monitor mounted on the wall beside the cage. The screen was filled with an odd constellation of multicolored octagons ranging from dark blue to red to pink to an orange-ish hue the color of Donald Trump's hair when it needs to be dyed. It was labeled "Right-Handed Fastballs from 94.5–95.5 mph Current Mvmt. Profile, Current Stuff+ of 113."

That was Yu's Blob, created by Driveline's Blob app, which is available to the public, as is most of their research, for free. "It's called the Blob because it just looks like a big blob basically," Jason said. "The Blob grades how unique your pitches are and how well they would perform on the field."

Jason pointed to a trail of octagons marching across the screen. "The further away from the middle, the better the pitch is. Because essentially that's what good pitches are, a deviation from the average. That's what guys are chasing in this pitch design process—unique characteristics that throw off a hitter's perception, whether that's the rise on a fastball or the sweep on a slider."

That reminded me of the night Cristian Javier of the Astros beat the Phillies in Game Four of the 2022 World Series. Javier was a great story, a story I knew how to tell—he had been a pitcher for all of three years when the Astros signed him out of the Dominican Republic for $10,000 at the advanced (baseball) age of eighteen. During the pandemic, he practiced his delivery on a weedy dirt path in the woods, throwing to a shoeless catcher. His father, who had never seen him pitch in the majors, was at the ballpark that night. His mother predicted that he would pitch a no-hitter. That's a story I could have written but it wasn't the story of the game.

It was a showcase for old and new baseball. The game was old-world in that it featured a dominant starting pitcher who relied primarily on his fastball. Fastballs have gone out of fashion in the era of stuff. Of his ninety-seven pitches, seventy were fastballs. He struck out nine.

It was new age in that old-soul Astros Manager Dusty Baker took Javier out of the game leading 5–0, having thrown less than a hundred pitches in six innings of no-hit baseball, a decision no one questioned. Three equally untouchable relief pitchers followed, collaborating on what the morning papers hailed as the first World Series no-hitter since Don Larsen threw a perfect game for the Yankees all by himself in 1956.

It was a thing of beauty, yes, but as Joel Sherman wrote in the *New York Post*. "There's a difference between a team allowing no hits and a no-hitter."

Indeed. Such an effort deserves a name of its own. "Half-assed" will do.

I thought Jason was going to be there and wanted to know if he saw it the way I did. I didn't know that he had just left the Phillies and had tickets for another game.

On the mound that night at The Bank, with a red roar reaching 105 decibels, Javier was implacable—his motion the consummate expression of biomechanical efficiency, beginning with a barely perceptible shift of his weight on the first base side of the pitching rubber. His fastball wasn't that fast; at 93.4 mph, it was three tenths of a second slower than the average 2022 fastball. His spin rate was good, not great. His delivery, as compact as his body, looked almost effortless until you saw the force with which his front right leg whipped around his midsection on his follow-through.

The secret to Javier's success, I learned the next morning from analytically savvy auteurs' coverage, was a new metric called vertical approach angle (VAA). That's like launch angle only from the other direction, the angle at which the ball approaches home plate. Pitchers with extremely high arm slots have high VAAs, and others, like Javier, with lower arm angles have low VAAs.

Because of the way the ball came out of his hand, moving east to west as opposed to Koufax's over-the-top, north-south delivery, his fastball crossed home plate three inches higher than the average fastball, disappearing from the plane of expectation formed by a batter's muscle memory. I have to say I felt a little jealous of their knowledge. I didn't tell Jason that when I finally caught up with him. Instead, I bragged. "That's why the Astros catcher Martín Maldonado called it the 'invisi-ball.'"

"Exactly," he said. "That's the illusion."

* * *

Driveline spawned a whole cottage industry of boutique coaches and training centers and proprietary team labs dedicated to scaling up the spin on your spin, the velo on your velo, the tilt on your tilt. Spencer Strider, the 2022 *Sporting News* Rookie of the Year, spent the following winter at Maven Baseball Lab in Atlanta learning to throw a devastating curveball to go with his devastating fastball and slider. "He's like a studio lab rat," said Dodgers Manager Dave Roberts. "They just kind of *made* him."

It didn't take long for Kyle Boddy to be imitated—and criticized—for using weighted balls to increase the heft of your heave, described as a form of ballistics training intended to enhance muscle strength and endurance at max intensity. "Back in the day it was like, 'You're either born with 90 or not,'" trainer Maxx Garrett said. "Kyle challenged that and put training protocols in place where you can actually train velocity."

The average 2024 MLB fastball traveled at a pull-me-over-$150-speeding-ticket-level speed of 94.3 mph, three miles an hour faster than it did when Kyle Boddy began writing a blog called Driveline Mechanics in 2008. When I mentioned this to Buck Showalter he harrumphed. I had never actually heard a harrumph before, but this was definitely a harrumph. Buck is not a fan of weighted ball training. "At what price for the player? At what price for baseball? You can't sell your soul to the game because guys who should be pitching 32 games a year are pitching three times."

The laws of physics are immutable. All the technology in the world can't change that. "It's still just a white baseball coming at you, right?"

said Rob Gray, professor in the Polytechnic School at Arizona State University. "You can't make a baseball break in any different ways than you used to, but you can teach how to make it break. The way that you can take an average pitcher and make their pitches play off each other now to give more gyro spin, you couldn't do that in the past."

Thanks to the thousands of data points—grips, angles, finger pressure points—stored in Driveline's massive digital archive, a trainer can show a covetous pitcher how to throw Griffin Jax's slider, which spins at 2800–3000 RPM. "We know how much that pitch moves, the velocity that it gets thrown at, the spin axis, and the efficiency of the ball, which is basically the tilt of the pitch after it's thrown," Mann said. "Then it's basically trial and error with the video until they get closer to it or better."

Which is why Yu stopped to confer after every pitch.

"Historically, pitchers have had to use subjective feedback from a coach or a catcher or hitters," Jason said, as Yu resumed throwing. "That's like what I did when I played in college. Like, 'Oh, I'm gonna try this new pitch.' And then you throw it in two or three starts, and that's your feedback. Whereas now they can do it in two pitches."

Whoa! Two pitches? It seemed improbable to my untutored eye that anyone, including" Yu "Freaking" Darvish, could master a new pitch in one pitch design session. Jason shook his head. "With these top talents, their body awareness and their ability to make adjustments and replicate the changes is their superpower."

This kind of practice with rep by rep feedback in real time may make perfect but maybe not inside the human elbow. Fleisig was intrigued by new MLB research showing a spike in UCL injuries during spring training and at the beginning of the season, suggesting that intensive training during the off-season when the sane thing would be to take time off is complicit in the epidemic. Orel Hershiser, who knows a thing or two about longevity, having set a record for 59 consecutive scoreless innings in 1988, told the Dodgers podcast *Talk Dodgers to Me*, "I think the injuries are really coming from the [fact that] practice is too hard. They know in super slow-mo what your fingers did and they know with that release point how much spin was created and what the angle of the spin was and then how the ball broke vertically and horizontally. And they can tell you that your six inches of break and your six inches of run is not enough. 'We need eight depth and six will be fine this way' And every time I change the grip it changes the pressure here, here, here, here.'"

He pointed to potential trouble spots from wrist to elbow to shoulder. "Now I want to do it at full velocity because I want to see what my spin's going to be like and what my pitch break's going to be like in the game. And if I can get the measurements that actually gets the ball off the barrel, then I'm going to go win a Cy Young Award."

So, the old guys are right?

"Correct," Fleisig said. "They knew what they were talking about when they say that training, particularly in spring training, is off."

Jason bristled when I repeated some of what I'd heard. "Weighted balls and bats work," Jason said. "Period. We're in the business of making players as good as possible within the rules of the game. And I think sometimes we're a wrong target for people that don't like the current baseball. It's like, 'fucking analytics and Driveline.'

"We're just trying to win, period. And if we want baseball to change the rules, then we'll adjust. We've evolved to optimize development for players in the game as it currently exists."

Or, as Mann says, "Hey, it works."

One hundred percent.

* * *

When the league considered lowering the pitching mound, as it did in 1969, or relocating the mound, last moved in 1893, to reduce stress on the arm and goose offense, they consulted Fleisig. Research suggested that the former wouldn't help the arm and the latter wouldn't hurt it unless the mound was pushed back at least two feet, maybe three.

A displaced New Yorker and beleaguered Mets fan, back when the Mets were particularly beleaguering—anyone seen Noah Syndergaard or Matt Harvey lately?—Fleisig has spent decades observing, admiring, and testing the best-known ligament in the human body. The ulnar collateral ligament is a one-inch strip of tissue the approximate width of one of those orange rubber bands affixed to lobster claws so they can't pinch you on their way into the boiling water.

It isn't meant to survive 100 mph fastballs either—of which there were 2,783 chucked in 2024.

What is baseball to do?

"Major League Baseball has leaked to the press a few possible things they are considering," Fleisig said. "You have to go six innings, or you can only have so many pitchers on your roster, or when the starting pitcher comes out, you don't have a DH anymore."

These trial balloons have not exactly soared.

"The ideal solution is to go back to a generation ago or one hundred years ago where pitchers varied their effort," he said. "If there's bases loaded, maybe you need to rear back and throw as hard as you can. But if the bases are empty, maybe you don't throw every pitch as hard as you can. That's the message we've been trying to get out."

Message sent. Message ignored.

Weary of sounding like a Cassandra issuing apocalyptic warnings—"the issue is throwing *all* pitches at *full* effort and throwing *a lot* of them"—Fleisig purchased twenty human arms from the cadavers of men in their twenties and thirties for dissection. He wanted to get a closeup look at the UCL and find out "whether bigger dead people have stronger Tommy John ligaments and whether it is proportional to body size.

"It turns out those little rubber bands don't seem to be bigger and stronger than the ulnar collateral ligaments of previous generations. So *that's* the problem. We have the old-model ulnar collateral ligament and new and improved humans!"

Legislating how hard to throw a baseball is almost as problematic as legislating morality but it can be done. "We *learned* how to pitch at 95 percent effort and hold back for when we needed it," said Tom Glavine, Hall of Fame practitioner of the ancient art of survival. "If you had to go there, you went there, but you went there four or five times a game."

Glavine was a member of the sublime Atlanta Braves rotation that flourished under pitching coach Leo Mazzone. As Leo recalls it, his top four starters made 537 starts in the years 1991 through 1993 without missing a turn because of injury. Team records don't go back that far but all four made more than thirty starts in each of those seasons.

"Today's pitching pretty much insults my intelligence," Leo said. "One year after he retired, Greg Maddux asked if he could talk to our young pitchers in spring training. He said, 'You know why I'm a millionaire? Because I can put my fastball where I want to. You know why I got beachfront property in LA? Because I can change speeds.' End of conversation."

Today, they'd laugh at him.

* * *

When the design session was over and it was clear Yu wasn't of a mind to talk, Jason and I went to find Brandon, who was at his desk manically texting grips and cues to Yu's agent. I said I had learned to like being able to explain things with his numbers; that you could teach a future Hall of Famer how to throw a new splitter in two hours with those numbers. I also said, "I hate that they dictate the way the game is played."

"Yeah," Brandon replied. "One hundred percent."

He was feeling good until I mentioned Maddux. He and Jason rolled their eyes in unison. *No way Maddux could play today. You know how many strikes he got off the plate?*

"He would've given up about nine runs if he was pitching now," Brandon said. "Because that 88-mph sinker's getting fucking crushed because he has to throw it over the plate now."

On the other hand, he still has his birth elbow.

"I don't think people realize that the game's changed," Brandon said. "These players are eight thousand times better."

"So change the strike zone," I said.

"If you go east-west, more strikeouts will even happen," he replied. "Stuff is too good. You either shrink the strike zone to lean into more offense and what ends up happening is now pitchers are going four innings versus five innings as starters. Because the strike zone's even smaller, walks will just go way up and games are even longer and what kind of offense is that?"

"Okay," I said. "No pitcher may be removed from a game during an inning unless or until he has been charged with a run allowed in that inning."

Force them to power down by forcing them to stay longer in the game.

"So that's interesting," he replied. "The only issue is workload management. So, if we were gonna go to that rule, you have to expand the rosters."

I wasn't ready to divulge my grand plan for bolstering the pitching staff while decreasing the number of pitchers available for each game. So I suggested this instead: "How about a rule that any starting pitcher removed before pitching six innings or giving up four runs is ineligible to appear in a game for five days."

"That's gonna make everyone else get hurt," said Driveline's youth impresario Deven Morgan, who joined the conversation just as Jason excused himself to meet the guys transporting his car to the Red Sox spring training camp in Fort Myers.

Before he got called up to The Show, Jason liked to sit alone outside the cage during pitch design sessions to see what he was up against. Every time, he came away thinking, “Oh, shit.”

What’s a hitting coach to do?

He thinks the future lies not in swinging from your ass but in bat-to-ball skills, putting the ball in play. The best outcome, he says, is a hard line drive. He reminded me, in case I had forgotten, that strikeouts have exceeded hits every year since 2018.

As Crash Davis told Nick Laloosh in *Bull Durham*: *Strikeouts are boring! Besides that, they’re fascist. Throw some ground balls—it’s more democratic.*

“If you really want to solve for the strikeout issue, they’re going to have to change the baseball to change the physics so that balls don’t move as much or go as fast,” Jason said. “To me, that’s the solution.”

Sounded good to me. “On the condition that players get to sample the options like brides and grooms at cake tastings.”

I once watched the Phillies’ official ball mudder, a lovely guy named Danny O’Rourke, manager of Equipment and Umpire Services, apply Lena Blackburne Baseball Rubbing Mud (sourced from the banks of a tributary of the Delaware River) while squatting in a truncated, Airstream-style humidor mandated by MLB in 2022 to ensure uniformity. At his side: an Official MLB Lucite Box containing one unmudded, one over-mudded, and one perfectly mudded ball for mud guidance.

Maybe the mudding guidance and humidors are working. I haven’t read many recent complaints about the ball. MLB tested a “universal tack” for two years in Double A, made with the help of Dow Chemical, but is not currently pursuing the project. Nor has there been any recent scuttlebutt about creating a new pre-tacked ball like the one used in Japan’s NPB league.

But "the little Tommy John Ligament," as Fleisig calls it with endearing familiarity, continues to pop and shred. Jon Roegele, whose TJ database is relied upon industry-wide, added thirty-eight names in the first five and a half months of 2025.

By the time I caught up with Jason in the spring of 2025, Darvish was back on the IL because of inflammation in his elbow, where he had taken up residence for large swathes of the 2023 and 2024 seasons. Spencer Strider, who underwent Tommy John surgery in 2019, had an internal brace inserted in his elbow in April 2024. Cristian Javier had Tommy John surgery two months later, the same week his teammate José Urquidy had a revision.

Acknowledging a problem—or if you're a scientist like Fleisig proving what is and is not the problem—is always the first step in finding a solution. I was gobsmacked when I heard Kyle Boddy Himself tell the hosts of a British baseball podcast called *Bat Flips and Nerds,* "Elbow injuries seem to be very difficult to solve. If it were the case that these motion capture labs and biomechanics labs and stuff we're working on could impact elbow injuries in a positive way, it hasn't happened yet. And so we need to do something completely different. And that's what we've been working on for about eight years, and we've been failing at for eight years. We have a new model of thinking about biomechanics, which we're pretty close on."

In the meantime I kept pestering Jason with ideas. "What about making any pitch clocked at more than 95 mph an automatic ball?" I asked.

I was sworn not to divulge the identity of the MLB honcho who shared this brainstorm.

Jason was speechless, which made me nervous. "And then you let them throw one pitch above 95 mph so the hitter never knows what's coming when."

Jason listened. I give him props for that. Then he laughed. "You're crazy—but I still love you."

CHAPTER 5

MAKING GOD LAUGH

Can the old school make nice with the new school?

The manager's office at Clover Park, winter home of the New York Mets, has the *je ne sais quoi* aesthetic of impermanence common to county facilities built with cinder block and appointed with what appeared to be rent-to-buy furniture.

Impermanence is the nature of employment for major-league managers. Sooner or later, someone else will occupy your chair. The skipper of the St. Lucie Mets Single-A team would have it when the Mets headed north for the season.

In early February 2023, Buck Showalter's future seemed assured. Surely, the Most Expensive Team in Major League History would go to the World Series, and Showalter would finally get his ring. But on the day before the regulars were scheduled to report, the reigning National League Manager of the Year, whose club had won 101 games in 2022, had a cold. Which as things played out would be the least of his problems.

The Amazins had not yet reinvented the June swoon as they would later that season, and big-pockets owner Steve Cohen had not yet invented Tanking for Billionaires—paying the Texas Rangers and the

Houston Astros to take aging Max Scherzer and Justin Verlander and their combined $78 million in salary off his hands and secure better prospects in return. So Showalter was busy planning the team talent show. As one does.

"You can learn a lot about a guy from a talent show," Buck said, like when Kodai Senga, the rookie Japanese pitcher, sang a Disney song in English. Or when Ryan Flaherty with the Baltimore Orioles rented two monkeys and had them throw batting practice to each other. It got Buck in trouble with the Humane Society, but it was worth it.

Buck was wishing he hadn't quit piano lessons with Mrs. Loveless and was reminiscing about the summer he won the Cape League batting title with a .434 batting average and the Most Valuable Player award. Ruefully, he accepted my congratulations on being recently voted "the sexiest manager in baseball."

"Look who I had to beat—Dusty and Tito," he said, referring to Baker in Houston and Francona in Cleveland.

Between them, the three pretty boys would have seventy-one years of combined managerial experience by the end of the 2023 season, which is no longer a recommendation or a guarantee of a job in Major League Baseball. Before 2024 dawned, Buck had been fired, Tito had retired, and Dusty, tired of being second-guessed by "the people upstairs," showed himself the door. Steve Cohen's corporate PR team would give Showalter the opportunity to announce his own firing. "Let me get this straight. I'm going to go down to announce I'm not coming back? Does anybody else find this strange?"

But before all that could happen, I wanted to ask Showalter how a sexy old coot such as himself managed analytics.

"You ever seen these Lindor chocolates?" he said, holding up a tiny foil-wrapped square of chocolate. "His daughter's coming tomorrow, and I got to have a Lindor chocolate for her."

Kalina Lindor, the ineffably effervescent two-year-old daughter of all-star shortstop Francisco Lindor, had last been seen in her daddy's lap searching the press room for the skipper after a Mets win during the 2022 playoffs.

"Papa? Where Buck?"

"She's a beauty," Buck told me. "And his wife is playing in our talent show."

He wasn't avoiding my question. He was answering it.

Bit by bit, predictive analytics devoured managerial prerogative and authority. Like Pac-Man eating the Power Pellets. It was one thing to use data to look for bargains like my mother pawing through the return rack at Loehmann's, but a whole other thing when the quest shifted from identifying talent to developing talent to deploying talent on the field and in the lineup, to rewarding talent for playing algorithm baseball, none of which is the purview of today's field manager.

"They don't really need your input. It's the ongoing castration of the American manager. The idea now is the manager runs the clubhouse. There's a guy for everything else. It's the only thing they think they can't do."

When a valued relief pitcher, Trevor May, melted down over the death of his cat and couldn't pitch for three days—that was in Buck's portfolio. "I couldn't tell the media that. So, I had to wear it. 'Why didn't you use Trevor May?' Was I supposed to say because his cat died?"

When Buck took himself to the Fall Instructional League to see the top Mets prospects, the muckety-mucks wanted to know, "What are you going there for?" "Hell, I got a ring about ten feet from me from the Yankees for winning Instructional League. That's how important it was. Now it's, 'What are you going to tell us that we don't know?'

"And if I said something that contradicted what their analytical evaluation was, it drove them fucking crazy and they hated that."

* * *

Daily-ness is baseball's defining characteristic, the source of bragging rights in professional sports. "This ain't a football game, we do this every day," Earl Weaver used to say. In the analytic age, that means every day brings a supermoon tidal wave of numbers to parse and dice and give up their inner truths.

Sometimes it seems the players exist just to generate more data.

I was gratified to learn that I'm not alone in that thought. Christina Kahrl, sports editor of the *San Francisco Chronicle*, who is a lot smarter than me, asks, "How did we get to this place where effectively people who don't play the game, but 'game it,' use it as an entertainment and then project the entertainment they've created back onto the original source?"

Obsolete metrics clutter baseball cyberspace like so much space junk orbiting the earth: Player Win Averages, Clutch Hitting Index, Win Shares, Linear Weights, WARP, VORP, MLEs, Brock2, Total Player Rating (TPR), Total Pitcher Index (TPI), Tom Boswell's Total Average because even when the subject was numerical, the writing was unsurpassed, and my personal favorite, just because I like saying it, Bill James's Pythagorean Winning Percentage.

Batting Average? Banished from Steve Cohen's 17,400-square-foot video board at Citi Field in favor of OPS—On-Base Plus Slugging—which frankly is also passé and surely will be replaced by a succession of proprietary versions of WAR (Wins Above Replacement) or something better.

Did I mention that I got a 320 on my math GRE when you got two hundred points for signing your name?

"Like the abbreviations . . ." Buck shuddered.

Or maybe he just had to sneeze.

Back in Baltimore, when he managed the Orioles at the dawn of the analytic revolution, Buck dispatched his right-hand man, Dom Chiti, to the front office to prepare a class on Analytics for Dummies for the coaching staff. "They go, 'DZR ratings, UZR.' I go, 'Stop, what does that stand for?' I don't care whether I look stupid or not."

Per the MLB glossary: "UZR quantifies a player's entire defensive performance by attempting to measure how many runs a defender saved. It takes into account errors, range, outfield arm and double-play ability."

My favorites are ones like xwOBA—Expected Weighted On-Base Average, which, according to the glossary, uses "a player's real-world data to *project* quality of contact instead of the actual outcomes."

So, basically, what a similarly struck ball with the same exit velocity and launch angle might have accomplished had it not been caught by the shortstop.

"We went over every abbreviation, had them take the cloak and dagger off of it. In other words, quit making it be the enemy," Buck said. "I said, 'Dom, show us what it means, tell us what it does, tell us what it doesn't do that can only be gotten from down on the field.' And what happened? These guys [coaches] start embracing it and saying, 'Oh, this is all it is? Okay. I got it.'

"I use this stuff to verify what my gut tells me. When the numbers agree with your eyes, then you really got something you can trust."

When Showalter returned to New York to manage the Mets in 2022, twenty-seven years after leaving the Yankees, he asked analyst Jack Bredeson, a former Driveline guy, to prepare a cheat sheet.

"Like Jankowski. How do you evaluate Jankowski?"

That would be Travis Jankowski, who played in forty-three games for the Mets in 2022. "I call them 'come to the rescue guys.' They'll come in and play as a utility infielder for two days, or for the backup catcher, and they bring an energy to the team. Those guys are key, and they have to have a certain makeup and a certain mentality. They gotta know who they are—the best fourth outfielder.

"He didn't fit a statistical evaluation that they wanted, and they thought they could get other people. He could play all three outfield positions. He could pinch-run. He could play a day or two and bring great energy. I said, 'Just sign the fucking guy.'"

* * *

Metric by metric, algorithm by algorithm, analytics asserted its prerogative, like the man-eating Tsavo lions in *Bwana Devil*, constructing rosters and lineups, setting the defense, and leveraging the angle on your swing and the pronation of your wrist. How you play, where you play, who gets to play, and, inevitability, how much you get paid to play.

The speed with which data supplanted judgment is astonishing, a point made forcibly by writer Will Carroll at the 2024 SABR Analytics Conference: "We have the spin rate of every single college pitcher, what their ball does and how much it spins, but not a single pitch from Nolan Ryan."

The degradation of Black-Ink statistics produces red-faced howls of rage from survivors of that generation for whom hitting .300 and not striking out meant something.

Take George Brett, the first player in major-league history to win batting titles in three decades and also to publicly discuss his hemorrhoids. "Nobody gives a shit about batting average anymore," he said, baby blues bulging with anger. "Do they give out Silver [Slugger Award] bats for OPS now? Tell me who led the league in OPS in 1986?"

The answer is Don Mattingly, George.

"And the greatest thing was you could compare your stats against every era. That's what makes the Hall of Fame so great. You go there and this guy's got a hundred more home runs, but I got three hundred more hits. Ironically, me and Mike Schmidt, when we both got inducted in the Hall of Fame, we had the same amount of RBI. About three years go by, and all of a sudden, some idiot lookin' through the books says, 'Oh, my God, we didn't count that RBI.'

"They called me up and said, 'George, you got one more than Mike Schmidt.' So, I called Schmidtty, and he says, 'You son of a bitch.'"

Earned Run Average (ERA), a former touchstone of pitching greatness, was supplanted by Dan Okrent's WHIP, then DIPS, then FIP, each a Neil Armstrong–sized step forward in the quant quest to determine a pitcher's value absent the stupid things that happen on a baseball field. Like a ball hitting a pebble on the infield dirt. (See Freddie Lindstrom, 1924 World Series.)

Francisco Lindor, Kalina's daddy and Buck's shortstop, saw the financial incentives shift. "It started my second year in the game." That was 2016, the second year of Statcast. "They don't pay for singles; they pay for doubles. Then it's, 'Oh, they don't pay for ERA, they pay for strikeouts.' They're not paying the starters for complete games. They want openers.

"If you stop the manipulation of players getting paid through analytics, then the game will fix itself," Lindor said. "If you are still valuing home runs, then I'm going to hit home runs. You want me to do this differently, change the game. See, it all starts with the top and how they want you to win games."

"Don't blame the players," Buck and Dusty say as if they are one.

To which Mr. National, Ryan Zimmerman, added, "Don't blame *just* the players."

"We're paying them for striking out 180 times and for hitting .210," Buck said. "If they were paying you three extra million dollars to strike out 180 times, you wouldn't have tried to hit it over the shift either."

"Try telling them you need a sacrifice fly. 'Oh, no, man. That doesn't go to OPS. I gotta get paid.' Makes it hard to teach."

Kahrl, a founding mother of the analytic age, acknowledges she has some atoning to do even as she puts things in perspective. "It all ended up leading to this germination where you put a dollar sign on your muscle, your career, your value, your life, your humanity, your place in the game.

"Instead of the language of the game being the poetry on the field, it became the gold we could spin out of the back of a baseball card."

* * *

Once, the accumulation of baseball knowledge about weaknesses and tendencies was known as The Book. Most managers kept it in their heads. Earl Weaver kept it in writing. He was modern that way. He started keeping index cards on opposing players when expansion forced him to take notes on what he once kept in his head.

Earl believed in "pitching, defense, and the three-run homer." He also eschewed bunts and sacrifices, platooned liberally, and sought hitters with a high On-Base Percentage. Pitching keeps you in the game, he said; home runs win the game. Outs are your most precious commodity. His 1984 book *Weaver on Strategy* remains a must-read for statheads.

He adorned the baby-shit-beige cinder block walls of his dressed-down office at Memorial Stadium with clipboards holding spray charts on opposing hitters, just to the left of his old wooden schoolhouse desk and easily seen from the threshold of the open door I once mistakenly construed as an invitation to visit.

Earl also had a small refrigerator filled with postgame cans of beer, in front of which he was squatting, naked, on the worst day of my sportswriting career. Confidently sashaying into his personal space, I took one look and burst out laughing. It wasn't the squat squatting Earl that amused. It was the perm on top of his wise, old white-haired head that reminded Jim Palmer of Little Orphan Annie.

That was the day I learned how many ways a baseball man can use the word "horseshit" in a single sentence.

Buck Showalter recorded stats sitting at the kitchen table. "My wife reminds me that I would bring home the pitching charts in the Florida State League in Fort Lauderdale. We had different-color pencils for different pitchers, and we would write where they hit the ball off them."

In the Era of The Book, data was small-sample, based on experience and observation rather than the "captured information" of the computer era. The difference between now and then is the difference between Picasso and cave art.

Laissez-faire Commissioner Bud Selig warned Phillies Manager Charlie Manuel what was coming. "He said, 'Baseball is gonna change and the manager would lose some of his power,'" Charlie said. "I didn't pay too much attention at the time."

As computers usurped the authority of cigar-chomping general managers who had been managers and managers who had been players, the once inviolable line between the front office and the clubhouse dissolved like hopscotch squares in a summer rain. The unseemly arrival of front-office guys and even owners in the previously sacrosanct precincts of clubhouse life was a reminder that the "skill set" required to run a baseball team no longer included actual experience.

Mark Lerner, principal owner of the Washington Nationals, kept a locker in the clubhouse with his very own Nationals uniform, his name stitched on the back, Oakley-style sunglasses, and spikes for shagging balls during batting practice. Players wondered, *Does he know this isn't normal? Getting dressed up like Halloween?*

On May 20, 2010, in full view of the media, the principal owner stationed himself in right field. Looking up into the afternoon sun, he was conked between the eyes by a fly ball off the bat of Mr. National, Ryan Zimmerman.

Blood flowed. Zim fretted. In the clubhouse, a phalanx of trainers attended to the fallen principal owner. When it was safe to move him, he was driven to the team's plastic surgeon in an unmarked police car with dark windows. Mending his pride was another matter.

Joe Maddon, former manager of the Los Angeles Angels, fumed when General Manager Perry Minasian and one of his top aides started using the coaches' room at Angel Stadium to change into workout attire. The assumption that they were just one of the guys was grounded in the reality that more and more they were calling the shots.

"*Shee*-it," Dusty said, turning a common expletive into a savory treat. "You know those guys can't play. They've never been on a team. They just want to be included."

Maddon was hardly an analytics denier. He pioneered the use of defensive shifts during nine years as manager of the Tampa Bay Rays. But during the twelve-game losing streak that cost him his job in June 2022, he was thwarted by a "proprietary algorithm" that determined which relievers were available to him when.

The coup de grace was a phone call to the dugout in the middle of a game. An assistant to the general manager calling to say Minasian wanted Mike Trout removed from the game. When push came to shove, Maddon told his boss which way to go where. He hasn't managed in the major leagues since.

"I had an analytics guy come in here and said, 'Uh, uh, hey, Buck, uh, this guy had two doubles and a triple last night,'" Buck said. "'I think he's gonna need a day off because he expended so much energy and he caught three balls in the gap.' I said, 'Let me get this right. He had a really good night, and I need to give him a day off? He's hot and he's one of our best hitters, and because he ran a lot he shouldn't play today?'"

The player in question was outfielder Brandon Nimmo. He played the next day.

"Nimmo plays the game right. He runs balls out. He's in every play. Nimmo was that energizer bunny, and I couldn't explain that to these people. I would get these charts—yellow, blue, green—he's in a red zone. So, they would make you think that he's more susceptible to injury if you keep playing him. That was their hook."

Buck sniffed and sniffled.

"You get to the point you don't want to be the old guy screaming at kids in their front yard."

* * *

"Have you heard about 'constraints-led coaching'?" I asked.

I told him the Red Sox, the Pirates, and the Cleveland Guardians were using it as a way around analytic glut. Mike Rizzo of the Washington Nationals opted for Peko's strategy: hiring noted left-wing left-hander and crime writer Sean Doolittle to be his analytics coach and conduit.

"With the way analytics have been able to quantify absolutely everything a player does, the player has been boiled down to an equation or a formula," Doo said.

Or, "a piece," shorthand especially useful around the trade deadline, as in "that's a nice piece to have."

It takes a whole lot of emotional intelligence to know how to speak to "a piece."

Showalter managed the surfeit of analytic offerings like a dietician limiting access to an all-you-can-eat buffet. At his first team meeting with the Mets, he pledged that no meeting would go longer than fifteen minutes, maybe eighteen in a pinch. "We're not going to be sitting around here for forty minutes while somebody's pontificating about useless shit," he promised.

* * *

I met Buck the day he managed his first game for the Mets. I told him what his old pitching coach Dave Wallace had to say about transcending the old guy/young guy schism. "Older guys like me have to stop being so fucking thickheaded and stop saying, 'No, that stuff doesn't matter, it's no good,'" Dave said. "And the young, pompous little assholes that come up and think they know it all have to get over themselves."

Buck laughed at that. I mentioned my father's allegiance to the Mets, as evidenced by his last words to me on this mortal coil. "Oy, the Mets."

Buck laughed again. Baseball makes fatalists of us all.

"I love how we're sitting here talking about something that might happen in April or May in February," he said. "The old expression my mother used to say: 'If you want to make God laugh, tell Him about your plans.'

"I try not to make too many plans."

CHAPTER 6

GOING BANANAS

What should we learn from the circus?

The last time Bill Lee had been seen in his Savannah Bananas uniform he was dead.

As in not breathing. Unresponsive. Dead.

A cardiac event had KO'd him in the bullpen at Grayson Stadium where he was warming up to pitch the bottom of the seventh inning. Luckily, August 19, 2022, was First Responders Night at the home ballpark, and every first responder in the joint wanted to attend to the Spaceman. First to reach him was his bullpen catcher and first responder Mat Wolf, who tossed the ball back to him and watched him go splat. "Caught it and went straight back," Wolf told reporters on the scene.

They paddled the Spaceman hard—"beat the shit out of me," Bill said later, which is how he knew he was alive. His teammates formed a prayer circle at second base, which, he told them later, is "where I get most of my outs."

Bill rose up and, having been emphatically dissuaded from going to the mound, walked to the ambulance, which took him to the hospital, where doctors told him he had a minor electrical problem in his ticker and fitted him out with a Medtronic device that is both a pacemaker and a defibrillator. That should have covered all the bases.

When I got him on the phone at the hospital, he was still wearing his iridescent yellow uniform pants, with electrodes pasted to his chest, and trying to get his nurse to dance.

Dying was a rush. Undying was better. He told me what he had told his teammates: "I wanna go on the field but not in the fuckin' bullpen."

* * *

He had looked swell when I saw him in the summer of 2021. Bette the Dog had brought him home from Eldredge Park for a sleepover, figuring she'd finally found someone who liked to throw as much as she liked to catch. But her well-masticated neon orange Chuckit ball remained at the Spaceman's feet. Unmoved by her silent entreaty, Spaceman remained doubled over on the deck of my house, mooning the pink sunset over Cape Cod Bay that perfectly matched the color of his shorts.

He wasn't doubled over in pain, mind you, but in the spirit of Gus Hoefling, Zen master of conditioning, whose combination of resistance exercises, stretching, and Northern Shaolin kung fu had whipped the Phillies of the Steve Carlton-Mike Schmidt era into shape. Schmidt likened Hoefling's training room in the basement of Philadelphia's Veterans Stadium to a "sweat dungeon."

One day, while pitching for the Montreal Expos, the Spaceman ran into Hoefling in the outfield at the Vet where he and Carlton were stretching. That's how the Spaceman became a lifelong Hoefling-ette. Soon thereafter, he was exiled from Major League Baseball by the Expos—black-balled, he says—after staging a one-game walkout to protest the release of his friend second baseman Rodney Scott.

Spaceman never got another shot in the big leagues, but thanks to Gus, he continued to pitch wherever and whenever he was wanted for the next four decades.

The Bananas were not yet the juggernaut they aspired to be. Nothing and no one could have helped to establish the brand more than Bill "The Spaceman" *Leeeeeeee* as Top Banana Jesse Cole crooned every time Bill took the mound. Toeing the slab, embracing the crowd the Spaceman said with every fiber of his yellow being: *We're not baseball. We're not normal. We're fun.*

He gave credibility to the goofiness and lots of good quotes.

Most people in the stands wouldn't know or remember that he was an all-star in 1973, won seventeen games three years running, and started two games for the Red Sox in the 1975 World Series. But the Spaceman? He's legend.

He began each appearance with a demonstration of his bonafides: touching his seventy-six-year-old toes and kicking his right leg above his wise old head. I accompanied him to Legends Field, home of the Kansas City Monarchs, the last stop on the Bananas' 2022 something-less-than-World Tour.

I invited Bill James, father of sabermetrics, and his wife, Susie, to join me for the game, figuring if the Bananas' wacky sacrilege made Bill smile, then they were really onto something. I decided not to include George Brett, who almost choked on his luncheon BLT—"the best in Kansas City"—when I mentioned the Bananas were in town.

* * *

A ragged dance rehearsal was in progress when I arrived at the ballpark. Kick lines, the first in baseball, formed and unformed in the base lines. Maceo, the breakdancing first base coach, was breakdancing in foul territory. Princess Potassia, the goddess of hydration, appeared in the stands in a ruffled yellow ball gown. A drone flying high over Home Run Hill beyond the outfield fence shot aerial footage for a forthcoming five-part ESPN series. There was a lot to take in.

"Places, everyone," shouted beleaguered entertainment coordinator

Zack Frongillo, sounding a tad fraught and for good reason. The two-game series in Kansas City was a Banana first, a test case of sorts, to see if they could incorporate a serious, real-life competitive baseball team into their chaotic looniness and manage a traveling party of 138 people.

Zack was having a hard time getting everyone's attention. Pitcher Kyle Luigs, who takes the mound in a straw cowboy hat and occasionally throws balls after lighting them on fire, bellowed, "Give a shit. Here we go."

A lot was riding on the weekend. If it worked—if Big City Matt Adams, last seen in a Washington Nationals uniform, former Cardinal Pete Kozma, and all the other Monarchs still hoping for a serious life in baseball bought in and played along—then owner and entrepreneur Jesse Cole, the man in the yellow tux, was going full Bananas in 2023.

He had fielded a respectable iteration of the Bananas in the Coastal Plain League in Savannah, a college summer league much like the Cape League. They'd won the league championship in their inaugural season in 2016 and again in 2021.

Roger Angell said baseball was a game of pauses and remembrances. Banana Ball doesn't allow for those. Jesse took the game he found boring once he was no longer able to play it and treated it like a washrag left out in the rain, wringing out of it everything he deemed tedious. Bunts—definitely bunts. And walks. And timelessness.

In its place: a frenetic facsimile of baseball. What I remember most about my first Banana experience is the inability to remember much of anything at all because the two-hour clock that commences with the first pitch makes any pause too short to allow for memory formation, but I do remember feeling grateful that somebody was doing something to shake up what first baseman Josh Bell called the "National Passed-Time."

"A beautifully orchestrated shitshow," Assistant Head Coach Adam "Viro" Virant said, admiring the chaos.

The Bananas had brought ringers to Kansas City: Jonny Gomes, who played thirteen years in the majors, the last bit with the Kansas City Royals; and Eric Byrnes, who played eleven seasons before retiring in 2010 to become a baseball gadfly and manager of the Bananas.

Gomes was playing catch in foul territory with a guy on stilts who is named Stilts.

"Why are you here?" I asked.

"It's fuckin' awesome," he replied, tossing Stilts a very high pop.

"What's the future of baseball?"

"You're looking at it."

Striding across the field toward us in a yellow plaid kilt, a knee-length faux fur vest, and orange shoes was Manager Byrnes. He bought the getup for a New Year's Eve party and wore it for the first game of the season when the weather in Savannah turned cold, then harvested the sleeves a couple of weeks later in Daytona when the temperature soared. He was wielding a neon green bat.

"I was just asking Gomes what he'd do if he was commissioner of baseball."

"Buy Little League," Gomes said.

"The kids would have their forever teams," Byrnes said. "You'd root for them for life!"

Yeah, and they could play in kilts!

"This decade is going to be figuring out who we are," he said, turning reluctantly earnest. "Baseball is at a crossroads as to figuring out how to bring the younger audience back into the game."

At that precise moment, the Bananas were the biggest, weirdest story in sports. Every news outlet from HBO to ESPN to *The Guardian* in London to *Southern Living* felt compelled to weigh in, and the verdict was pretty much unanimous. "Baseball Will Never Be As Fun As Banana Ball," *New York Magazine* declared.

Jesse Cole was anointed marketing's new top Banana.

It is never hard to find the Man in the Yellow Tux. It is hard to keep up with him. Hyperkinetic, long-legged, and athletic like the player he had hoped to be, he bounced back and forth across the field in a yellow blur while I trotted after him.

Cole always thought big. He was a batboy for the Red Sox when he was five years old and an assistant coach for the Cotuit Kettleers of the Cape Cod League the summer after he graduated from college in 2007. In between, he was a pitcher recruited by Division 1 colleges and was scouted by major-league teams until he tore his labrum while pitching for Wofford College in Spartanburg, South Carolina. Three surgeries later, he needed to think big about something else.

When he had to quit pitching, he joined the college theater club and studied the Great American pitchmen: Bill Veeck, P. T. Barnum, and Walt Disney, whom he quotes a lot. Thus, his first words to me, and I suspect a whole lot of other people: "Walt Disney said, 'I wish there was a place where parents and kids could have fun together.'"

He learned to speak in cheerful aphorisms. *If you market like everyone else, you're going to get the same result as everyone else. All innovation is about falling in love with a problem.*

And most importantly: *Fans First, Entertainment Always.*

It was while sitting on the bench in Cotuit that he allowed himself to think the unthinkable. *I'm bored.* Though truth to tell, lots of people are bored in Cotuit.

A year later, he signed on as an intern with the Gastonia Grizzlies of the Coastal Plain League, and they reciprocated by making him general manager. He found out why no one else wanted the job. The team had $268 in the bank.

No idea was too bad to try. On "Underwear Night," they lobbed Grizzlies underpants into the stands. Then they gave out free bean burritos. They staged grandma beauty pageants and "First Pitch Midnight" games with Jesse in the dunk tank. He told the owner, *We're gonna be a circus, and maybe a baseball game will break out.* Then he bought the team.

The Grizzlies' uniforms involved some purple and yellow in those days, which explains why Jesse was wearing a pre-Bananas yellow tuxedo when he got down on one knee mid-game on a soggy field to propose to the woman who would become his second Banana. Emily McDonald surprised him with a trip to Savannah to celebrate their engagement.

They fell in love with the derelict 1925 ballpark, Grayson Stadium, where Babe Ruth once played, and decided they had to have it. When the existing tenants, the Class A Sand Gnats in the Mets minor-league system, moved out, taking everything but the seats, the Coles made their move, buying a new Coastal Plain League franchise scheduled to begin play in Savannah in 2016, and signing a $20,000 annual lease on the stadium.

They sold their home in North Carolina, sapped their bank account, and moved into a garage turned ground-floor apartment where they slept on an air mattress. They were $1.8 million in debt five months before opening day.

That fall, they announced a Help Name the Team contest in conjunction with the *Savannah Morning News.* A local nurse, Lynn Moses, who worked nights and had trouble sleeping, saw the announcement, thought about it for two minutes, and submitted her name—the Savannah Bananas—and waited for sleep to come, picturing a smiling banana.

They gave her two season tickets and two T-shirts bearing the likeness of the menacing new banana mascot, Split, which was not at all what she imagined. "It's kind of a scary-looking thing," she said.

These days she pays her way. She's noticed that the free buffet that comes with every ticket has been "streamlined and they're putting it away earlier." This is a rare Jesse Cole fail. This woman should have tickets for life and free passage on their new annual winter cruise.

Out on the base paths in Kansas City, they were rehearsing a Jack Sparrow bit, called "Run Like Jack Sparrow," in which each of them circled the bases doing their best impression of Johnny Depp.

"We just go for whatever is trending on TikTok," Jesse said.

Silly me. The TikTok post of yellow men running the bases like Jack Sparrow has gotten 3.2 million hits since then. Those numbers are important in Bananaland, and Jesse mentioned the most important of them, other than sellouts. "Ninety-eight percent stay till the end," he said. "That doesn't happen."

I sensed his attention wandering and followed his gaze to the home dugout. The Monarchs are a proud franchise, winner of the 2021 American Association of Professional Baseball Championship. They also bear the mantle of the Negro League team for whom Ernie Banks, Cool Papa Bell, Satchel Paige, Jackie Robinson, and Toni Stone played.

With so much riding on their good nature and cooperation, Jesse asked to address the team. "I know you guys are wondering what's about to happen tonight," he said, enumerating the ten rules of Banana Ball. No bunting. No stepping out of the batter's box. No walks, no mound visits. No game longer than two hours. "There are a lot of unwritten rules of baseball we don't really play by, all right? We play by having *fun*."

* * *

Baseball used to be funny. Nobody in baseball is funnier than the Spaceman, who claims he learned everything he knows from Disney movies and Mel Brooks.

Baseball had bloopers, the celebration and acknowledgment of which distinguished it from sports that give and take fouls instead of embracing human error. Baseball understood that bloopers was just another word for the human condition. Also, unlike football, baseball didn't maim children's brains.

Baseball had rain-delay stories and nicknames like Tomato Face (Gabby Hartnett, Cubs), Catcher Face (Norm Sherry, Dodgers), Penitentiary Face (Jeffrey Leonard, Giants), and the Gerbil, the *nom juste* the Spaceman hung on his chubby-cheeked, metal-headed Red Sox Manager Don Zimmer. When management demanded an apology, Spaceman apologized to gerbils everywhere.

Bill Lee is everything modern baseball lacks. He is outrage and opinion, flakiness and "character." He calls himself "a big old left-handed shit baller." He ran for governor of Vermont and for president, declaring "I'm so left, I'm right," a reputation that scored him an invite to appear at the grand opening of the cannabis giant Curaleaf's first adult-use dispensary in Massachusetts. He purchased a bottle of cannabis oil. "I'm a dropper guy now," he confessed.

He carries a beat-up, laminated Graig Nettles baseball card in his back pocket so that the SOB who wrecked his shoulder during a 1976 Red Sox–Yankees brawl in the Bronx "can kiss my ass all day long."

Baseball used to laugh at itself. Players understood that entertaining was part of the gig. That's what infield tarps were for. MLB.com erroneously credited Milton Bradley with the first soggy tarp dash in 2008, some thirty years after the debut of Rick Dempsey's bravura performance as The Babe, preparing to hit one off the Green Monster at Fenway. Pillow-stuffed in his uniform pants, he high-stepped around the bases in his stocking feet, splashing into every base.

A decade later, on August 8, 1988, the evening of the first night game at Wrigley Field, Greg Maddux and three coconspirators did what came naturally on the tarp, entertaining themselves and everyone else as they turned it into a Slip 'N Slide. For this good trouble, they were each fined $500. "That's $125 a slide," one of them calculated. "No, wait, it's $167 a slide."

Robin Ventura's star turn as Mets catcher Mike Piazza enlivened a soggy Sunday Subway Series doubleheader at Yankee Stadium in June

2000. It had already been a long day when the rains came in the third inning of the night game. "We weren't going very good," he said. "We were bored to hell. Like, it was a *long* delay. Al Leiter and John Franco were going, 'You gotta go out on the tarp and do like Rick Dempsey.'

"I just kept walking around and would pick something outta Mike's locker and put it on. And then I started walking like him. And I just started acting like him. And I just kept adding stuff on."

He helped himself to a Piazza jersey in which he found it easier to ape his mannerisms and his gait. The final touch was a Fu Manchu drawn with eye black.

It was a less serious time.

* * *

I found the Spaceman and Mrs. Spaceman lounging in one of four modular "pit" seating groups arranged on the main concourse: a comfy L-shaped couch, a cushy singleton chair, and a coffee table. An idea we'll import when I'm in charge.

The Bananas were practicing a line dance, and it wasn't going well. When players missed their marks, veteran catcher Bill LeRoy barked, "Pay attention!"

The Spaceman doesn't dance.

"I mean, these guys are out there at one o'clock practicing," he said. "I'm going, 'That's not major-league.' They work really hard. We did a couple of stretches, had a cigarette, and warmed up. You think Dean Chance did that?"

Jesse recruited the Spaceman in February 2022, inviting him to come to Savannah for a tryout, which in my family is called *chutzpa-dik*, especially coming from a guy whose dream was to pitch for the Red Sox. Before the tryout, Bill told Coach Viro he was throwing 83 mph. He had told me the same thing. "He throws 60, but he knows how to pitch," Coach Viro confided.

Having pitched continuously and competitively in five decades, he'd earned the right to exaggeration.

"So," I said, "when did baseball stop being baseball?"

"Designated hitter, '73," Spaceman said. "'Specialization breeds extinction.' Buckminster Fuller, *Operating Manual for Spaceship Earth*, Chapter 1 on comprehensive propensities: 'rely on yourself, to your own self be true.'"

Baseball, in his view, has quit being true to itself. "It's all specialized. It's based on numerology. It's Bill James. Statistics, statistics, statistics. Damn statistics."

I chose that moment to tell him that Bill and his wife would be joining us for dinner. He pretended to mope.

I told him George Brett's answer to my question: aluminum bats. "The whole bat's a sweet spot. You get rid of aluminum bats, you go back to all wood—Little League, high school, and college—and people playing baseball would become artists. They wouldn't be swingers. They wouldn't be painters; they would be artists."

But Spaceman had taken off on a flight of fancy, a seemingly untethered tangent, about two Israeli psychologists, Daniel Kahneman and Amos Tversky, who were so intellectually simpatico that they thought like one person and changed the way people thought about thinking, upending baseball, Wall Street, and the Israeli military in the process.

With the Bananas Pep Band blasting its horns in preparation for the game-day parade, and the no-dead-air Banana soundtrack blaring, Spaceman offered a barely audible explanation of cognitive psychology, behavioral economics, and the respective responsibilities of Kahneman's Brain #1 and Brain #2 as applied to baseball.

"Okay, you have your fast brain and your slow brain. If you're driving a car and you see a cat and your slow brain takes over, that cat is dead."

Fast and intuitive, Brain #1, the automatic brain, will save your cat. Slow and analytical, Brain #2, in Spaceman's telling, is Bill James.

"What happened is the game is being controlled by the #2 side of the brain, and the #1 side of the brain produces all the great things in baseball. In other words, James is analyzing everything and coming up with statistics that Brain #1 will not accept.

"In other words, there's a conflict in our duality."

"Why is Brain #2 controlling baseball?" I asked.

"Because of the analytics and because the academic brainiacs are taking over. What did Yogi Berra say?"

I pointed out Yogi never said any of the things he said.

But I knew which Yogi-ism he meant—"You can't think and hit at the same time"—which turns out to be true. I quoted Jason Ochart on the subject: "Expert hitters are using less of the deliberate, conscious decision-making part of the brain because it's slower; and, in hitting you have the blink of an eye to make a decision. The experts are using more of the motor cortex, which is subconscious. Like Yogi said, the better hitters are not thinking."

In a 1974 paper, "Judgment Under Uncertainty: Heuristics and Biases," Kahneman and Tversky explained that when faced with uncertainty (such as whether a phenom is really a phenom, my example, not theirs), human beings fall back on *heuristics*—mental shortcuts that enable quick or snap decisions but that can lead to serious errors in judgment. Say a female sportswriter walks into a baseball clubhouse full of naked men she does not know and has to choose one to interview. She picks the guy with a tiny towel draped over his package because she assumes he shares a cognitive bias for modesty. That's a liking bias. Or she picks the guy who is naked except for his glasses because she thinks he must be smart. That's a stereotyping bias. (They assume she's there to gawk at their particulars, which is just plain old bias.)

Because baseball scouts can't remember every play, they fall back on those that are memorable. If a scout sees a flashy young shortstop make a Derek Jeter jump throw on the edge of the outfield grass, it can occlude his memory of all the errors the kid's made. That can distort his evaluation, the report he writes, the general manager's judgment, and the owner's decision whether to use a first-round draft choice on the kid. Whereas: Data has no bias. It is agnostic and remembers everything equally, and therefore, presumably, it's trustworthy.

Kahneman won the Nobel Prize in Economics in 2002, six years after Tversky's premature death at age fifty-nine. Kahneman lived longer, Spaceman explained, because he was a pessimist, and "pessimists live a lot longer than optimists."

"I'm glad to hear that," my fast brain said.

* * *

I met Bill James in 2016 when he addressed a decidedly underdressed group of baseball fans in a barn built in 1907 by painter Charles Webster Hawthorne atop a sandy bluff in Provincetown at the tip of Cape Cod. The barn was a wooded idyll, home to an iconoclastic art-and-music center presenting interesting and sometimes unlikely speakers in Provincetown. Ever proper, Bill wore a black blazer.

We were introduced by Dan Okrent, the man who made Bill James famous and who was Bill's host for the weekend. Bill and I had stayed in touch since then and had been yakking of late about the rules MLB was testing in the minor leagues, what they still needed to do, and what they had failed to do that caused them to arrive at their precarious position. I was honored when he asked my opinion of the new rules and more than a little surprised that he agreed to see a Bananas game.

Bill met his wife, Susie, at the Stokely-Van Camp's Pork and Beans Cannery in Lawrence, Kansas, where he was responsible for making sure the boiler didn't blow up and she was in charge of laying in the fat. They met me behind home plate. One thing about Bananas games—and it's no small thing—all tickets are the same price, except on StubHub, and all seats are first come, first served. I had saved seats in the front row, directly behind the plate, practically touching the protective netting. Also, I was able to buy a Bananas sweatshirt before they sold out and join in my favorite Bananas innovation—a pregame parade when the Pep Band leads players and fans into the ballpark singing "Hey! Baby."

I had hoped to be able to continue the Big Issues conversation with Bill during the game, but the Bananas made that impossible. Like Bette the Dog, they'll do anything to please. They staged stunts in the stands like "Banana in the Pants," which is exactly what it sounds like—though they no longer chuck 'em from the upper deck. They presented Mother's Day roses to every mother in the crowd. I was surprised they didn't offer to babysit and change diapers too.

As his readers know, Bill is a consummate researcher and historian, not to mention a beautiful writer and a profoundly original thinker whose ideas upended the game and offended many of the people in it, including the Spaceman. Because the Bananas made conversation impossible, he later sent me a seven-thousand-word letter—a treatise, actually—explaining what he would have said had the Bananas been less entertaining.

"I am always afraid of coming off as a cranky old bastard, which I really am not, but most of modern sabermetrics does not have any idea how to wrestle with ideas, like 'How do we measure whether a proposed innovation would help the game or hurt it?'

"Most modern sabermetrics is just directed at small issues, like 'How do we increase the percentage of time we have a fielder in the right place for this hitter from 71.4 percent to 71.6 percent?' There's nothing wrong with that, but what I was trying to establish was a community of people who worked on thinking through the bigger issues. But that community doesn't really exist.

"The game always changes; it is immensely different now than it was when you and I were young. So, to me, it is really a question of choosing between deliberate and accidental or random changes. Yes, you can make deliberate changes and miscalculate and lose standing, but I'd a lot rather take my chances with deliberate, organized changes than with just-whatever-happens-that-the-owners-make-money-from changes.

"There are many, many, many places in any baseball game in which a player or a manager must choose between the entertainment value of his action and a competitive advantage for his team. By allowing players and managers to re-shape the game without any concern for the entertainment value of their decisions, the game ITSELF has chosen to ignore the issue of the entertainment value of the product. Of course, players and managers MUST focus entirely on gaining a competitive advantage for their team. They must always choose that. That is 100 percent of the problem: Relentless pressure on players and managers to find competitive advantages, on the one side, versus a complete lack of action by management (ownership and league officials) to defend against the negative consequences of that in the entertainment value of the sport.

"It's like leaving an oil painting in the sunlight because it is a perfect oil painting. In the course of ten years, twenty years, thirty years, you might hardly notice the difference. Over the course of one hundred years, the colors fade, and the artwork is no longer the same."

"Brilliant," Okrent said when he read the letter.

* * *

When the bell rang for the official Banana weigh-in on a Banana-yellow scale, Big City Matt Adams stepped up, flexed his muscles, and sneered theatrically at his Banana opposite. Some of the Monarchs even attempted Banana dance steps. Three actual Banana Mamas were ushered to the field for Mother's Day hugs from their boys in yellow. Two diapered babies raced down the third base line to their waiting moms.

When the Spaceman's number was called in the bottom of the fifth inning, he was sitting in the front row behind the Bananas' dugout. "Now coming in to pitch! Coming out of the crowd!"

He snatched a Budweiser from a fan's hand, toasted the crowd and the BananaTV cameras, chugged half the purloined beer, and tossed the rest of it over his shoulder as he stepped onto the field. He climbed the mound to Harry Nilsson's "Spaceman" song, the refrain of his life: "I wanted to be a spaceman. . . . I wanted to make a good run / I wanted to go to the moon / I knew that it had to be fun."

"Went out on the field," he said later. "Did my stretches. Did my bend down. Did my round kick up over my head. Got ready and then 'Bang! Bang! Shoot 'Em Up, Destiny.' And I was seventeen years old again. And I threw the shit out of the ball and won the ball game."

Not quite. It wasn't a five-inning game.

When he was done, setting them down 1-2-3, he headed straight for home plate. In fact, he headed straight for me and planted one on me through the netting.

* * *

Everyone behaved. Spaceman Bill was his most exultant self, recording a birthday greeting for a friend back in Washington whose Big Birthday I had missed. "Gloria, I'm seventy-five years old. I threw 78 mph. Which means I have three more years on my life."

He cackled loudly at himself, which attracted attention, not that he minded. Sabermetrics Bill was Midwestern-dry and polite. He liked Spaceman Bill and Spaceman's wife, Diana, even though none of us could get a word in edgewise.

Spaceman Bill bragged that he had just finished reading a book that no one else had read about two Israeli psychologists and how they changed baseball and everything else.

Sabermetrics Bill mentioned, mildly, that he and Amos Tversky had corresponded in the early 1980s. "Before either of us was famous," he told me later. Tversky was a baseball fan and saw the similarities in their work. Kahneman, who lived in Israel, was once asked by the

Foreign Minister how much more likely was all-out war with Syria if Henry Kissinger's 1974 peace mission failed. "Ten percent," Kahneman calculated. *Big schmear*, the minister said. This was an aha moment for Kahneman. If a 10 percent increase in the likelihood of war was meaningless, then something was wrong with his thinking. No one ever made a decision because of a number. They needed a story.

* * *

When the Spaceman's heart doc vouchsafed his return to the mound in February 2023, I booked a flight to West Palm where he was scheduled to make his first appearance since undying at the spring training complex shared by the Astros and Nats built on a landfill. The complex then known as the Ballpark of the Palm Beaches is nowhere near even one beach. The long driveway leading to the bifurcated facility is cleaved by a narrow pond with a sign warning baseball fans to beware of alligators.

The regulars had not yet reported. Pitchers and catchers and a few stalwart spring training scribes had arrived. On the Nationals' side of the divide, Manager Davey Martinez convened his annual spring training circle of trust. On the Astros side, minor leaguers were working out on the back fields when the Bananas showed up for batting practice.

Cool as it is to be a Banana, Coach Viro was overcome by the real deal, Dusty Baker. "I felt this gravitational pull, like a Greek powerful god. It was almost like he was floating. Then he crossed his legs and leaned on a fungo bat. This magnificent human."

After their success in 2022, the Bananas went full carny. Their schtick got schtickier, their trick catches got trickier. They even looked yellower. Their much-expanded World Tour featured a team of foils called the Party Animals, who were fond of taking off their neon-pink jerseys.

Looking for a seat behind the Bananas' dugout, I saw ESPN baseball man Tim Kurkjian. He was in West Palm to interview Dusty. We sat together for a couple of innings, and it didn't take Timmy long to come to an informed opinion. "It's the stupidest thing I've ever seen," he said. "But I love it."

He told the Bananas privately, "You guys, this only works if you can actually play baseball."

Bill Lee had a new catcher, Eric Jones, who'd given up a job with the Seattle Mariners to play for the Bananas. I was curious whether Spaceman had lost anything on his fastball since his near-death experience. "What's he throwing?" I asked.

"Seventy... ish, when he reaches back," Jonesy said generously. "He's effective because he can throw it 50-ish on a lob and then come back with 70."

That night, as Bill made his way to the mound, teammates davening at his feet, the Bananas cranked up his other favorite song, Warren Zevon's ode to Bill Lee, called "Bill Lee," a lyrical celebration of his refusal "to sit on your ass and nod at stupid things."

His Bananas jersey glistened in the stadium lights. Though made of polyester, it looked like the satin worn by the Brooklyn Dodgers when television was new in hopes of making players easier to see. "It has something to do with the sublimation process when they're dyed yellow," Coach Viro explained.

So what if it's not the real stuff? Bill and the Bananas had given baseball back its shimmer.

I wasn't there the next night when one of the hunky Party Animals took the Spaceman deep. I'm told he hit the next guy up, who had removed his jersey in a celebration of studliness.

"Nailed him in his nakedness," Spaceman crowed.

CHAPTER 7

OLD SCHOOL-ISH

Janie gets a dose of reality testing

No one ever accused Mike Rizzo, president and general manager of the Washington Nationals, of being cuddly. He's a serious baseball guy who discourages unnecessary chitchat in the general manager's box. "A baseball man in full," Tom Wolfe would have called him, which used to be the biggest compliment you can pay someone in the game. It's like when a big-city sports columnist announced, as did the late Ken Denlinger during my first days at *The Washington Post*, "She can play."

News to me.

The morning after the Banana takeover, Riz was especially cheerful. Maybe because he was the proud poppa of an infant son, Santino, back home in Washington with his mama. So no diapers to change. Yes, the sixty-something baseball lifer does diapers.

His expansive president-and-general-manager office has a wall of glass overlooking the field at the seven-thousand-seat ballpark. He had caught some Bananas action the night before. Enough to take note of their merchandising chops. "They sold more damn T-shirts during that game..." Riz said.

Looking out at the deserted field, it was hard to believe it was the same place. Groundskeeping rituals had erased any trace of Banana exuberance. "So, what can Major League Baseball learn from the Bananas?"

"Well, like fan engagement."

"Okay, what kind of fan engagement?"

"You know, fan engagement."

Okay.

"I like the, uh, the liveliness stuff of it. It's a carnival kind of atmosphere. They do a great job in between innings, and they do stuff on the field during the game. You can't do that during a real game. But what they do in between innings, that's what we do a lot in the minor leagues. But they've taken it to, uh, the next level."

"But what specific things could MLB do?"

"Between innings, pregame—the carnival-type atmosphere where it's upbeat, loud, lively, lively music."

"Like in Latin America," I said.

"Exactly," Riz said.

Riz jiggled and twitched like his grandpa Vito, the boxer. Sitting still is not his thing. Thick and fit, with two new hips, he's a Chicago guy with a graying goatee and a bowling-ball shaved head.

Downstairs, pitchers were warming up with newly installed pitch clocks mounted on fences behind them. Like pretty much everyone else, Riz was praying that the pitch clock would do for Major League Baseball what Jesse Cole's two-hour clock did for Banana Ball.

"Baseball doesn't have to do what Jesse does," I told Riz. "They just need to think like Jesse thinks."

Fans First. Entertainment Always.

One of the new rules limited players to ten seconds of walk-up music in an effort to hustle their shimmying butts into the batter's box.

"What about music throughout the game?"

"Throughout the game? Noooooo."

"Make it a party, for God's sake," I said.

"Can't do it during the game."

Riz is who he's always been, which is no small deal. There's a bigness about him that dwarfs his corporeal self. He's the son and grandson of baseball guys who worked full-time jobs for the city of Chicago by day and bird-dogged at night. (Bird-dogging is the scouting equivalent of stringing for a big-city newspaper when there were still such in circulation.)

They brought Mike up to know what's what. He learned the fundamentals of the industry the hard way—at every level of the game: minor-league washout, area scout, director of scouting, and assistant general manager before being named vice president and general manager of the Nats in 2009.

Now he's an outlier: an actual baseball guy in charge of a baseball team. Nine of the majordomos in charge of major-league teams in 2024 had Ivy League degrees, two were former players with Ivy League degrees, and four had postgraduate degrees. Riz got schooled at Triton College, Saint Xavier University, and the University of Illinois, where he got his BA and coached baseball.

While other baseball geniuses were learning analytics in their playpens, Rizzo was driving the byways and highways of the Upper Midwest as an area scout for the Chicago White Sox, the absolute lowest rung on the scouting ladder. "I don't know if there's a lot of thirteen-year area scouts that are general managers now," he said.

* * *

Confession: I have a thing for scouts. Riz wasn't my first. My first was Frank "Blackie" O'Rourke, who played beside Ty Cobb in 1925 with the Detroit Tigers and had the best season of his itinerant fourteen-year career. When I met him in the late 1970s, he was living alone in the house he had shared with his late wife, Elizabeth, in Elizabeth, New

Jersey, and bird-dogging for the New York Yankees. On the grandfather clock in the diminutive parlor, time stood still, the immobilized hands where they stopped after she last wound it.

I was once his plus-one at a game at Seton Hall University for a *Sport* magazine story. Blackie dressed for the game—jacket, tie, tie tack, fedora, and white socks. He sat behind the backstop in a folding beach chair in a row with other scouts in folding chairs, a chaw of tobacco in his cheek. He spit and talked and spit and talked. By the end of the game, Blackie's white socks were brown.

By the third inning, he had accounted for each of his signings, the biggest being Yankees pitcher Johnny Kucks, remembered for pitching a three-hit shutout of the Dodgers in the final game of the 1956 World Series and nothing else. Blackie also signed pitchers Jack Cullen, who appeared in nineteen games for the Yankees, and Bill Henry, who lasted sixteen years because he was a lefty who could get lefties out. What riled, though, was not getting credit for signing Al Downing, the first Black Yankees starting pitcher, because the brass wanted a Black man to get the credit, Blackie said.

"Those old guys showed up in a dress shirt and a sports coat, sometimes a tie, and I'm sweating through my golf shirt," said Riz, whose sartorial disarray earned him a rebuke from Larry Himes, the scout who drafted him for the Los Angeles Angels with the 554th pick in 1982 and hired him as a scout after dropping him as a player. "Don't make me look bad again," Himes said.

The art of scouting was passed down from his grandfather Vito to his father Phil to Mike. Vito was a boxer who played shortstop for the semipro Chicago Trouncers for five dollars a game while Grandma made wine in the bathtub. They called it Rizzo Red. He greeted Mike, the only one of Phil's four kids who went into the business, with two short rights and a left hook until six months before his untimely death at age 104.

Phil signed a minor-league contract out of high school and played six years, reaching Class B baseball before quitting to drive a cement truck for Mayor Daley, a job with a pension and benefits. He'd drive all day and bird-dog at night. After he retired, he scouted full time for the Los Angeles Angels. By the end of his career, he had done work for six major-league teams, including his son's, and was elected to the Professional Baseball Scouts Hall of Fame.

Riz was the Lerner family's first hire when they acquired the Montreal Expos from Major League Baseball. His first hire was his father, who told me not long before he died that his father had taught him "what to look for, how a pitcher moved on the mound before the pitch or how a guy acted when he went from the dugout to his position, and how he put his bat back in the rack after a strikeout."

Vito also said, "Look at his face: Does he have a quick face?"

I asked what "face" meant. "Face means: Something happens through the course of the game, guy looks at you. Some guys have a big, mean-looking face."

Talk like that is the reason for the *Moneyball* revolution.

"There was no radar guns, no stopwatches," Phil said. "You just watched a guy run. You went to a ball game and watched his actions. Did he have guts? Did he have balls? That was my scouting—heart, guts, and balls."

Is it any wonder that Riz's older son, Mike Jr., asked permission before buying a ticket to see Brad Pitt in *Moneyball*?

"Yes, it's true, I boycotted the movie, my dad too," Riz said. "Because scouting is my life and it's near and dear to me. It depicts baseball people as dummies that just sit in the room, spit tobacco, and say stupid things. And I don't like it to be depicted in that regard."

The first player Riz signed for the White Sox who made the majors was future Hall of Famer Frank Thomas. Phil scouted Cy Young Award–winner Brandon Webb and signed second baseman Mark

Loretta. "Loretta has the last bottle of Rizzo Red," Mike told me. "My dad gave it to him. They were fighting over $2,000. Dad offered $26,000. Mark wanted $28,000. Instead, he gave him the last bottle of Rizzo Red. I ran into him sometime back and said, 'You didn't drink that, did you?'

"That stuff would take wallpaper off the walls."

In Phil's capacity as special assistant, he scouted high schooler Bryce Harper and reported back, "Can't catch, you're buying a bat." Phil also hit Mike upside the head in the draft room after more than one pick he didn't agree with. Finally, Mike told him, "Dad, don't call me anymore. You give me agita. It's the only time ever a scout hit a GM in the draft room. When he died he was still smacking me in the head."

I met Riz in 2012 when the Nationals finished first in the National League East, reaching the playoffs for the first time since baseball returned to Washington. He was named Executive of the Year by baseball writers in Boston and Chicago. I'm pretty sure the first thing he told me about his team was: "We need some more tough guys."

That was the year he declared Stephen Strasburg's season done before the playoffs, a career-defining decision that was no doubt the toughest and most progressive Rizzo ever made. He showed me a six-inch-thick binder tracking how every pitcher in the league fared the year after returning from Tommy John surgery. According to his statistics, a pitcher of Strasburg's age should pitch no more than 160 innings. Strasburg had thrown 159 one-third innings when Rizzo shut him down.

Manager Davey Johnson was pissed. Pitching Coach Steve McCatty, a wonder boy for the A's until Billy Martin wrecked his arm, was pissed. "How did that work out for you?" Riz asked.

Phil was really pissed. "My old man said, 'You dummy, this is your chance to win.'"

That decision led to Strasburg re-signing with the Nats in 2016 and, despite recurring and ultimately career-ending injuries, leading them to the 2019 World Series championship, making up for the playoffs he had missed.

* * *

Now I was giving Riz agita, and I was starting to feel guilty. But not *that* guilty.

"Okay. So, what specific Banana thing can you see happening at a major-league game?"

"As far as rules? I don't know all the rules that they use."

No bunting. No mound visits. No walks. No game longer than two hours. No stepping out of the batter's box, which MLB was going to emulate by limiting a player's God-given right to call time-out to one. Foul balls caught in the stands count as outs.

I mentioned I kind of liked that on the grounds of fan engagement.

"Come *on*," Riz said.

I didn't really expect him to go for any of that. Nor do I ever want to see an MLB relief pitcher on stilts, or a "Flatulence Fun Night" with giveaway whoopie cushions, one of Jesse Cole's earliest promotions.

"The game of baseball is the carnival for me," Riz said. "The confrontation of pitcher and batter, or a fielder and a runner—that's the carnival."

Yeah, for me too, but we're not six-year-olds raised on dopamine hits.

"How about players walking through the stands kissing babies and signing autographs?"

What I had seen the night before that Riz hadn't was a storm of little humans careening down an aisle of his ballpark begging for autographs and high fives when a couple of Bananas climbed into the seats just behind home plate. It didn't matter that they weren't wearing the regulation see-through Major League Baseball uniforms that debuted in 2023 and disappeared in 2024. Or that they weren't major leaguers. When they reached out to touch the yellow sheen, the kids were touching baseball.

"Those kids just became baseball fans," Coach Viro said.

Then a security guard arrived, armed with MLB protocols, and spoiled all the fun, shooing the kids away with a tight-lipped admonition about clogging the aisle.

"So . . . ?" I said.

Riz was obdurate. "Can't do it during the game."

"Joey Votto did it in Cincinnati."

Votto, then in his sixteenth year with the Reds, was on the injured list following shoulder surgery in September 2022. Before the Reds took the field on September 21, he was honored (for the second time) as the team nominee for the annual Roberto Clemente Award, presented only to baseball's best guys. Votto had his picture taken on the mound wearing Clemente's number 21 jersey and rushed off the field to the clubhouse to change. It didn't feel right being in a Pittsburgh jersey.

It occurred to him, as he was changing, that he had seen players in Atlanta, Anaheim, and Chicago go into the stands to greet fans. He thought, "You know, I can make someone's day."

He put on a reproduction Reds Barry Larkin jersey, grabbed one of his own plus the Clemente replica, and headed for the grandstand. "I thought, 'I'll just head upstairs and give them away.'"

He wandered through the Great American Ball Park, going places he'd never gone before, walking the concourse behind home plate on the 500 level, giving high fives, and posing for pictures. He thought he might be scared, which says a lot about the estrangement between public persons and their public. Instead, he was charmed and disarmed and surprised by how normal it felt.

"I thought, 'When does an everyday player in the middle of a game have that option? It's few, if ever.' I just wanted to say hi."

He spent ninety minutes among his people. It took a while for fans to recognize him, or believe what they were seeing, and for the team's TV cameras to find him. When they did, the voice of the Reds asked, "What's wrong with him?"

"Nothing," broadcast partner Barry Larkin replied. "He's making friends!"

No surprise to me that Joey Votto was the number-one choice among baseball fans to dine with in a survey conducted by *The Athletic* in 2023.

"Yeah, but," Riz said.

"Yeah, I know, it's Cincinnati."

"Can you see Bryce Harper walking through the fans, the New York crowd?"

Yes, as a matter of fact, I can, but, as I pointed out, he doesn't play in New York.

"You're just waiting for something to happen," Riz said. "Now, do you want to get these guys to be available before and after games to do something, that's something that you could ask them to do."

Yeah, and you could ask them to do pregame clinics as Mickey Mantle did in the fifties. And stick around after the game as a designated autograph signer as Cal Ripken did after every Baltimore home game.

Back in the day, the Pirates, the Dodgers, and the Nats hosted kids for free in sections set aside for them. In Pittsburgh, the kids had their own entrance. In Washington, grade-schoolers in mini Senators uniforms sat upstairs above the third base line. At Ebbets Field, they clogged the center field bleachers on Saturday afternoons.

"Weren't there businessman specials?" Riz said. "On a Wednesday or Thursday afternoon?"

These invitations to play hooky worked particularly well in urban ballparks, like Griffith Stadium, and especially on getaway days. "So," I said, "let's insist on at least one weekday game every week in every ballpark and make them students get in free days."

"Love day games," Riz said. "You're talking about the biggest day-game guy ever."

Sensing an opening, I decided to try out a few of my own ideas on him. "In Jane's MLB, all weekend games will be day games except four designated showcase games on Friday and Sunday that MLB can put on all their fucking platforms," I said.

"You gotta have a Sunday night game. You have one game, that's the game, and one backup game if it gets rained out. It should be a marquee game like Sunday night football. But the rest of 'em we play at 1:30 p.m. I love it. Saturday 1:05 p.m. is my favorite time to play a baseball game on the weekends. Players like playing at one o'clock because the four o'clock game, they don't have the morning or the night. One o'clock game at least they have the night."

Like everything else, it's revenue determined. "The commercial is worth more at four o'clock than it is at one o'clock," Riz said.

Maybe the smartest of Jesse Cole's innovations—one born of desperation when the Bananas weren't drawing—is a flat-fee ticket for home games with all you can eat. In 2024, the price was thirty-five dollars.

"How about if at every home game every club designates a section in the upper deck, first come, first served for thirty-five-dollar tickets and all you can eat."

Maximum four tickets.

"Hey, that's a good idea," Riz said.

"All kids ten years old and younger accompanied by an adult get in free."

Riz brightened. "Especially in designated sections of the ballpark in the upper deck. We wanna fill that thing up. So, okay. I like that."

Also: Commercial breaks are too long. Instead of taking two more seconds off the time a pitcher has to throw a pitch with men on base or cutting the time a manager has to challenge a play, let's get rid of guaranteed two-minute commercial breaks—what the commissioner calls "commercial load."

I was on a roll. Riz didn't dare interrupt.

"Let's go back to seventy-five seconds between half innings—which is basically the attention span of an average human—and add two long, six-minute breaks after the third inning and sixth inning. Kind of like hockey, but shorter. You could cut down further on mound visits, give guys a chance to get looked at by trainers, and try some Banana action down on the field. Let the babies crawl. Let a high school catcher warm up the pitcher. Let elementary school kids compete against (pick one) Washington's Racing Presidents, Pittsburgh's Racing Pierogies, or Milwaukee's Famous Racing Sausages."

If you want them to love baseball, you have to let them touch baseball, steal a blade of grass from one of those lush green carpets, rub some dirt on their hands, feel the enormity of a major-league stadium from behind home plate, give them purchase on the game.

"So, you in with all that?"

"I would have to see it in a big-league atmosphere. The minor leagues, I get it. And the Bananas, I get it. I don't want to minor league it up to the point where it's detracting from the pro product."

"Don't you think baseball's gotten a little bit too much invested in its dignity?"

"You think so?"

"Yeah, I think so. I think decorum is overrated."

Riz and I are one about the ghost runner instituted during the COVID-19 pandemic so that the cardboard fans yakking it up in premium seats behind home plate didn't have to get home late. "Let's just say it was the right rule for 2020," Riz said.

I hate the ghost runner because starting a runner at second base in the tenth inning of a tie game is inimical to everything that made baseball quintessentially American. First, no one gave you anything.

You had to earn your way around the bases. And you stayed until the job was done. Even if that meant thirty-three innings at a minor-league game in Pawtucket. Wade Boggs and Cal Ripken Jr. were opposing third basemen in that 1981 game that began one night and ended, officially, two days later. And they survived to become Hall of Famers.

Would baseball have been better off without the sixteen-inning scoreless duel between Juan Marichal and forty-two-year-old Warren Spahn at The Stick in 1963? A game that ended with a Willie Mays home run.

Without Ed Armbrister's sacrifice bunt in the tenth inning of Game Three of the 1975 World Series when he froze in the basepath, interfered with Carlton Fisk's throw, and enabled the Reds to advance the winning run to third? (Abso-fuckin'-lutely, BoSox partisans say.)

I get why managers, general managers, and traveling secretaries embrace The Ghost—it doesn't lay waste to a pitching staff or flight plans. But nothing is more pathetic than seeing a team built to slug trying to play small ball in the tenth inning. You ever see Giancarlo Stanton try to shorten up on his swing? What's more, Roger Angell hated it. Anything that Roger hated is hateful to me.

Last year, 75 percent of extra-inning games were decided by the end of the tenth inning. And 97 percent went twelve innings or fewer.

"When I'm commissioner, we're going to give games the chance to end the way they are supposed to end. We're going to bench The Manfred Man until the thirteenth inning or until both teams have a chance to go through the batting order one more time. While we're at it, we're going to station that Ghost at first base when he gets stationed at all."

Call it divine inspiration from an Angell.

* * *

It seemed only fair to let Riz get a word in edgewise. "We need to market the stars like the NBA does and the NFL does their stars," he said. "We do such a poor job of that, it's crazy."

It is crazy. Dodgers Manager Dave Roberts attributes the craziness to the institutional animus between labor and management. Riz concurs. "Of the three big-three sports, we do the worst job of marketing our players because we don't work with the union," Roberts said. "We need to make this pie bigger. How can we make this pie bigger? We need more eyeballs watching our game."

Memo to billionaire owners and union heads: Making us care more about the players is good for business.

This year, only eleven baseball players made the *Sportico* list of the one hundred best-paid athletes in the world. Ohtani ranked 29th. The ink on Soto's contract wasn't dry enough to include him. Only A-Rod and Jeter make the list of the top-paid athletes of all time.

Upon hearing this, The Babe rolled over in his ample grave.

Ohtani also dwarfs the MLB field in social media presence with nine million Instagram followers, according to *Sportico*, which is not that much less than MLB's twelve million followers. The Savannah Bananas, who had zero clicks in 2021, have more followers than Mike Trout, who is a distant second to Ohtani with 2.2 million followers.

"We have all these new rules, pitch clocks, but the young generation won't watch baseball," Bananas Manager Emeritus Eric Byrnes said.

Not his kids, anyway, who love baseball and play on the travel team he manages but never watch a whole game. TikTok clips maybe.

Here's a marketing idea. Hire a public relations czar who gets why it's stupid to schedule Opening Day on the same day as the NCAA men's basketball round of the Sweet Sixteen.

If baseball really wants to grow a newer, younger audience, it needs to grow a pair and market the game spikes-high. Sell the game to parents as the sane alternative to tackle football. It's no coincidence that flag football is now an Olympic sport as well as the fastest-growing sport in the youth market. Somebody at MLB gets it, or there wouldn't have been flag football advertisements on the Home Run Derby broadcast.

I asked Ryan Kutscher—founder of Circus Maximus, the advertising agency that created the 2019 baseball campaign for "Roman," the online dispensary of male health aids and once a proud partner of MLB—what he'd do to lure kids back to baseball. "It's not necessarily honorable or moral, but play off the fears of the parents. So, maybe 'Teach them the game they're gonna remember forever.'"

Consider it a public service.

I was about to suggest a Mother-Daughter Day and day care at the ballpark to attract new parents, but I could see Riz was about to bust a move. I didn't know he could sit still as long as he had.

"And then you'd make me commissioner?"

"Yeah," Riz said, giggling. He actually giggled. "And then I would back away and let the players play the game."

CHAPTER 8

PAID TO DREAM

A washed-up catcher demonstrates how to be

It helps that Scott Hatteberg has a good sense of humor.

He calls himself Patient Zero, which implies contagion, which is one way to look at analytics. He was the washed-up catcher in whom the washed-up phenom, Oakland A's General Manager Billy Beane, saw value where nobody else did. "You're looking for the most bang for the buck," Scott said. "I was the bang for the buck."

In the Hollywood version of his life, his signing on January 2, 2002, was the warning shot in the battle between numbers and judgment, causing the expulsion of Beane's scouting director, Grady Fuson, who actually left to accept another job. Hatteberg was played by Chris Pratt, who took up intermittent fasting after being told he was too fat for the part.

I found myself telling Hatty that he reminded me of the drop-dead-gorgeous, two-piece lavender organza and sequined Halston number my mother found, mismarked but marked down, on that blessed rack of returns and seconds behind the Back Room in the Loehmann's off Queens Boulevard and which she wore proudly to my wedding. As a result, I now only pay full price.

Scott didn't bat an eye.

My grandfather, the immigrant tailor, pronounced this legendary Loehmann's bargain "good goods." My mother said I could bury her in it but opted instead for cremation, sitting in a kosher salt Grecian urn in my front closet for five years.

Scott Hatteberg is good goods. A quality guy.

Signed because of his stellar on-base percentage at a time when nobody cared about on-base percentage, Scott is now, yes, a scout for the vagabond Oakland A's.

"It is very ironic that I end up where I am," he said. "Actually, it's pretty funny."

I met him in Cary, North Carolina, home of USA Baseball's National Training Complex, for the tenth annual National High School Invitational, a sixteen-team single-elimination tournament featuring some of the best schools and the best talent in the country. "It'll be elbow to elbow behind home plate," Scott said, as we walked up the path to Field #3.

A group of more scouts than I knew still had jobs had gathered to see T. C. Roberson versus Doral Academy at 1:30 p.m. Like everyone else, Scott wanted to see a skinny shortstop from Florida and a blocky catcher from California, who looked old enough to be the shortstop's father.

"F-1s," he calls them. As in Formula 1 race cars. "Peak specialized, tweaked out. Top-of-the-line engineering." Sipping bad coffee out of paper cups, the scouts were waiting on Adrian Santana, the diminutive shortstop with advanced defensive chops and a whole lot of filling out to do. "You're watching agility," Scott said. "I know his reaction time off the bat. Is he twitchy? Who is he going to be in five or six years?"

The A's were well-represented. They had brought four scouts plus their scouting director. "We can't sign Mike Trout," Scott said. "We have to draft Mike Trout."

So how do you see Mike Trout before he becomes Mike Trout or Adrian Santana before he grows into being Adrian Santana?

"Ya gotta dream on them," Scott said.

Which is maybe the best job description I've ever heard.

Except for the standing around and the waiting. Adrian was due up first in the bottom of the first inning, but the top of the inning lasted seventeen minutes. "Gotta get back in standing shape," a guy muttered. The season was young.

"I saw Anthony Volpe here," Scott said, apropos of shortstops. Volpe was the thirtieth pick in the 2019 draft and was recently anointed as the Yankees' starting shortstop. "He's a nice player. Jack Leiter was here."

The seats at Field #3, one of four at the complex, each 330 feet down the lines and 400 feet in center field, were almost empty. Those that were filled were occupied by parents, siblings, maybe a girlfriend or two.

When Adrian finally stepped into the left-handed batter's box, a whole row of paunchy guys with the exception of Hatty, who still looks like a ballplayer, reached into their team windbreakers for stopwatches, a nod to old technology that made me smile. "He's an athlete," Scott said, from his dream state. "Framewise, how much will he put on?"

Adrian, who had been picked off twice the night before, put a quick end to the much anticipated at bat, striking out on four pitches. Disgusted, the amoeboid mass of visionaries headed down the path to Coleman Field, the stadium field, with an actual press box where games were filmed by the scouting combine. "Mechanically the swing works," Scott said. "Decent quickness. He got pitches to hit, but he didn't touch them."

The USA Baseball National Training Complex occupies twenty acres gouged out of old red North Carolina soil. From the air it looks like a four-leaf clover plunked in a bed of grass. It sits within the 221-acre Thomas Brooks Park on land donated by his descendants with the stipulation that the town restore, and preserve, the remnants of what's called "The Old Slave Wall." It was fashioned from sandstone and bricks made by a slave named Pompeii, who was owned by Thomas Brooks. Pompeii used clay dug from the estate to build the wall that kept him within its perimeters.

The baseball facility was expanding. A new forty-thousand-square-foot indoor practice facility was on the boards. Two of the four existing fields were being converted to artificial turf—just the thing for young knees—to increase the number of days a year they can be in use. Also, the 1,200-square-foot merchandising facility was undergoing renovation.

"There are no secrets anymore," Scott said, as we found our seats along the first base line. Nobody is finding F-1s like Mickey Mantle in an environmentally condemned town full of sinkholes these days. "That's not gonna happen with social media. The advantage is taking the players you have already and making them better. Can we take a pitcher that throws 90 mph and make them throw 95 mph? Then, it's wow, we made something out of nothing."

Liam Peterson—"a big white guy with a big body"—was on the mound for Calvary Christian High School from Clearwater, Florida. He walked the first batter and the second, almost hit the third, gave up a run on an infield grounder, and walked in another run. Altogether, he gave up four runs on three hits. At the end of the inning, he went to the dugout and got an infielder's glove.

"Go back to high school, kid," a scout sitting in front of me muttered.

"I've seen enough," Scott said. "Good body. Good breaking ball. Tops out at 90–94 mph on his fastball, but he's not getting his fastball over the plate."

Position players are graded from two to eight on the still-sacrosanct tools of the game: hitting, hitting with power, speed, throwing, and fielding defensively. The only problem is they get to use maybe two of them and have little chance to develop them.

Add those scores together and you get your Overall Future Potential (OFP). A score in the mid-sixties or higher means: stardom. Under forty means NP for "No Prospect." Pitchers are graded on the same scale pitch by pitch: fastball, curveball, slider, changeup, splitter, cutter. Scott decided not to file a report. "It wouldn't be fair," he said.

The scouting combine gave Peterson an overall score of forty-five. He went back to high school and then to college at the University of Florida.

Sometimes you dream on them; sometimes you wait on them.

* * *

Hatteberg never wanted to be a scout. He remembers thinking, after he retired in May 2008, "I don't want to do this." What he wanted was to learn the language of scouting. "Because it's basically the language of baseball. I did it just to educate myself and fell in love with the lifeblood of it."

Every spring, he travels the country seeing, timing, and grading the top eighty to one hundred amateur players. He does it because he loves baseball but mostly because he loves the A's, the team that dragged him off the salvage pile and paid him $1 million when he and just about everyone else thought they were nuts.

The legend of Scott Hatteberg begins at home plate in spring training 1999. He was the Red Sox starting catcher the year before and was getting ready for the season with mundane catching drills, making throws down to second and working on pitchouts. He remembers that the ground was really soft in front of the plate. His foot slipped, and he hyperextended his elbow. "I ended up smashing my ulnar nerve and hurting the ligament. They had to move the nerve and fix the damage to the ligament."

He never threw right again. What had been so natural became unpredictable, unrepeatable, undoable. "I just didn't come off the ball the same," he said. "I don't have full extension. The precision velocity wasn't there."

He played in only thirty games in 1999 and became Jason Varitek's backup in 2000, remaining in that unlovely role until Varitek broke his elbow diving into the stands in 2001. In one game that year, Hatty grounded into a triple play and hit a grand slam. He says his story is a lot like baseball, defined by luck and failure.

Meanwhile, that year the Oakland A's won 102 games thanks to equal measures of pitching and slugging and faced the Yankees in the American League Division Series. But Billy Beane knew he was about to lose his two top run producers in 2002, not to mention his closer. He also knew he had to replace them on the cheap.

He found what he was looking for in Hatteberg, who possessed an uncanny ability to draw walks, to get on base, and to create runs. Other teams had expressed interest, but the A's were ardent. They never explained their fervor, Hatty said, "but they were giddy at finding a chink in the business. I thought they were dumb and crazy, and they were giving me too much money, and I was jumping at it."

Third base coach and infield savant Ron Washington was charged with the responsibility of turning him into a first baseman.

How did *that* happen? I asked Wash. "I have the skill set to teach it. He had the skill set and the genes to learn it and apply it. That's how that happened."

They worked daily in spring training until exhaustion precluded more. "I got blisters on my toes," Scott said. "My feet hurt. I'm sweating and losing pounds a day. And, you know, he's not a young chick. He wasn't at that time."

It was Infielding 101. Starting with tiny, little, short hops fielded barehanded from three feet away.

"He wanted me to be pretty. Being pretty allows you to play bigger at the position, meaning expand the position. I played it smaller. He would get real excited about me playing freer, more one-handed, going to read hops, being aggressive, trusting my hands."

"He put in the work, and he got consistent," Wash said. "He turned himself into a heck of a first baseman."

The A's did okay in April, nose-dived in May, and were ten games out of first place at the end of the month. "The team was coming off a great year, so *Sports Illustrated* was going to do an article on us," Hatteberg said. "And then they scrapped it because we sucked so bad."

Then they started winning and kept winning, winning twenty consecutive games from August 13 through September 4. That was Dollar Night at the ballpark in Oakland. The A's sold fifty-five thousand seats. Everyone wanted to see them set an American League record for consecutive victories. It was the biggest crowd since owner Charlie Finley packed them up and left Kansas City, whose new franchise was their opponent that night.

The A's led 11–0 after three innings, then allowed eleven runs to tie the game. In the bottom of the ninth, Manager Art Howe sent Hatteberg to the plate to pinch-hit. He brought with him a beautiful hunk of maple carved into a bat by a garage company—not one of the big manufacturers and most definitely not a Louisville Slugger, with whom he was under contract.

After he hit the game-winning, streak-setting home run, a man from the Hall of Fame appeared at his locker requesting the bat for Cooperstown, which is usually a gimme. Hatteberg gave him a Louisville Slugger.

The season ended with 103 wins and 59 losses. Paul DePodesta, Beane's *Moneyball* man, now chief strategy officer of the Cleveland Browns, calculated that the A's would have scored 940–950 runs, more than the mighty Yankees, had Hatteberg batted for the entire lineup.

Published in June 2003, *Moneyball: The Art of Winning an Unfair Game* sold a billion copies and transformed an industry. The one thing it didn't do was make an unfair game fair.

"It had more of an impact on owners than it did on GMs," said former A's General Manager Sandy Alderson. "Gradually you started to see a turnover in personnel from traditional to more contemporary based on those principles."

* * *

An invite to the National High School Invitational Tournament in Cary is a big deal. The uniforms were as ebullient as the kids wearing them. My favorites were purple-and-orange pinstriped zoot suits worn by the team from Brother Rice on the South Side of Chicago.

The dugouts were alive with practiced cheers, whoops, and hollers that had some of the undulating quality of soccer crowds. "Olé, olé! Do a job!" for Ralphy Velazquez, the chunky, clunky catcher who caught Scott's eye. "If you dream on him, maybe in three years he's Kyle Schwarber," Scott said as we made our way back to Field #3 for Adrian's last at bat of the afternoon. "This is a quality high school kid. If you're dreaming."

The scouts were ready for him to do something, anything. I, however, had looked down to write something in my reporter's pad and therefore can't say exactly how it was that Adrian arrived safely at first base, and I was too embarrassed to ask.

I did see him take off for second. And saw the pitcher throw crisply to the first baseman, who handled the ball cleanly and threw to second.

Caught stealing.

Scouts with stopwatches still in their clutches had come a long way for this.

"What the fuck?"

"That shit is dumb."

"No fucking point."

"Stupid."

"Is that trying to show off?" I asked Scott.

"No," he said. "He's obviously extremely fast."

A seven runner on a scale of eight.

"I think he just was betting, even if he did throw over, he could beat the throw to second base. It was him just being a little cocky, a little overconfident, one of those 'I'm faster than everybody. I'm gonna go.'

"I bet he gets away with it a ton because he is so fast. People do that in the big leagues. I wouldn't have marked him down for it. It's basically a young mistake."

As the shadows lengthened, players began to nod off on unoccupied benches and patches of ornamental grass connecting the fields, reminding me they are just boys. One kid in dusty white pants and a royal blue jersey hid under the brim of his cap, curled into a fetal position around his bat and glove.

* * *

Hatteberg calls himself Grandpa Scott, though he hardly looks the part. He says he wouldn't mind at all going back to a time when managers wore street clothes. "Do we need to see their fat asses?" he asked as we sat down to dinner.

We had been talking for more than a year when we met in Cary. He had seen the trickle-down effect of analytics on the kids he scouts and on the high school coaches who work with them. He bemoaned a world that wouldn't have a place for slugless Tony Gwynn and Ichiro Suzuki. "There's a new voice in the room on what makes great baseball. I saw averages plummet to levels I've never seen before. I've been told batting average doesn't mean anything."

I'd recently been told by a prominent new-age baseball thinker: "Batting average is Santa Claus. Most baseball fans still enjoy watching baseball as if they are kids."

"I'm so sick of hearing it," Scott said. "I get that in the quantitative world, it doesn't maybe mean everything, but it does define a lot of who a player is, who he is capable of being."

The baseball ops guys are deputized to project a kid according to his numbers. "They're the smartest people in the room. We're the baseball contingent. I would argue we're doctors of the game of baseball that didn't come from MIT. I think there's a marriage."

Children ape their elders until they get old enough to switch to oppositional behavior. That's why there was so much eye black smeared on so many teenage faces. And that's why twelve-year-olds are chasing velo and calculating launch angle.

"Whatever you value at the big-league level trickles down to college, high school, and Little League," Hatty said. "So you've got kids swinging forty-five degrees up in the air. We've got ten years coming of that.

"The young kids, it's astonishing how little they know. Josh Donaldson, he was the MVP one year, and I remember him saying now he wants to swing up, and I'm like, you just ruined one hundred thousand Little Leaguers."

To be clear, Scott knows analytics are vital. "We're still trying to figure them out as far as really what they mean and how they can be used. Major leaguers who have mastered their skills and incorporated the metrics are as good as they're going to get. That's where feel comes in. It's hard to explain. It's primal. It's instinct. It's voodoo. It's like they see around the corner. The kids? They have no feel. It's all robotics. It's like running across rocks. Some people have to look down."

* * *

The 2022 season did not end happily for the A's. The highlight of the year was an investigation launched by the Oakland police into a public act of fellatio committed in the upper deck, section 334, as far down the left field as the left field grandstand goes. Law enforcement released a surveillance image clearly showing the faces of the couple at the late August game and sought community support in nabbing the duo who were not keeping score.

"Not a first," Scott said. "Could have been more exciting than what was happening on the field."

The A's attendance was less than ten thousand per game that year, the worst in the league. In 2023, they had the worst attendance and the lowest payroll. Hatteberg knew his beloved A's were not long for Oakland.

Avaricious ownership and craven MLB thinkers didn't want to be left out of the good times in Sin City. In 2024 came the announcement: The A's were moving to Vegas, where a new ballpark with all the attendant sequins and spangles, including a covered roof, would be built—after a layover in a Triple-A ballpark in Sacramento.

I asked Scott at dinner whom he'd be dreaming about that night. Adrian? Ralphy? Both were projects. Ralphy had to find a position. Adrian had to grow into his body.

"Ralphy, he's a strong kid who can find the barrel. He can find the ball. You can dream on the catching part."

(In the spring of 2025 he was the Cleveland Guardians' sixth-ranked prospect.)

"You weren't that impressed with the shortstop?"

"I think we gotta wait on the physicality," Scott said. "It's too much of a gamble right now for me."

(Adrian was the nineteenth-ranked prospect for the Rays.)

I'd been too absorbed in the calculation of Scott's OFPs to notice that it was Opening Day of the season. The first games of 2023 had been decided. My Yankees had won with Anthony Volpe at shortstop.

"I just feel so much better when it's the baseball season," I said.

"Yeah," Scott said. "It feels right. The alarm went off. Time to come out from hibernation."

CHAPTER 9

BLACK OUT

Watching baseball 2.0 from the bleachers on Opening Day

Baseball has a complicated relationship with the past. Never is this truer than on Opening Day, when the slates are wiped clean, every team has the same record, and, theoretically, though not financially, the same right to dream.

Opening Day was a national holiday when I brought Sammy Esposito home from Saks Fifth Avenue. Later in life, I learned that pretty much everyone else celebrated Opening Day by getting shit-faced, and I learned it the hard way—from a greasy, schvitzing, beer-guzzling, wifebeater-wearing, bald, Buddha-sized Red Sox enthusiast sitting behind me at Fenway Park who observed the occasion by projectile vomiting into my fleece hoodie.

No one knows the fraught relationship between past and present better than Janet Marie Smith, the architect and urban planner, whose imprimatur informs modern baseball. Five of the top-ranked ballparks in a 2024 *USA Today* survey were conceived by or improved on by Janet Marie, including Fenway.

She invited me to Opening Day 2023 at Pittsburgh's PNC Park, her latest project, and the only one of her labors of baseball love I had yet to see. PNC Park finished first in that *USA Today* poll, and it was easy to see why, though I'm still partial to Camden Yards, where no one has thrown up on me. I like to think I had a hand in the design thanks to the dismembered ballpark book with blueprints that Larry Lucchino borrowed during the planning stages of Oriole Park. I told that story to five hundred people at a Great Fenway Park Writers Series gathering. Lucchino, who died in 2024, tried to buy me off with a genuine Red Sox warm-up jacket. I'm not that easy. I gave it to a legit Boston fan.

Janet told me to meet her upstairs before the first pitch for an Opening Day party where VIPs were being served troughs and troughs of everything but ballpark food—Canapés! Charcuterie boards! Mini lobster rolls! "A really big spread," George Solomon, my sports editor at *The Washington Post*, would have said.

Grateful as I was for the invite, and impressed as I was to watch Janet Marie work the room, spreading thick Mississippi charm and turning chat into an art form, I felt really guilty about the mini lobster rolls, an abrogation, on my part, of Opening Day decorum which requires a beer and a dog, not lobster. I did not wear my party shoes.

Opening Day harks back to spring rituals of regeneration, religious and pantheistic. It is as much about the past as it is about starting over. Unless it's your first Opening Day, it's also about your last Opening Day—who accompanied you, what you ate, what you spilled, and maybe who won, and who lost.

This Opening Day marked the debut of MLB's new rules in Pittsburgh, a declaration of a new beginning if ever there was one. But it was also a day that demanded the willing suspension of disbelief in the home of a team that hadn't sniffed the playoffs since 2015. If you were a Pirates fan, you had to hope the sun would come out from behind the clouds and shine fiercely enough to block out the odds, posted everywhere, against the Bucs reaching the postseason.

"The landscape today is one where you have a system that works with teams that are in strong geographical markets, such as New York, or have owners willing to spend on the theory that leads to a World Series trophy," said Roy Eisenhardt, who ran the Oakland A's for his father-in-law, Walter Haas, from 1980 to 1986. "The rest of the teams are tied for first on Opening Day but have no chance as the season evolves. It's a 'known-known' that half the teams or more are not going to be competitive.

"If you're a fan of baseball, you're going to immediately not pay attention to probably ten or twelve of the teams because they just have no chance."

So what's a team owner to do with fatalists and empty seats in the grandstand?

If you're Bob Nutting, owner of these once-proud Pirates, coming off four straight last-place finishes in the National League Central, you bring back the homegrown guy, the last connection to the last playoff team, five-time all-star Andrew McCutchen. And you hope for headlines like the one on TribLIVE, a Western Pennsylvania news website: "He's Home!"

And you bring back his mother, Petrina, too, a former volleyball player with a great set of pipes, to sing the national anthem just as she did at playoff games in 2013 and 2015.

In case that isn't enough, you summon 2013 batterymates A. J. Burnett and Russell Martin for the ceremonial first pitch and choose as your Opening Day starter Rich Hill, who at age forty-three was the oldest pitcher in baseball. He didn't survive the fifth inning. Sometimes old is nostalgic, and sometimes old is just old.

McCutchen engineered his return to Pittsburgh—where his family lived throughout his five-year big-league diaspora—by texting Nutting. *I want to come home.*

Three days before the opener, Cutch took to Twitter to call for a PNC Blackout: "If you want to wear black you can; not saying you have to."

A blackout is when Pittsburgh fans show up draped in black. It was a kind of call-and-response between Cutch and his fans. So when I stepped outside, away from the mini lobster rolls, onto a patio facing home plate, the ballpark was buzzing black and yellow like a gigantic beehive.

Chants of "MVP!" greeted him when he stepped to the plate in the bottom of the first inning and the newly installed pitch clock began its relentless descent. Overcome by an aural embrace 39,167 souls strong, McCutchen stepped out of the box to compose himself. Home plate umpire Ryan Wills ignored the clock, allowing Cutch the moment. Then, unwilling to be consigned to nostalgia, he singled.

* * *

Taking a break from schmoozing, Janet Marie showed me around. Her mandate in Pittsburgh was to complete what the architects had left undone and to do it without mucking up what made it perfect—the postcard view of the three sister bridges spanning the Allegheny River named for Roberto Clemente, Andy Warhol, and Rachel Carson. The river is just 443 feet from home plate.

She led me through the lower third base concourse, where two staircases had been removed in order to open it up to the field and the light and then back out into the sunshine of PNC's new backyard, tucked behind the outfield bleachers and the river.

In the new world of ballpark design, this is called an "outfield experience," which is different from the outfield experience of Yankee Stadium bleacher creatures. Or from early twentieth-century urban immigrants like Vin Scully's Irish parents, for whom a day in the bleachers meant a day in the park with greenery and sunshine and a way to feel American.

Janet Marie's new company, Canopy, had been hired to upgrade and renovate the twenty-year-old park to accommodate the way fans actually watch baseball these days, which is to say, they don't sit still for nine innings marking their scorecards and waiting for the beer guy to come by.

Architects from HOK Sport (now Populous) in Kansas City and L. D. Astorino & Associates in Pittsburgh created a two-deck ballpark on the north side of the Allegheny, importing the buff-colored limestone and decorative terra cotta suggestive of Forbes Field and the steel trusses supporting Pittsburgh's bridges. "You had beautiful views of the river and downtown, but there wasn't anything going on over here on the Riverwalk," she said, leading me through a happy thicket of guzzlers and gourmands.

They filled the Riverwalk with café tables and cheerful yellow umbrellas, open bar rails, and a stand-alone bar facing home plate, where you can pull up a stool and watch the action. They added a pirate ship climber—no vacancy when we were there—and a miniature yellow bridge for kids to cross. "Right here in the middle of the action because one of my pet peeves is putting the playground off in the corner as if you're penalizing parents for bringing their kids."

By removing a section of the outfield wall and six rows of bleacher seats, they opened the ballpark to its full potential. "Before, you were either in the bleacher section or you were on the Riverwalk," she said. "Now you can live in the view."

Reinvented PNC Park reminds me of my nose job. Bear with me. It's a baseball story. In fifth grade, I was conked in the nose by a line drive off the bat of my fifth-grade teacher, Jim Rogan. I went home and told my mother, "I think I broke my nose."

She said, "Oh, Jane, don't be ridiculous."

Within months, my nice little pixie nose turned into a honker with a speed bump, which had no business being in the middle of my face.

As soon as I was of an age, I got it fixed. Midway through the operation—yes, I was awake—the doctor, who also doubted my story, told me he had to inject more anesthetic because it was going to take all day to get rid of an avalanche of scar tissue.

Now I have the nose I was supposed to have, and I look the way I was meant to look. So does revised PNC Park. Like my nose, it looks like it's always been there.

* * *

More than anyone in baseball, Janet Marie is responsible for the look of the modern game. Her paws and her exacting aesthetic are all over it. This matters because how baseball looks is inextricably linked to how it is viewed, by which I mean regarded, and how it is played.

Baseball lives at the intersection of history, memory, and nostalgia, which are "different things," Janet Marie reminded me. She is clear-eyed about the pull of the opposing constituencies that makes her job complicated. That is: to preserve and celebrate the past without wallowing in it. She knows that nostalgia is death to something trying to live in the present. "So, there are things about these old ballparks that live on long past their normal life expectancy," she said. "But they give insight into what is memorable.

"Baseball looks forward but with a big old hefty rearview mirror hanging off that windshield. We look back with nostalgia at the old ballparks, which is probably not the right word because many of us never knew those parks. So, we're pining for a past we never knew.

"I can say I love the way Ebbets fit into the neighborhood. I can say I love the way the angles of the ballpark were formed. But I didn't know Ebbets Field, so I can only say what I might have loved about Ebbets."

I couldn't offer any insight because, you will recall, my father left me home when he took my older sister to Ebbets Field in 1957.

* * *

Janet Marie Smith grew up in Jackson, Mississippi.

There was no TV in the Smith household until the Kennedy assassination. She learned to love baseball through her father's telling of it. Thomas Henry Smith, a Southern gentleman and a Yankees fan, told her about the childhood baseball games he constructed with sticks and pebbles. The sound of his transistor radio "on full bore" while he mowed the lawn—a game in progress in some distant city delivered to their yard via a crackly AM signal—still rings in her ears.

She was ten years old when she saw her first major-league game on a family trip to Houston in 1968. What she remembers about the visit to the Astrodome is a popcorn-filled cardboard cylinder that turned into a megaphone. "*Chaaarge!*" She says she'd like to save the Astrodome, the first domed stadium and the last example of concrete donut ballpark construction, now an abandoned hulk standing opposite the shiny new home of the Houston Texans.

Like every successful female professional I know, she is a multi-multitasker: construction supervisor, architect, urban planner, preservationist, baseball historian, real estate developer, project manager, mother of three, and wife of a very patient man.

She came in over the transom, which means nobody asked her to apply for a job to work in the development of Camden Yards. She received a polite kiss-off from Orioles team Vice President Calvin Hill. Undaunted, she put on her big-girl pants and wrote again. Lucchino saw that letter, noting her experience in the public-private sector working on the development of New York's Battery Park City and Pershing Square in Los Angeles. "Bring her in," he said.

Since then, she has supervised over $1 billion in baseball construction at Oriole Park in Baltimore, Turner Field in Atlanta, Fenway Park in Boston, Dodger Stadium in Los Angeles, and Polar Park in Worcester, not to mention the Orioles spring training complex in Sarasota and the Dodgers youth academy in the Dominican Republic.

The decision to build a downtown ballpark in Baltimore was an inflection point for baseball in design, aesthetics, and location. It sparked a boom in urban stadium construction that rivaled the concrete-and-steel age that began with Shibe Park in Philadelphia in 1909. It inspired envy, urban revitalization, and a slew of Camden wannabes that, ironically, are now cited as evidence that baseball is stuck in the past.

Imitators followed in Cleveland, St. Louis, Denver, San Francisco, and Pittsburgh, creating the retro boom in ballpark design. Nostalgia was not the intent in Baltimore. "Camden Yards was the first in several generations to go into a center city and use the urban environment to guide everything from the shape of the playing field to the way the B&O Warehouse engages with the ball on Eutaw Street," Janet Marie said.

Once the longest brick structure in the United States, the 1,116-foot warehouse was just down the block from where George H. Ruth Sr. kept a saloon on Eutaw Street. "The outfield dimensions of Camden Yards were born in response to the site." As were the stylistic finishes and details.

Eutaw Street is now home to Boog Powell's BBQ, to brass disks embedded in the street marking the landing spot of every home run to clear Boog's pit beef, and to a sculpture park and flag court that informs onlookers as to who is in what place in the American League East.

"The rest of the world looked at it and said, 'Well, that's cool. I think I'd like to have an outfield experience.' And I remember shuddering the same way I shuddered when people said, 'Maybe we should also build a retro park' because we were not looking to create a retro park. And we were not looking to create an 'outfield experience.' We were looking to create something that was authentic to Baltimore and that responded to that particular site."

That's what architecture is supposed to do.

At Lucchino's insistence, they set aside a percentage of tickets for game-day sales because he wanted people to be able to walk up Eutaw

Street and buy a ticket on the spur of the moment as he had as a boy at Forbes Field.

The warm orange glow of the brick warehouse at sundown camouflages what makes Camden Yards radical. Within its old-timey shell, it contained all the appurtenances of modernity and luxury that have become de rigueur. Large, comfy clubhouses, a vast underground complex of batting cages and pitching mounds, medical facilities, family facilities, and wellness opportunities (massage, hot tub, cold tub, meditation suites) are now pro forma. And for noncombatants, luxury suites, a seating bowl close to the field, and an urban esplanade open 24/7, 365 days a year.

"The evolution of all of that over the last thirty-plus years is that now the 'outfield experience' has become a thing. My own personal opinion is that its allure has been exaggerated by the fact that the netting now goes foul pole to foul pole around home plate. So, the notion of showing up with a glove on your hand and taking home a souvenir is all but gone unless you're in the outfield."

Another reason to live in Janet Marie's view.

* * *

After Camden Yards, Lucchino brought her to Boston to preserve and improve upon Fenway Park, rescuing baseball's oldest stadium from the teardown it was thought to be. They turned a rabbit's warren of old streets and quirky passageways into concourses with modern dining facilities. They even reimagined the Green Monster as a place to sit. Those seats on the top of the wall are a signature Janet Marie move. "If it's me," I told her, "I park my ashes up there. And I'm a Yankees fan."

In 2012, Stan Kasten, president and CEO of the Dodgers, summoned her to LA to supervise the ten-year, $400 million rehab of the mid-century stadium jewel, now baseball's third-oldest ballpark. The plan that she oversaw rendered the limitations of the site surrounded by mountains and the original design moot. They removed the seats behind home plate and dug down to create a zeitgeist clubhouse hailed by Sandy Koufax, a onetime architecture student, as an ingenious solution to an intractable problem. People-moving escalators, considered an unnecessary luxury in 1962, were added at either end of the main concourse.

She gave the park the front door it had always lacked, a transition from the swaths of circular parking lots that surround the ballpark. Sculptures of Jackie Robinson and Koufax grace the plaza along with corporate meeting rooms, climbing structures, batting and pitching cages, a virtual photobooth, a vintage ice-cream truck, and an eighty-two-foot-long digital baseball information board.

As architecture critic Paul Goldberger said, "They made it better than the original, almost like channeling what it could have been and should have been."

Like my nose.

* * *

While Janet Marie went in search of a beer and a schmooze, I basked in an in-and-out sun and considered the competing interests of history, memory, and nostalgia and my friend Hans Gumbrecht, who knows a lot about each of them. Gumbrecht, who goes by Sepp, is a literary theorist who grew up playing soccer in Germany and came to America to teach Important Things—philology, philosophy, semiotics, literary and cultural history. He is also a sports guy. He likes everything except "explicitly aesthetic sports" like gymnastics and ice skating, which I understand.

He saw his first baseball game in 1980 in Oakland when he was a visiting professor at the University of California in Berkeley. Despite the A's throwback uniforms, which he abhorred for their explicit appeal to nostalgia, by the end of the game, he thought, "I like this pastime."

After he returned to the Bay Area in 1989 as a full professor at Stanford, he became a baseball fan. His European sensibility, formed by soccer's rhythm of touches and rushes, acclimated to baseball's unique delivery system of lull and spectacle, the "all of a sudden" moments that baseball gifts to its most patient and knowing fans.

"I don't know who said, 'What is baseball? It's a long, hot Sunday afternoon in the bleachers.' You're sitting in the stadium for four hours, and then all of a sudden there's this seismic, charismatic moment—*something* happens."

Those languid afternoons allowed for time to breathe, to daydream, to look away, to think, to imagine, to write a complete sentence if you were upstairs in the press box, to go get a hot dog. "So, my wife, tragically, always buys hot dogs when that moment happens," he said. "I already know when she buys a hot dog, something good is going to happen. In football you don't get up to go get a hot dog.

"The distribution of drama is different in baseball. And the beauty of baseball is you can never predict the real great moments. But then this unbelievable home run happens. In the Giants stadium, the ball flies into the bay."

I never did find that quote about Sunday afternoon in the bleachers. Maybe Sepp was remembering Roger Angell's defense of the pace of the game, now so deplored, that allows those Sundays to be replayed in winter when the bleachers are bare. "... it is a game of recollections, recapturings, and visions. Figures and occasions return, enormous sounds rise and swell, and the interior stadium fills with light and yields up the sight of a young ballplayer—some hero perfectly memorized—just completing his own unique swing and now racing toward first."

One night on his way back to Palo Alto, Sepp realized he had not gotten from the game what he had come to cherish and expect, something alive that kept him company on the forty-five-minute drive home. "Something was missing."

He decided it had to do with those seismic moments that are the reward for loving baseball, or rather the absence of them. He began to think about the "retro" ballparks, including Oracle Park in San Francisco. "The Giants stadium is a beautiful stadium in every sense, but it is too explicitly historical."

Easy for him to say. His cathedrals are older than ours. And baseball's cathedrals are almost all gone except for Wrigley Field, Fenway Park, and Dodger Stadium.

If you want an example of a deliberately historical neogothic baseball cathedral, I said, take the opulently overdone redo of Yankee Stadium—perfectly described by the late Frank Deford in a 2009 NPR commentary as having "something of a mausoleum aspect to it" what with the gold-inscribed lettering on its oversized limestone palisade. Its grandiosity extends to its hamburgers: The "99 burger" features two four-ounce patties of Wagyu beef, a $19.99 homage to Aaron Judge.

Sepp wondered if "the moment baseball deliberately started to feature itself as historical was the beginning of a crisis, a melancholia for something important in your life that has passed."

I realized with a gurgle of ballpark frank–induced indigestion that I knew how he felt. I had felt it too. Luxuriating in the bleachers at PNC Park, I wondered where those moments had gone.

* * *

In the march toward analytic optimization, baseball lost its narrative thread. Analytics devoured the plot points like so many Dippin' Dots, imposing its own irrefutable logic on the way the game is played. Pitchers get hit hard after twice through the lineup. You score more runs with a walk, a strikeout, and a home run than with station-to-station baseball.

As a result, home runs have become so ubiquitous that I barely look up: 5,862 of them in 2023 and 5,453 in 2024. Same with strikeouts:

41,843 in 2023, 156 more than in 2024. Used to be even a strikeout could inspire awe.

Did you see The Mick swing so hard he fell down?

Hell yes. I practiced how to do it.

Twenty strikeout games? Twenty game winners? Perfect games? You can't win thirty-one games, as Denny McLain did in 1968, if you only start thirty-one. Hard to throw a no-hitter, or a perfect game, when you only pitch 5.2 innings, the average in 2024. Complete games are almost as rare: just twenty-eight in 2004, the same number thrown by Rick Langford in 1980. League leaders last season threw two complete games. Two!

Baseball knows it needs storylines. "People don't come to see velo," said Morgan Sword, MLB's emperor of the diamond. "They come to see a story."

Storytelling was baseball's gift. Entertaining is its (legal) obligation. (See 1922 tax exemption.) Analytics made it hard to deliver on either. "Entertainment is 'I watched this for two or three hours,'" said Mike Fast, chief analytics guy for the Atlanta Braves, who gets the need for narrative. "A story wraps you up in the season and its people."

I know analytics aren't going away and that I have to get used to them and to using them. The truths mined from data are too entrenched now, too valuable now (economically and otherwise), too useful in too many ways now: think of the physics behind the Torpedo Bat.

Even as I find myself adopting the language and logic of metrics, the loss of the familiar narratives is disorienting and alienating. It's as if the topography of a path so familiar I could walk it sure-footed on a moonless night has become foreign terrain, dirt crumbling beneath my feet where once there was a soft pine needle trail.

* * *

How did Major League Baseball get so stuck? Why was it so slow to enact the new rules I was seeing for the first time at PNC Park? Why had it failed to react to the challenge the NFL and the NBA posed in the seventies and eighties?

Michael Lewis offered a compelling explanation on a December 2023 episode of Stephen Dubner's *Freakonomics* podcast: "Baseball has a peculiar problem. Baseball is simultaneously selling a sport that you are watching and a history of the sport.

"People are so invested in the continuity of the game. It's an old and aging fan base. They're attached to the game being played pretty similar to the way it was played. They want the statistics, the accomplishments, to be comparable. Baseball is going to have to make a decision between the future and the past."

These days he'd rather watch women's softball. Maybe that's because, unlike baseball with its dueling constituencies, softball lives resolutely in the present. When you go to a baseball game, you're watching what's happening on the field while looking for reminders of the past: players chasing records, breaking records, filling the shoes of former greats. "Some of the moments we get are engineered," Sean Doolittle reminded me, as well as the font of a potent revenue stream. "Nostalgia has been commodified. Every part of the game, whether it's team uniforms, even primary uniforms, are harkening back to some previous version of the team's history.

"Nostalgia is also constraining. It creates these artificial barriers where things should be the way they are just because, 'Well, it's just always done it that way.'"

Economists have a name for this: path dependence. Luckily, I have my own personal baseball economist, Michael Haupert, professor at the University of Wisconsin-La Crosse, who specializes in the economics of sports, especially baseball, and entertainment. He laid it out for me while driving to a Toledo Mud Hens game because he's the kind of baseball fan who will drive 976 miles from La Crosse, Wisconsin, to Washington, DC, and back if he can stop at least twice to see a ball game on the way home.

"You remember in the seventies when gas was cheap and American cars were huge and heavy and then all of a sudden, all these small Japanese cars came on the market? American manufacturers had no idea what to do. So they just kept doing the same thing.

"That's path dependence. Now think about baseball. For seventy-five years, it was *the* sport in the United States. Throughout the sixties and seventies, football and to a lesser extent the NBA start to encroach on baseball. They're attracting younger fans. They have more action. They're marketing their superstars. Baseball is on a very different path that's based on team autonomy. That's how William Hulbert built it."

William Hulbert, one of the nineteenth-century founders of the National League and president of the Chicago White Stockings, was the driving force in organizing the league, giving clubs exclusive territorial rights—rights that are at the root of today's economic imbalance.

"He said, 'You guys get into this league, and you have a monopoly over your own market.' So baseball teams always had their own territorial rights for radio broadcasts. When television started to come along, the same model applied because that's how they've been doing it forever.

"In the seventies and the eighties when cable TV (Turner Broadcasting, WGN, WOR) and regional sports networks (RSNs) started to get big, baseball started to fall behind, splitting the market into haves and have-nots. And by then it's really hard to change that television model.

"Now if you want to undo that and start sharing television revenue, you're gonna have to convince the Dodgers to abandon the $8.25 billion path they embarked on when they signed a twenty-five-year deal with Spectrum Charter.

"Why not change the game to the ideal form that would attract large numbers of fans of all ages? Because of path dependence. Instead of starting over from scratch, baseball is attempting to gradually move the game toward its ideal marketing format through incremental changes."

Meanwhile, the battle between proficiency and wonder goes on, leaving far fewer stories to tell, except about money and injuries, and not nearly enough moments to build stories around, leaving a yawning chasm for nostalgia to fill.

"Baseball sees its fan base eroding because of sabermetrics," Mike said. "And one way to try and capture that is nostalgia. 'Let's bring back those pleasant memories.'"

So, you bring back Andrew McCutchen. You put on the black. You live in Janet Marie's view.

"When analytics makes it impossible for what was great to be repeated or exceeded, you have no choice but to wallow in the past," Mike said. "But the problem with that is we're all gonna die, and they need to cultivate younger fans to replace old ones like you and me, who fell in love with a different game."

* * *

Janet Marie was vexed that I hadn't seen the postcard view from upstairs behind home plate. Not just because it's gorgeous, or because it survived the changes she had made; she wanted me to see it so I could understand the parable of "the preferred view." When Camden Yards was on the drawing board, she ran smack-dab into a heretofore unknown maxim that a stadium must be laid out so that the third base line is true north. "I don't want to call it a sacred cow, but I think it probably was a sacred cow," she said. "I can remember great anguish in the room when we proposed moving it five degrees off true north. 'Gee, we're going to screw up the sun.'"

This vestige of a time before stadium lights that had lived on into the present is a perfect example of path dependence. She assured all concerned that baseball would survive the alteration needed to use the warehouse as a backdrop and create the Eutaw Street promenade. It was a tough sell. Such are the demands of baseball's past.

In order to secure its postcard view, PNC Park's architects used what's called "the second preferred position," first base south. This was the view Janet Marie wanted me to see.

I didn't want to disappoint her, but time was growing short given the 4:00 p.m. first pitch. What I wanted to see was Phil Coyne's view.

Phil was a Pirates usher for eighty-two years, from age eighteen to age ninety-nine, from 1936 through 2017, with four years off to fight the Good War in Germany, Italy, and France. He accompanied the team from Forbes Field to Three Rivers Stadium to PNC Park, where he reigned over sections 26 and 27, field boxes along the third base line, ushering some six thousand home games.

I met him near the end of his run when I was finishing my book on Babe Ruth and heard about a guy who had seen his last three home runs at Forbes Field, which is why I wanted to see the plaque presented to Phil on his one-hundredth birthday, now affixed to a concrete wall behind Phil's section, and see if anybody remembered him.

In his later years, he sometimes shepherded the grandchildren of fans he had helped to their seats at Forbes Field, where he forged a lifelong relationship with the team in the lower right field grandstand, set aside every Saturday afternoon for neighborhood kids. They had their own entrance, the run of the section. The tickets were free. With that touch of grace, the Pirates made them at home in the game.

Many of the boys, including Phil, became ushers as soon as they graduated from high school, escorting people into the world they inhabited for free, easing the way with some chat and a nice, clean seat. Phil brought a purple rag from home every day in a plastic grocery bag for that purpose.

You know where else there are ushers? Weddings, the White House, Broadway. You know who doesn't have ushers? The NFL. It is a word that comes with the unspoken connotation of being conveyed into something utterly other, something rare. That's how we used to feel about baseball.

Phil was in the lower right field grandstand on Saturday afternoon, May 25, 1935, when The Babe hit his number 712, 713, and 714 home runs. "The first two home runs we really didn't pay attention to," Phil told me. "We just run around a lot. But the third one we paid attention to. A miracle happened, and he hit it all the way over the fence. We got a little excited and stopped playing around when he hit the ball out of the ballpark."

He hit it over the roof of the extended right field grandstand and into the Oakland neighborhood where Phil was born, raised, and died. The ball was never found.

Phil was working behind the visitors' dugout at Forbes Field in 1960 when Bill Mazeroski hit the home run over Yogi Berra's head, and over the ivy-covered brick wall behind him, that joined The Mick and me in misery. That portion of the wall—inscribed with the painted white numerals 406—now resides at PNC Park beside a statue of Maz.

Phil never married or had children. Pirates Manager Danny Murtaugh was his pal. Fans became his family. He knew the wives and children of Pirates players. They sat in his section.

Jordy Mercer, a Pirates infielder from 2012 to 2018, recalled, "One time, my wife said somebody was chirping a little bit, you know what I mean? Phil took care of it real quick. My wife said that he wasn't gonna have any of that."

As the glum 2017 season came to an end, Phil's regulars fretted. The Pirates were rebuilding, again, and that meant they would be selling off their assets. By Opening Day 2018, Andrew McCutchen, Gerrit Cole, Tyler Glasnow, and Phil Coyne were gone. He quit because he was afraid of falling. "Something's wrong up there," he told reporters. "I tried to make it to one hundred but I just couldn't."

Like Cutch, Phil refused the seductions of nostalgia. He even worked a Pink Floyd concert or two. He remained resolutely in the present, respectful of the past, for as long as he could and was glad to do it.

That's why I needed to visit his section. I needed to live in Phil's view.

On April 27, 2018, the Pirates threw him a one-hundredth birthday bash on the field. Phil wore his usher's uniform. More than a hundred members of his family came from all over the United States and Ireland, County Galway. Nine nieces and nephews posed with him in the visiting dugout.

The Pirates fell behind 5–0 that day. Mercer drove in the tying run, and the Pirates won in the eleventh inning. Phil stayed until the last out. When Mercer was summoned to the field for a postgame interview, he asked for the microphone. "Just want to give Phil a shout-out," he said.

Phil Coyne died on April 9, 2021, at age 102. The uniform and badge he wore to his birthday party are now at the Hall of Fame.

CHAPTER 10

RICH HILL'S MIDDLE FINGER

The oldest working pitcher in baseball gives art lessons

Rich Hill extended his middle finger. The left one that's been the source of all the trouble. He wasn't being rude. He's not that guy. I had asked to see the finger that wrecked perfection.

"Right now, I have some blistering," he said, holding the finger up for inspection. "I pickled it. I pissed on it. Put rodeo rub on it that they had in the clubhouse. The one thing that I found that really helped was the laser that they have now that actually heals the wound."

I didn't see much except some redness. Kind of like Mount Vesuvius before it blows. Nothing like the bloody mess Dodgers Manager Dave Roberts described to reporters after he pulled Rich at the end of seven perfect innings in Miami on September 10, 2016.

In the dugout, Hill made his feelings known. In the clubhouse, he told reporters, "I get it." It was his first start for the Dodgers after arriving via an August 1 trade with the Oakland A's. He'd been unable to pitch for more than a month after a blister ripped off his left middle finger pad in mid-July.

"What did you say to Roberts?" I asked.

"We spoke our piece. But we're always playing the maybe game—'maybe he gives up a hit, maybe he gives up a double, maybe he gives up a home run.' As opposed to the positive side and saying, 'Go get 'em.'"

The second time he approached perfection, in Pittsburgh in 2017, he was sabotaged by a ninth-inning error by his third baseman. Hill hadn't allowed a ball to leave the infield for five innings.

Zeroes piled on top of zeroes, but the Dodgers managed not to profit from eight hits and four walks. With a no-hitter still in the offing, Roberts sent Hill back to the mound for the bottom of the tenth. Josh Harrison was the first batter he faced. With the count 2-1, he hit Hill's ninety-ninth pitch just over the letter *c* in the AAA Auto Insurance banner plastered against the low left field wall. Skimmed it is more like it. Outfielder Curtis Granderson draped himself over the six-foot wall, practically falling into a woman's lap before letting go of hope.

Statcast compounded the pain, calculating that a ball hit with the paltry exit velo and launch angle Harrison mustered had a one in ten chance of clearing the fence. "I didn't get it all," Harrison said.

Six years after the fact, Hill was philosophical. "I mean, hey, what are you gonna do?"

He was forty-three years old now, the oldest player in the major leagues, old enough to have perspective on his peculiar fate, twice losing perfect games after seven perfect innings; twice undergoing a surgical repair to his left elbow. The first thwarted effort in Miami in 2016 helped him secure what he had never before had in baseball—financial security. He signed a three-year, $48 million contract with the Dodgers that winter.

His twenty-four-year baseball itinerary reads like a TripTik for a fifties shoe salesman: Boise, Lansing, Boise, Daytona, Iowa, West Tenn, Peoria, CHC, Iowa, CHC, Iowa, Daytona, Cubs (Ariz), CHC Aragua (Venezuela), Norfolk, Frederick, BAL, Pawtucket, Memphis, BOS, Pawtucket, Portland, Salem, Greenville, Red Sox (Gulf) BOS, CLE,

Pawtucket, Scranton/Wilkes-Barre, LAA, NYY, Syracuse, Pawtucket, Long Island (Ind), BOS, Stockton, OAK, LAD, Rancho Cucamonga, LAD, Rancho Cucamonga, LAD, Rancho Cucamonga, LAD, MIN, TBR, NYM, Portland, BOS, PIT, SDP, Worcester, BOS, Omaha.

Maybe twelve times in all those cities and all those games, Hill had the feeling he had that night in Pittsburgh. "Like I was able to put the ball wherever I wanted to without even thinking about it," he said.

What's stayed with him is the effortlessness of the ball coming out of his hand. "It's like a painter having a brush and just being able to look at the canvas and go, 'It needs a little bit of red here.'"

Somewhere around the sixth or seventh inning, the sounds of the game receded. "Like the organ that's still playing while the batter's getting in the box. All that stuff goes away. You don't hear anything. You're really just so locked in on the moment and it's so visceral.

"So, you stay in the moment. And you keep yourself in that moment because as soon as you let yourself go to thinking about a no-hitter or a perfect game, you lose it."

For such moments to reach a happy denouement, luck and skill must collude with circumstance. Wind, for instance. A bad bounce. A close call. A botched call.

These moments are rarer now. Seven times in 2024, a pitcher was removed from a no-hitter after seven-plus innings; ten others were yanked from their purpose after six-plus no-hit innings.

In today's "probabilistic" world, the forever plays that run on a loop in baseball's collective memory are an endangered species. There's no metric for measuring what's lost by making the improbable impossible. But every time a pitcher is hauled off the mound as Hill was in Miami, baseball retreats a little more from what it was and the drama it uniquely delivered.

Winning isn't everything. That's for football with the merciless exigencies of a seventeen-game season. Every year, baseball grants 162 chances to win, to lose, or maybe to be perfect. Surely among them there must be a way to grant Rich Hill et al. permission to explore the dimensions of the possible.

* * *

Thirty-one times since the mound was moved to its current distance in 1893, pitchers carrying no-hitters through the seventh inning have not been around to finish the job, according to the Elias Sports Bureau. Twenty-eight of those thwarted attempts have occurred since 2015 and the advent of the Statcast era.

Moments that aren't getting a lot of ink these days.

Game Six, 2020 World Series, Tampa Bay Rays versus Los Angeles Dodgers: Rays pitcher Blake Snell dallied for five innings with the Dodgers, striking out nine of them and allowing hits to just two of them, when with one out and one on in the sixth inning, Manager Kevin Cash crow-barred him from the game. It's what the Rays had done all season. The Dodgers were delirious; everyone else, including Snell, was incredulous.

"Oh, Cashie," Joe Torre remembers thinking.

Three years later, in his next-to-last start for the San Diego Padres before free agency, Snell was seven innings into a no-hitter when Manager Bob Melvin came for him. Forty thousand Padres fans had shown up for a team that repeatedly stunk up the joint. Couldn't Snell and the Padres have given them something to remember?

Game Two, American League 2023 Wild Card Series, Toronto Blue Jays versus Minnesota Twins: After throwing three shutout innings to begin a must-win elimination game, Jays starter José Berríos made the mistake of walking the first batter in the bottom of the fourth. He was unceremoniously relieved of duty in favor of another starting pitcher, masquerading as a reliever. Yusei Kikuchi promptly loaded the bases and allowed two runs. The Jays were cooked.

Baseball at its best is drama the way old Westerns are drama—with a guy in a white hat and a guy in a black hat standing seventy-five paces apart on a dusty dirt street in front of Miss Kitty's saloon in Dodge City. It's a storyline so central to the American narrative that fifty years after she shut down the Long Branch Saloon and *Gunsmoke* was killed off by CBS, we're still arguing about the meaning of the Second Amendment.

These duels between pitcher and batter or pitching ace and pitching ace were called matchups. Head-to-heads. Jim Kaat's father drove three hundred miles round-trip on his only day off each week to see Cleveland's Bob Lemon and Bob Feller face the Yankees' Vic Raschi and Allie Reynolds at Municipal Stadium. Don Newcombe of the Dodgers and Robin Roberts of the Phillies faced each other seventeen times in the fifties. Madison Bumgarner of the Giants and Clayton Kershaw of the Dodgers met eleven times between 2010 and Bumgarner's retirement in 2023. Bumgarner also had five hits off of Kersh, two of them home runs, and named his strongest horse after him.

In the era before analytics, matchups gave shape to seasons, decades, careers. They formed relationships between protagonists and antagonists, central characters as in Shakespeare and Aeschylus. The crux was always the same: Who would get whom? Who *owned* whom?

Would Koufax ever figure out how to pitch to Bad Henry? (BA .362, OPS 1.077 in 116 AB over twelve years.) How was it Tony Gwynn never struck out in 103 plate appearances against Greg Maddux? Why did Willie Davis torment Bob Gibson with forty hits and twenty-one RBI in 125 at bats?

A single at bat could be a one-act play; the last inning of a perfect game could be operatic. Listen to Vin Scully's impromptu poetry from the broadcast booth at Dodgers Stadium when Sandy Koufax struck out the side in the ninth inning on September 9, 1965. "On the scoreboard in right field, it is 9:46 p.m. in the City of the Angels, Los Angeles, California."

Gone, too, is the thinking man's pitcher, who saved something for the third time through the order that he hadn't shown the hitter before. The pitch he kept in his back pocket, maybe all season. Also gone, the delicious anticipation of the next encounter.

* * *

The Spaceman woke me up early on April 14, 2022, screaming into the phone. "Did you see that? Did you see *that*?"

I saw it. Clayton Kershaw, the Dodgers' sublime left-hander so often compared to his mentor, Sandy Koufax, had been removed from a perfect game in his first start of the season at the end of seven innings. "You know what Ferguson Jenkins said?" Bill bellowed. "'I don't care if I had to roll the ball to home plate. I'm not coming out of a perfect game!'"

Kershaw did hard time on the injured list in 2021 and had been unable to pitch in the playoffs. He hadn't thrown much in spring training either, delayed as it was by the lockout at the expiration of the collective bargaining agreement in December. His longest outing of spring training, except in a "sim" game, was five innings.

That was of no consequence to the Spaceman, who sneezed in a vain attempt to muffle a sob. "Why are you crying, Spaceman?" I asked.

"Because the guy wasn't allowed to find out how good he could be."

It was 34 degrees at game time on April 13, 2022, at Target Field in Minneapolis. Kershaw's mastery over the young Twins was complete. He was far from the pitcher he was when he came armed with a 96-mph fastball. Age, injuries, and mileage had forced him to remake himself into the "complete" pitcher of baseball cliché.

This was no secret to anyone, which made his thorough domination a work of art. He struck out thirteen Twins on eighty pitches; eleven of the strikeouts, and seventeen whiffs, were on his slider. No one hit a ball harder than 90 mph until the last batter grounded out in the bottom of the seventh.

And then the grim reaper came again. Dave Roberts took him out after the seventh inning, making himself the first manager in MLB history to preempt two perfect games in progress. Kershaw became only the second player in MLB history to complete at least seven innings and get removed with a perfect game still intact. The other was Rich Hill.

* * *

"Clayton and I were just talking about you," Kershaw's best friend and former catcher A. J. Ellis said when he answered the phone.

Wait, what?

"I wasn't just talking about you; I was bragging about you," A. J. said.

Ellis was Kershaw's main catcher during their eight seasons together in Los Angeles. He caught the 2014 no-hitter, perfect but for a teammate's fielding error. He was at home in Milwaukee when Kershaw faced the Twins that day in Minneapolis. He had retired at the end of 2018.

"I'm watching that game. I'm sitting in my house, I'm just enthralled. My best friend is on the mound, and he just keeps rolling and rolling through this Twins lineup. Just the way that he was just commanding the baseball, the weather, everything started lining up.

"His weapons were so nasty that day. These perfect games tend to evolve over time. The hitters get antsy and want to get the hit as fast as possible. They don't want to go deep in the count. So, even though he was at eighty pitches, and he had six more outs to get, it was the bottom two-thirds of the Twins lineup."

What the moment called for, what baseball in its current iteration lacks, what the future demands, is what Ellis called "situational dexterity."

That may be the best call he ever made.

There have to be allowances. In the moment, for the moment, for the person of the moment. "Metrics means that there's no deviation ever for what's not the norm," said Rich Hill. "And when you have a great player like Kershaw, it's never the norm."

This is why Joe Maddon held a preseason no-hitter meeting with his starting pitchers in spring training. He thinks it was Theo Epstein's idea. He told them: "When you're going for a no-hitter, go for the no-hitter, and we'll make it up on the next start."

And what of the impact on the team? Should that have been a consideration? "Is this gonna be a rallying cry for our team?" Ellis said. "'Oh, my gosh. Clayton's first start coming off injury. This is gonna be a special year, guys. I mean, can you feel it? This team is destined to do something special when Clayton throws a perfect game in his first start coming back. This is our year: 125 wins and a World Championship and a parade in LA.'"

Situational dexterity would require planning and contingencies and trusting baseball eyes. Intuition used to be relevant information.

"They could have found a way to get Clayton extra off days to recover, and he could have gotten his perfect game."

After the game, he texted Kershaw. "Come on, man."

"He wrote back, 'Yeah, I know I should have went for it.' He wishes he would have fought to go get those six outs. From the mood in the dugout he knew there was no way they're gonna let him fight for it. He knew right away, walking down those steps, that he wasn't gonna be allowed, he wasn't gonna be encouraged, to go for it.

"I think that sometimes what gets lost in the shuffle is what our responsibility is in this game. We need stories, we need heroes, we need narratives. We need to retake some of the ground that basketball and football and soccer kind of stripped away from baseball. And this was an opportunity to do that."

The day we spoke he had just seen Kershaw pitch against the Brewers. Sitting in the stands, he thought about the obligations that talent brings, the responsibilities that attach to the cost of a ticket. "We're entertainers. We're escape artists trying to give people an opportunity to get away. I like watching him up close and seeing in the people around me the joy he is providing. I think that sometimes gets lost in the shuffle."

And then he said the most amazing thing. "I'm sorry for just talking too much right now, Jane."

* * *

I met Dave Roberts for breakfast at the Dodgers' swanky team hotel in the Buckhead section of Atlanta. I told him right off I had examined Rich Hill's middle finger. "Did you really?" he said. "That's amazing. I had to deal with his blisters his entire time with me."

I asked about the 2016 game in Miami. "The trainer's telling me to take him out like two innings prior," Dave said. "And I'm trying to let him go longer, and we're, like, fighting. I'm just like, dude, 'If you do this and...'

"If he can't pitch in September, let alone October...and the guy had a bloody finger, and it was like the skin was coming off.

"It was brutal."

Then, he suggested ordering.

Dave had lots to say about the devaluation of starting pitching, "I'm guilty of it," he said. "I don't know if you saw the game the first night..."

In the first game of the three-game series against the Braves, rookie Bobby Miller more than held his own in his major-league debut against the usually unhittable Spencer Strider. "Couldn't get him through the fourth inning," Dave said. "No. He couldn't get through the fifth inning. He had one out in the fifth inning, and I brought in our highest-leverage reliever."

I hadn't seen the game, so I didn't know that Dave was wrong. You can't be expected to remember everything when you've played and managed in as many games as Dave has. But it was telling, reflexive, to assume the kid got himself in trouble and had to be given the hook when in fact Miller pitched five complete innings and left with a 4–1 lead.

Upon consideration, Dave said, maybe he should have been penalized. Maybe every manager should be penalized. "Once the starting pitcher comes out of the game, you lose the DH," he said. "A manager would have to weigh the likelihood of a starter getting pummeled in late innings versus the loss of his DH. It would incentivize the value of the starting pitcher going longer into the game."

"They've been talking about that."

Manfred got slammed for talking about that.

"Have they? I like that idea."

"Here's one you're really gonna hate. Ready?"

"Yep," Dave said.

I call it the Roberts rule.

"Any manager who takes a guy pitching a perfect game out in the seventh inning loses his managerial challenges for the next three days."

"That's fair," he said. "I like it. I like it. Just with the context on how much he pitched and all that stuff."

I showed him the numbers on aborted no-hitters and perfect games and named all the managers who said they'd have done as he did. But I was dancing on the head of a pin trying to avoid the harder, more pointed question.

"Who speaks for the game? Somebody has to say, 'What are we losing? How do we balance this a little bit?'"

"I love that question. I *love* that question!"

"You understand. I'm not saying there's a right and wrong here. I can argue it both ways."

I understand all the reasons Kershaw is a bad test case: weather, injuries, age, not to mention his importance to the team. I also understand why he is the best test case: because he's Kershaw. If anyone could have done it, should have had leave to do it, it's him.

Dave paused. "That's why I'm so . . . because to be honest with you, I one thousand percent agree with your thoughts."

* * *

Mike Rizzo, the stubborn old coot who still believes in building a team around starting pitching, was unmoved by my appeal to sentiment. "I want the manager to manage to win that game. That's the drama I want. The romance of it like you're describing, the Willis Reed moment, if you will, we have them occasionally. It's just more rare now, and it's something we have to embrace when we see it."

Dave Smith—founder of Retrosheet, a microbiologist by training, a baseball historian, and an occasional sentimentalist who named his daughter Sandy because his first date with her mother was on the day of Koufax's perfect game—was also unmoved. One thing he's not sentimental about is cell structure.

"How many great pitchers blew up their arms before they were thirty? Warren Spahn wasn't a human being. He doesn't count. And Nolan Ryan was ridiculous besides being an asshole. Those extraordinary three-deviations-away-from-the-mean kind of people don't say that the mean was wrong. It says, 'Those are really special.'

"But what's the cost of getting them? Yeah, you lose Sandy Koufax pitching on two days' rest. It was pretty cool. But it wasn't a good thing to do to him, and I think it probably set some trends for other people to do foolish things like that."

Nor does he lament the loss of complete games and the machismo that came with them. "'If you don't have 30 percent of your games be complete games, you're not a real man.' 'You gotta pitch three hundred innings to show you got balls.'

"Well, that was stupid in 1915. It was moronic in 1965, and happily enough, they don't do that anymore."

Kevin Cash wasn't having it either. "How do I think today's pitching has changed the character of the game? For so many years, a starting pitcher [would say], 'It's my day, it's my start day.' Fuck that. We're about winning."

"Players just don't understand the consequences," Dave Roberts said. "They're in the moment." They have to be in the moment. "But as a manager you have to look at the micro and macro. He was a viable member of the team. If we were out of contention, it wouldn't have mattered."

In the fullness of time, Rich Hill achieved a kind of equanimity about his losses. That's because he's suffered bigger ones: the loss of an infant son, for example. That's also because he's as much a competitor as he is a pitcher. That's why he was still pitching at age forty-four. "The playoffs were coming down the road. Any manager, or any general manager, any owner, that's what they want in a player," he said. "A guy who's out there in the moment, who understands how to compete, but also sees the future."

Roberts didn't sound as resolute about Kershaw. His regret was palpable. "It killed me," he said. "It *killed* me... Kershaw was only supposed to go five innings."

Yeah, *but*, I said. "What if the next-day story wasn't 'Kershaw removed after seven perfect innings' but 'Clayton Kershaw, who was too injured to pitch in the playoffs, who barely threw in spring training, who has accomplished absolutely everything else in his Hall of Fame career—four Cy Young Awards, a World Series ring, a no-hitter blemished only by an infielder's error—threw a perfect game in his first start of the 2022 season.' Wouldn't that be a reason to go out to the ballpark?"

"Absolutely," Dave said.

"So what do we do?"

I winced at "we." So much for reportorial objectivity. I was too busy punking myself to register Dave's reply.

"I'm kicking the can on that one."

* * *

The way Rich Hill sees it, every game is a symphony, and when he's on the mound he's the conductor. "As the pitcher you're on center stage. That's something that people see and can feel. The starting pitcher gets top billing, top spot on the marquee. And he should be the name on the marquee."

Some moments called for interpolation, some for ritardando. He would step off the rubber, walk around, tell himself, "I'm gonna let this moment build."

He gets that this is about more than appealing to sentiment. It's about appealing to your audience. "Fans buy the ticket for the emotion. They want the emotion in the stadium. So, buying that ticket is connected to something within us when we were little kids. But it's also connected with that player you came to see. The player brings the emotion, and the fan can resonate with that because they want to get away for two and a half hours or three hours from whatever is going on in their life.

"And what I think baseball is trying to do is remove that and say, 'You need to just come and watch the organization,' which is the brand. And I think that takes away from that human element of what that player is accomplishing. I've always been a proponent of the human element."

He has devoted himself to the exploration of pitching possibilities, the art of keeping guys off balance, understanding how to change speeds, and the efficacy of slow, slower, and slowest. "I threw a pitch yesterday at 64 mph and got an out," he said suddenly and started laughing. "Would I like to throw a hundred miles an hour? Of course. I think that would be amazing."

But velo was never his calling card. Maybe once he threw a ball 96 mph, or maybe the radar gun at Wrigley Field was faulty.

In 2015, the Red Sox signed him and sent him to Triple-A Pawtucket, where he met the new director of pitching, Brian Bannister.

"This is where everything changed," Hill said. "He said, 'You have a really good feel for spinning the baseball. How much do you think you could change the shape of it?'

"And I was like, 'Holy shit.' It was like this explosion of creativity. Before, creativity was a thing guys had to be comfortable enough in their own shoes to take the chance to throw something obscure and use a different arm angle, use a different shape."

Eight years later, he was center stage on opening day at PNC Park with a 64-mph curveball in his back pocket.

"And I'm going to use it because I have conviction behind it. And I have an aggressiveness behind it, and I'm gonna be creative with it."

His stay in Pittsburgh did not last long or end well. He was traded to the San Diego Padres on August 1. That didn't go well or last long either. But there was a moment in September after he lost his spot in the rotation, when he was fooling around with different grips, because that's what this pitcher does, and because that's how he indulges his curiosity and explores his imagination.

So he kept throwing, and the ball did something interesting. And he thought to himself, *I think I found something.*

CHAPTER 11

A WAY TO DO THINGS

Learning how to keep the faith and how to cut the bases

Ron Washington, "Wash" to anyone who knows him at all, was hanging by the railing next to the Atlanta Braves home dugout, all cackles and nervous energy, waiting for his pupils to show up. In their absence, laughter would have to suffice. It's his default position. "Another day, another dollar in The Show," he said.

Wash was then in his seventh season as third base coach, and drill sergeant, instilling in his pupils a respect for the craft of the game. If God is in the details, Wash is His Minister of Particulars. But he was also seventy-one years old, an old man in a young man's industry.

He had spent close to a quarter century drilling players in the exacting science of tags and pivots, teaching and talking about the little things that no longer seem to matter, watching and filing away details about the way the game was being played and managed, and thinking about what he'd do if he got another chance to manage again.

He'd spent fifteen years in the minors; parts of ten years in the majors; then ten years as third base coach for the Oakland A's, as well as eight years as manager of the Texas Rangers, taking them to the

World Series in 2010 and in 2011. Twice in Game Six in 2011, they were one strike away from winning the whole shebang.

Then the downfall: a fifth-place finish and an admission of infidelity in 2014 after admitting cocaine use in 2009 proved insurmountable. They are sins common to the baseball life but not easily forgiven when you're sixty years old and Black. He resigned from the job and resigned himself to the life of a baseball lifer doing what he could, instead of what he can.

In more than a decade with the A's, he turned Marcus Semien and Eric Chavez into Gold Glove Award–winners. Chavez presented him with one of his trophies, inscribed, "Not without you, Wash." When Hurricane Katrina destroyed Wash's New Orleans home, and the trophy along with it, Chavez had another made for him.

He turned Scott Hatteberg, the decommissioned catcher, into a respectable first baseman. "I'd watch him go through these drills exhaustively in spring training with so many players because everybody wanted to work with him," Hatteberg said. "I mean, his reputation was like an Ivy League type. He was this savant, and he gave everybody the exact same effort if your number was 98 or the freaking starting shortstop. He would come into the coaches' room at the end of the day and—he's an older guy, exhausted—just sit on his stool and almost wilt. He's one of those foundational guys."

Two months into the first season under MLB's new rules, I wanted to get Wash's take. "We'll give you a quick game but it's not normal baseball," he said. "I don't think I'd leave my house to go see it."

You forget how much horseshit there is in the game until you meet an honest man.

He just can't help himself. "The game of baseball has gotten to the point where they want to give these kids advantages because they don't take the time to learn the advantages. So, what the fuck are they doing?

They can't break up a double play because they don't want to take the time to learn how to protect themselves. So, what happened? The game protects them. That's this generation.

"We was taught how to steal bags. So, now you can't teach them how to steal bags. You gotta do things to give them an advantage to steal a bag? Like having a pitcher can only throw over there three times? Pitcher should be able to throw to first base as much as he want."

The advantage produced 3,617 stolen bases in 2024, the most since 1915, which with the increased pace of play made the game feel faster still.

We were standing not far from first base and the new and improved official Major-League Pizza Box bags, three inches bigger than the old ones. "Have you felt them?" I asked.

Naw, he said.

Well, I had. I wondered about their hard, crisp edges. They felt slippery. "Well, you know, in the day when you was back there with Babe Ruth and them, they had those leather bags," he replied.

There's nothing better than a baseball guy giving you shit. That's how you know you've done something right.

"You know what Dusty said about these bags?" Dusty looked after Wash when he was called up to the Dodgers in 1977, the way Hank had looked after Dusty a decade earlier. "He said, 'They're making it conducive for nonathletic white players occupying the game.'"

Wash snorted and chortled, which is not something you hear every day.

"That bag can give you an advantage if you know how to use it. All they see is [it's] a couple inches bigger. If you really run the bases to perfection—and there's no perfection in baseball—those couple of inches, if you hit the bag right, it's a difference of being safe or out. You gotta make sure you let them know that when they hit that corner, they gotta lean inside."

Then one of his pupils arrived. "Gotta go to work. One of my boys showed up."

* * *

His office was a patch of perfect grass perhaps fifteen feet from the Braves' dugout. The sound system came alive briefly, just long enough to play a ballpark standard, "Celebration."

He opened for business, as is his habit, four hours before game time, when the ballpark gates were still closed and the stands were empty. The tools of his trade were packed into two medium-sized soft-sided coolers, Braves logo prominently displayed, one filled with baseballs and the other with thin white towels and two training gloves, one a smaller version of a regular glove, one that looks like a pancake.

Wherever Wash goes, a fungo bat goes with him. I couldn't see if it was a "Ron Washington Proven Brand Fungo Model, 36-inch, 24 oz., with a slight flair on the knob and his signature on the barrel."

Third baseman Austin Riley was first to show up, just as he had at age nineteen, having just finished his first year in A-ball, when he would appear in the Braves' clubhouse at 7:00 a.m., a half hour before anyone else—except Wash—and ask without asking to do some of Ron Washington's famous infield drills.

Wash's regulars go through the familiar motions in half an hour. Riley had long since become a regular and finished with dispatch. Two more regulars arrived: Ozzie Albies, the voluble second baseman, who accessorized his black athletic tights and baby blue T-shirt with a gigantic diamond-encrusted "A" dangling from a chain about his neck, and his silent sidekick, shortstop Orlando Arcia.

He came for drills. Instead, he got an argument. Wash was displeased by the way Albies had applied a tag at second base, allowing a runner to advance into scoring position. Wash demanded a reckoning.

"All I had to do is tag him," Albies said cheerfully. "Get off. Because I didn't wanna be in the spot. Monster's coming in."

"Right," Wash said, skeptically.

"I'm 170 pound, he's probably 240," Albies said with high-pitched incredulity. "I ain't gonna take that. He's gonna kill me. So, I had to just tag him, go quick, and get out of the way."

Wash turned to me. "See, that's a form of playing scared."

"No, no, no. No scare here," Albies said. Arcia giggled.

"I'm trying to get it out of you," Wash said.

"There's a whole big heavy truck coming in," Albies insisted. "I ain't staying there."

Skinny as he is, Wash has a big, deep, throaty laugh that rises like an express elevator and opens up into a penthouse cackle. "Look at me!" Ozzie chirped, pretending to have done it right. "*Pow!* I'm out."

"No, you was like this, dawg."

"How was I?"

"Your head was never in there."

"Should it be?" I asked.

"Yes."

"Why?"

"You got to see where you're taggin' the guy," Wash said. "If you tag without seeing you're tagging blind. Now tag with it."

"Sometimes I ask dumb questions on purpose."

"It's not dumb," Wash said, "I got the answers for you."

"I know you do."

"You will learn," Wash said. "It's not dumb."

"Not dumb," Ozzie agreed.

"You got to be seeing what you're doing," Wash said.

"You have to in everything," Ozzie added, cheerfully. "That's the game of baseball."

"That's the game of life," I said stupidly.

Upon reflection, I realized Wash was teaching that too.

* * *

Arcia kneeled on a folded clubhouse towel five feet from Wash—Albies jabbering nonstop—while Wash bounced strategically placed one-hoppers his way alternating right, left, and center, varying the speed and direction without giving notice. Then they took turns trash-talking and using Wash's small infield glove.

Wash grabbed the fungo bat, halfway up the shaft, and kneeling on one knee, peppered each of them, one after the other, with harder-hit balls. Astonishing how quickly each fell into an established rhythm with him, like base liners exchanging balls in an extended rally. Back and forth, click and catch, click and catch. Their reflexes were almost hypnotic.

Neither missed until Arcia butchered a backhand that bounced up and hit Albies, who was minding his own business, crouching on one of Wash's duffel bags. "Washhhhh!" he cried. Arcia laughed.

Next, they glided side to side, reaching for harder-hit balls, this time with Wash's pancake glove. Arcia, who is taller, bent his knees more. Albies laughed more. "Beautiful," Wash said.

Wash moved farther back and hit the ball harder. They moved now with greater urgency but no less grace as if the ball was in play, adopting a ready stance, stretching out one leg, then the other, practicing getting low to the ball. Their dexterity and quickness were riveting. Dr. Strangeglove, these guys are not. If you don't know, look him up.

* * *

Ron Washington is an exception in so many ways. And exceptions matter. First: He's old and he's employed. Because he is employed, and because he demands it, he carries the imprimatur of authority that distinguishes him from all the other old-timers brought to spring training as special assistants who specialize in telling old baseball stories.

Jim Palmer told me about a visit to the Minnesota Twins spring training complex—you gotta have a complex—by Hall of Famers

Jim Kaat, Paul Molitor, and Rod Carew where they were kept in virtual quarantine, Kaat said. "They weren't allowed to talk to them," Palmer said. "Carlos Correa walked by and said, 'What can they tell me?'

"Kaat said, 'I wanted to deck him.'"

Kaat pitched in four decades without a major arm injury. He learned conditioning from one of his elders, Warren Spahn, who pitched until he was forty-four. He took Kaat to the outfield with a little leather bag full of balls. "He picked one up and did a little hop, step, and a jump and threw it to second like an infielder," Kaat said. "I probably started at forty feet, then moved back to fifty feet. By the end, Luis Tiant and I were doing one hundred feet. We'd do it three or four days in a row, then take a day off, then increase the velocity. Probably had twenty-five or thirty balls in that pile. The first time I did it in spring training, the coaches said, 'That can't be good for you.' They didn't realize I'd gotten it from Spahnie."

* * *

One June day in 2022, I joined former Phillies Manager Charlie Manuel and his predecessor, Larry Bowa, in a luxury suite behind home plate at Citizens Bank Stadium. A TV monitor hung from a wall over a faux wooden desk the width of the suite with a row of ubiquitous black office chairs that swiveled, leaned, and rolled. The refrigerator was empty. The windows were fixed in an upright and locked position, sparing us the sounds and the smells of the game.

Waitresses devoted to Uncle Charlie ducked their heads in the door to ask if he wanted something to eat or drink. He didn't. But he did need one of them to use a badge to swipe open the door to the press area some ten feet away, off-limits to "special assistant to's" such as himself, where the closest men's room was located. "Bo and I still like to go to minor-league games, talk about baseball, teach," he said. "But they look at you because you're old and push you aside. And they want you out. That's the message they send."

"Well," I said, hopefully, "baseball still looks like baseball before the game starts. What happened, Charlie?"

"What's the name of that movie, Bo?" he said, swiveling to face Bowa at the other end of the row.

"*The Bad News Bears*," Bo said.

"...And the one that was supposed to be the Cleveland Indians, and the owner was going to move 'em to Milwaukee?" Charlie said.

He meant Miami.

"Wait, wait, slow down," I said. "You think the Hollywood treatment of baseball eroded the—what's the word?—the authority of baseball managers?"

"Yes," Charlie said. "Because they made fun of them."

"'*Major League*!'" Bo interjected.

"You seen people on there talk about how dumb the managers and coaches were, and it was all like a joke, comedy, and I think a young generation they get caught up into things like that. And all of a sudden here comes fantasy baseball."

I made a note to tell Dan Okrent he had broken Charlie's heart.

Charlie had a good run in Philadelphia, managing the Phillies from 2005 until he was fired in August 2013, winning the World Series in 2008 and losing it in six games the following year. The Phillies brought him back to fill in as hitting coach in August 2019, five years into the Statcast era. "I like Statcast. Hey, it gives me information. From a hitter's standpoint, it shows you that he's improving his plate discipline, getting better pitches to hit. He's walking more and he's swinging at good strikes. But that guy that's showing you that Statcast, he's not the teacher. That old coach sitting over there is the teacher. And when we go look at our last four or five years in the minor leagues, we fired every hitting coach we had, and we had some good ones, but they get fired for the analytics people."

The next morning, I was half an hour late for breakfast with Charlie, who was sitting in the hotel lobby, brooding and waiting, with a cup of coffee for me.

"How did you sleep?" I asked, instead of apologizing, which was rude.

That was the least of my offenses.

"Not well," he said. "I was up all night thinking about what you said about the changes we're making, and the questions you asked about whether we've improved the game. It's deteriorating. I love baseball so much. I want it to be played the way it was."

In a lame attempt to make amends, I pointed out that the Phillies had won the game the old-fashioned way—without hitting a home run.

"There was a way to play," he said mournfully.

He missed that way and his place in it. "I've never been to work. Never had a job in my life. If anyone laughed more than I did, I'd like to meet them. I can holler, I can cuss, I can do anything I want to in a locker room. And I miss all that. I miss all the BS-ing, and also I miss the real guys that you got to be kind of serious with and understand everything about.

"I miss being who I am."

* * *

One morning in December 2023, when surely I had better things to do, I was watching the *Hot Stove* on the MLB Network and heard Ron Washington's New Orleans laugh. Harold Reynolds and Matt Vasgersian were interviewing the newly named manager of the Los Angeles Angels and showing photos from his fifty-two-year career in baseball. A photo of Milwaukee pitcher Odell Jones flashed on the screen. The date was May 28, 1988. "I broke up that no-hitter!" Wash crowed. "Tried to flip me a breaking ball. Didn't work."

Jones had held the Cleveland Indians hitless through eight innings when Charlie Manuel, Cleveland's hitting coach, sent Ron Washington up to pinch-hit. "And Charlie Manuel called on me! The real thing about that is we had guys who were better pinch hitters than me. Charlie Manuel called on me because he knew in the minor leagues I wore him out."

Wash managed an opposite-field line drive just over the second baseman's head to break up the no-hitter. Now I knew why I was watching the MLB Network.

Long before he got the job in Anaheim, Wash was thinking like the manager he had been. He saw too many players not watching the game. Not staying in the dugout. If he had his way, the clubhouse would be closed.

He saw too many young managers not even seeing what's happening on the bench. "More concerned about their job than they're concerned about the power that they have to not see something that they don't wanna see."

Thinking about analytics led him back to the dugout, where too much technology resided. "These young kids, they just keep going up there doing the same thing over and over and over and over, every pitch, every at bat. They don't make adjustments that fast because they'll go back and look at that iPad and see on that iPad what they wanna see, and not what's really happening.

"Experienced eyes see what's happening in real time. I try to get Ozzie and all those guys to figure what's going on in real time and not on this iPad because that's gonna make you feel good, and how can you feel good about what you did because you didn't get the result he was looking for?"

He shook his head and sighed. "We feed 'em too much."

You mean like force-feeding geese to produce foie gras?

"What really happens in the game right now is we've taken their thought process away from them." He reminded me a bit of Jason Ochart. "We've given them thoughts instead of letting them think for themselves and help them get through challenges by themselves."

Red Smith taught me how to ask a question guaranteed to elicit a good quote. It had become as reflexive to me as hitting fungoes is for Wash. "So, how does one man counter that entire avalanche of stupidity?" I asked.

Wash looked askance. "I don't think one man can conquer that avalanche of stupidity. I just think that one man when he's involved in something makes certain that those things are done with detail, but some people don't understand what detail is."

I apologized for being a noodge, for pushing him, repeatedly, to explain the specifics of Ozzie's "headless" tag until I could see it. I told him why it mattered in writing to be facile with details and how, when I taught journalism to undergraduates at Georgetown University, students could never answer the question: What is the color of the sky?

"Blue," they'd say.

"But what kind of blue?"

They looked at me dumbfounded.

"Light," one wiseass said.

"Robin's egg," said another.

"Okay," I said, "how about the color of my grandmother's eyes on the day she died?"

I could see her holding my hand on the CC local on the day we went to Saks Fifth Avenue to buy me a baseball glove, which made it necessary to tell Wash about Sammy Esposito. How I tracked him down on an Opening Day when there was no baseball in Washington and how we commiserated over the loss of our Sammy Esposito gloves.

"I'm just trying to do the same thing as you," Wash said.

CHAPTER 12

DIPPED IN SHIT

To style or not to style: Is there a right way to play?

In elementary school, I learned that the Mississippi River was big and wide, separating these United States east from west, and was the way to go if you were lightin' out for the territory.

Imagine my surprise, upon lightin' out for Oklahoma State University on Route 35, heading north from Edmond, Oklahoma, in Jordy Mercer's tricked-out Ford F-150 Raptor, to learn that this was yet another East Coast canard. The Great American Prairie of the west and the Black Prairie of the east were cleaved by an impenetrable, ancient forest called the Cross Timbers, running north-south from southern Kansas through Oklahoma into central Texas.

Pioneers were rebuffed by them. (Wagon trains went around them.) Indigenous people sought cover in them. So thick was the vegetation that different species of bugs set up camp on either side of the divide.

This ornery growth—coarse-branched post oak, bristle-lobed blackjack oak, thicket-forming rough-leaved dogwood, flowering buckbrush, and fragrant sumac—imposed "vexations of flesh and spirit," easterner Washington Irving wrote in 1832. It was as if "struggling through forests of cast iron."

Those Cross Timbers wouldn't have stood a chance against Jordy's Raptor. Even with the cool retractable power step, illuminated by a strip of neon blue running lights, I had a hard time hoisting myself into his new ride. All pickup trucks are monster trucks to me.

"It's a beast," Jordy said, extending a hand. "My kids call it the Storm Trooper because it looks like a Storm Trooper from *Star Wars*."

Stillwater, home of the Oklahoma State Cowboys, sits on the eastern edge of the Cross Timbers at the junction of two streams, Stillwater Creek and Boomer Creek. The town was founded there in 1893 in advance of the land grab that ensued when the unassigned Indian territories were opened to the acquisitive. Nobody in town could tell me where the now ecologically "impaired" streams met. "There's not much water left," Jordy said.

He had returned to Stillwater after retiring from baseball to complete his college degree. Head Coach Josh Holliday, son of former head coach Tom, brother of MLB all-star Matt, uncle of number-one draft pick Jackson, heard he was taking classes and sweet-talked him into serving as a student-assistant coach. The NCAA only allowed two paid assistant coaches. A loophole had allowed Josh's brother, Matt Holliday, to serve as a volunteer coach, a loophole the NCAA closed just as Jordy arrived in 2023.

Jim Kaat had tipped me too to a boomlet of former major leaguers going back to college to finish their degrees and volunteer as much-needed student-assistant coaches. He mentioned Troy Tulowitzki at the University of Texas and Robin Ventura at Oklahoma State, who succeeded Matt Holliday, which is how I ended up riding shotgun in Jordy's beast. "So did you see what happened yesterday with the Rays and Wander Franco?" Jordy said.

The night before, Tampa Bay shortstop Wander Franco had broken one of baseball's cardinal unwritten rules: he failed to take it seriously. In the top of the seventh inning, with the Rays leading 6–1, Franco fielded a one-hopper traveling at 103.2 mph and flipped it up in the air to himself before throwing to first for the out.

If a Banana had done it, he would have gotten extra points for the effort.

"Did he just do that?" Rays' color man Brian Anderson asked TV viewers. "He tossed the ball up to himself!"

MLB.com highlighted it in the roundup of big-league plays: "...6-3 putouts don't come any cooler than Wander flipping the ball to himself."

SB Nation asked: "Who needs a bat flip when you BALL FLIP?"

A sports radio jock exclaimed: "You know if old-school baseball fans are getting irate then something awesome happened."

Rays Manager Kevin Cash, Josh Holliday's roommate in the minor leagues, didn't seem put out—publicly. "As soon as I get home, I know my son, J. D., is going to look at me and tell me to go out there and practice that play with him. Unfortunately, I won't be able to do that."

Jordy was aghast. "So, do you think that's the right way to play?" he demanded. "Or do you think that's the wrong way to play, Jane?"

"I know what the right answer is," I said.

"I think the reason why he did that is he wants to get noticed 'cause he wants it to be about himself."

"I think he did it because he could."

And because he comes from a baseball culture that is as effusive—"colorful" and "flashy" in baseball code—as American baseball has been hidebound by unwritten rules. He quickly became the talk of sports radio and social media, exposing a generational and cultural divide every bit as ornery as the Cross Timbers.

"I think there's a right way to play," Jordy said. "I think there's a wrong way. I do. The rebuttal's gonna be 'let the kids play.' It's fun. It's exciting. I understand that.

"Your guy and my guy, Mickey Mantle, ran around the bases with his head down 'cause he was humble and he didn't wanna show up a pitcher."

This was something I knew about. "Sorry to disappoint, he ran around the bases with his head down, not because he was humble—which he was—but because he didn't want to trip over the bag and make his knee worse."

Jordy wheeled the Beast into a parking lot that was the only unimproved part of the Cowboys' spanking new $75 million baseball facility, O'Brate Stadium, all orange and black, with black metal silhouettes of cowboys on horses ringing the concourse, O'Brate is a magnet—George W. helped open the place—and a recruiting tool as potent as having ex–major leaguers on your coaching staff. The 7,400-square-foot locker room is plenty big enough for the ping-pong table showcased at the entrance where recruits are sure to see it.

"It's funny because a couple guys up here in Oklahoma State will want to do the flashy play," Jordy said, unable to let go of Wander Franco. "I said to them, 'You know how to get noticed? You make the play. You make the play every time. You make the routine play every time. And then the great play will just happen.'"

* * *

In a lot full of pickup trucks—a whole state of pickup trucks—Jordy's was the baddest, cleanest, and undoubtedly the most expensive. Base price $72,350, and there was nothing base about Jordy's ride. Jordy had coordinated it with a black-on-black Louis Vuitton backpack and matching duffle bag he had purchased on one of the last road trips of his ten-year big-league career. The whole look said, "big league."

Trust me, the players noticed. A jabbering posse of Cowboys made its way from stretching on the grass of the thirty-five-hundred-seat stadium (with eleven suites and four hundred premium seats) to the artificial turf for drills with Jordy. I could make out only three words: "backpack" and "Wander Franco."

Parker McCollum, the country singer and 2022 winner of the Academy of Country Music award for New Male Artist, was lifting weights in the gym. (Who says there's nothing to do in Stillwater?) His latest release circulated throughout the complex on repeat. "Oh, my God, we've heard this song like eight times!" a voluble red-headed Poke moaned.

That's how I met Roc Jack Riggio, the Cowboys' cock-of-the-walk second baseman, who was named for stardom and raised to expect it. I followed him to the half diamond where Jordy was preparing for bunting drills. In Stillwater, bunting is still a thing, a weapon, a skill to be perfected.

"What about Franco?" I asked Roc.

"Being an outside viewer of it and being a baseball player, it's something you probably shouldn't do," Roc said carefully. "I don't think I'd ever throw the ball to myself. But, also, being a baseball player, I understand that you have to have a lot of confidence to throw the ball up to yourself before you throw it to first base. And so, being a baseball player, it says a lot about Wander Franco, I think, in a positive way. "

It was an interesting response considering he was the guy Jordy had alluded to in the Beast. Roc had adopted Jack Sparrow's *Pirates of the Caribbean* tippy-toed gait somewhere between second and third base during a home run trot in the 2022 NCAA Tournament Regional series. His teammates had dared him to do it.

It didn't go down well in some parts, but Roc likes when people talk shit about him. "Let me hear it. Give it to me. I know I can handle it."

He responded to criticism from the unamused Arkansas Razorbacks with another home run the following day. Declining any manner of trot, he sprinted around the bases like a bat out of hell in sixteen seconds.

Wander Franco was hardly the first player to test MLB boundaries of propriety. Miguel Sanó kissed a baseball he fielded at third base before throwing the hitter out at first. Willie Mays deliberately wore a cap one size too small so that it would fly off when he ran. "People like that," he told John Shea, his coauthor in *24: Life Stories and Lessons from the Say Hey Kid*. "They want to see the hat fall off."

* * *

Stillwater, Oklahoma, is smack-dab in the middle of Tornado Alley. It's twenty-five miles northwest of Cushing, the "Pipeline Crossroads of the World," where a hefty percentage of the US crude oil inventory is stored. It's sixty-six miles north of Oklahoma City and sixty-three miles west of Tulsa, which is the answer to every prospective student's first question: "What do you do in Stillwater on the weekend?"

Stillwater was also smack-dab in the middle of the conversation about a population that is both rapidly aging and diversifying. A huge demographic shift is in progress in baseball as it is in the rest of the country. By the end of the century, America will no longer be a predominantly white nation—a reality that can't help but fuel the roiling rage about immigration as well as attitudes toward preening ballplayers.

That shift was reflected on 2025 Opening Day rosters: 28 percent—or 265—of all players were foreign-born, the vast majority from Spanish-speaking countries. I was surprised the number wasn't higher. Maybe that's because they make themselves so noticeable. "They play with a joy and an abandon that is sorely lacking from too much of baseball," Buck Showalter said. "And if we're gonna get kids in America back to loving baseball the way you do—"

Who, me?

"—we're gonna need some of that kind of excitement."

According to Playfly Sports, which supplies audience data to professional sports leagues, 67 percent of baseball fans are white; 12 percent are Hispanic; and 11 percent are Black. White as baseball fans may be, they are getting younger—half are younger than forty-four, same as the NFL—and perhaps they'll be more tolerant of exuberance. MLB reports that the median age of ticket buyers has dropped from fifty-one to forty-five since 2019 with a 10 percent increase in ticket buyers in the coveted eighteen-to-thirty-five age bracket.

The need to get younger and cooler was at the heart of MLB's "Let the Kids Play" advertising campaign launched in 2018. Cycle Media, the production company, gathered all the coolest kids in baseball at a table for a postgame gabfest showing how cool baseball players can be.

"Baseball is fighting a stigma that it's an old and boring game," the creators declared. "As traditionalists often criticize the new school about 'the right way to play,' the MLB knew it needed to step into the modern age, and embrace young talent who are reshaping the league through a new campaign."

One of the ads gave the last wiseass word to Alex Bregman, Houston's Jewish, Spanish-speaking third baseman: "It's faster, younger, harder. The kids are here. And we play loud."

The campaign didn't exactly go over big with the old guard. "We're well beyond loosening up," Mike Rizzo snapped. "It started with 'Let the Kids Play.' Now they're flipping bats . . ."

"Why does that offend you so much? Because Mickey Mantle didn't do it?"

"Then you get mad when I strike you out and I pump my chest and you get pissed off about it."

"I think that's a culture clash," I said.

"It's a generational clash. And we've let it get that way."

"It's only gonna get more that way."

"Jeter never did it."

"Jeter's almost forty-nine years old."

And, by the way, Joltin' Joe is dead.

"I'm talking about hitting it five hundred feet, turning to the opposing dugout, pounding your chest, flipping your bat in the air," Riz said. "Because this is not the Bananas. This is freaking real shit where people make real money and get hired and fired."

After talking to Riz, I went downstairs to the visiting locker room in search of the Mets' stylish shortstop Francisco Lindor, who commissioned a one-off glove from the House of Gucci, employs a style coach, and likes to vary his silhouette every day. I wanted to ask how baseball should negotiate this transition in its fan base and its player population. He had tinted his cornrows lime green to match the glove he was using that day. "Embrace the culture," he said. "The culture has shifted. It's not the same game it used to be," he said, pausing for an important *but.* "But you gotta respect the game."

In fact, he said it four times. "But you gotta be yourself, because the moment you're not and try to be somebody else, you're not at your best."

And then I blurted out the single most unprofessional sentence I've ever uttered, one I couldn't finish as soon I realized what I had said. "It's like what's going on across the board in this country. If the old white guys would just die already..."

Lindor looked at me, eyes as wide as his magazine cover all-league smile, and said, "That's a great opinion, but I didn't say that."

Andrew McCutchen laughed when I told him the story. "I don't know if these people have been watching minor-league games lately. We got a whole tandem of people that have a flair for the dramatic, and they're not afraid to showcase it on the field.

"That's coming. Man, that's not gonna slow down any time soon."

To which Lindor added: "You gotta have the freedom to play the game how America is: free. Show emotions; it's okay."

It's more than okay. It's necessary.

* * *

Tom Holliday, father of Josh and Matt, grandfather of Jackson and 2025 first round draft pick Ethan, greeted me sitting down in the living room of his rental house in Cape Cod, where he was midway through his sixth season as coach of the Chatham Anglers. He was welcoming, and very generous with his time, but a bit glum, I thought.

He made one source of his unhappiness clear right off. The Orioles were racing Jackson through their minor-league system. He was about to be moved up to Double-A baseball, his third team of the year. "I don't know what's wrong with baseball today," he grumped.

Tom was proud to be the coach who never left Stillwater. He raised seven-time all-star Matt and College World Series champion and former Orleans Cardinal Josh in Stillwater. He was a Cowboy coach for twenty-six years, the last seven as head coach before being fired in 2003.

Stillwater became the nexus of his recruiting pitch. "The strength of Stillwater, Oklahoma, is that when you let your kid go there, you can go to bed at night and not have to worry about drive-by shootings, drug dealers, everything that could take your kid away from you. The safety of Stillwater became my number-one selling point. When I signed Pete Incaviglia, Pete lived in Monterey, California—I flat out told him, I said, 'Pete, I'm going to tell you right now, your dad just took us to dinner. You're not going to have a place like that to eat in Stillwater.'"

I couldn't find a place to get a sandwich.

"Stillwater was *Happy Days*," Tom declared.

Happy Days went off the air in 1984.

"And you could be somebody instead of being at UCLA and you walk right by a movie star and nobody knows who you are. Well, in Stillwater, you could be a movie star."

No doubt he was referring to Roc Riggio, the California kid, who had played for him in Chatham in 2022 and hated it—the fields, the umpires, the heat, and especially the quaint white houses beyond the outfield fence where a batter's eye ought to have been.

When it got to be around 2:00 p.m., I wondered, "Don't you have a game today?"

Tom said he had a doctor's appointment. He said he had never missed a game in forty years of coaching. Unbeknownst to me he had submitted his letter of resignation, citing health concerns.

Also, he had given an interview to Anglers TV expressing unhappiness with some of his "today" players. What had been a development league had become a summer drive-by for agents looking to get their clients a last look-see by scouts gathered behind backstops. "Everybody is playing for a different purpose," Tom lamented in his Anglers interview. "I got kids here who are not here for the right reason. Our team is not a team. It's just a collection of thirty people. They're setting target dates to leave. I gotta get kids who want to be here."

* * *

Roc Riggio knew where he was going to go to college before he knew where was attending high school. He committed to play for UCLA when he was in the eighth grade and decommitted during his sophomore year of high school.

"De-commit?" said Buck Showalter. "You mean, de-promise?"

Not that Roc wanted to go to college. He didn't. "I wanted to be done with school. I just wanted to play baseball." But when the Milwaukee Brewers drafted him in the eleventh round of the 2021 draft and offered eleventh-round money, he started making the rounds of big-time college baseball programs. Then Josh Holliday saw him at a tournament played at MLB's Compton Youth Academy.

"When I came to Oklahoma State, it checked off everything on my checklist. I had no idea there were gonna be this many major leaguers and guys with the knowledge that they have at the school."

Some elder scholars, like Jordy Mercer, return to college to keep a promise to themselves or to Mom or as an object lesson to their own kids. It was good for his three boys to see him sweating over the computer for a presentation to his class.

Troy Tulowitzki, now a full-time assistant coach at the University of Texas, wanted players to see "the other side from what the big league portrays," he told me. "I want to open their eyes."

Robin Ventura, Jordy's predecessor, returned to Stillwater in 2020 seeking a new life in a place where life had been sweet: He still holds the NCAA Division 1 record for a fifty-eight-game hit streak.

After sixteen years as a big leaguer and another five as manager of the Chicago White Sox, he went home to California. "Then I went through a divorce. I lived in kind of a small town, and I was probably there a year, and I was coming back here to football games. I just got this feeling like I need to get outta here. My kids were all grown. 'Cause she had left me for another woman. I was kind of like the guy around town that had cancer. Everybody was like, 'Hey, how you *doing*?'

"I'm like, fuck this."

He moved to Edmond, an hour from campus, and met with the Athletic Department's academic advisor, who advised him almost none of his old college credits were good. "She's like, 'Well, what do you want to get your degree in?' I said, 'Well, I'm here to really coach,' but I'd like to get my degree. I just picked classes, management classes, one of 'em was a science class, and one was in beer making."

"I got two points from Columbia for a class in bartending," I said. "I made a mean Grasshopper."

Unfortunately, I had to drink whatever I mixed.

Robin listened to class reading on the drive back and forth to Stillwater, where he taught Cowboy hitters old-fashioned flow drills, how to reset their bodies when their swings got out of sync, to check the flags when they got to the field, letting the wind inform how to approach at bats.

He used two old tires, one lying flat, the other standing inside the hole, to create a batting tee, forcing players to keep their swings flat. "They go, 'How'd you know about that?'" Ventura said. "And then they realize that I've been around a long time."

The emphasis on fundamentals was refreshing. "Granted, there's fundamentals in the big leagues," he said.

"Yeah, some," I replied.

"But this is taken to a whole 'nother level. This is kind of playing like old baseball."

The work ethic was equally refreshing. "They can work a long time. You know, a pro player—they do a little bit and, like, 'Yeah, I'm done for the day.'"

I was sitting just behind the backstop at downtrodden Ed Smith Stadium in Sarasota, Florida, winter home of the Baltimore Orioles, when Ventura slid into home plate, breaking his tibia and his fibula. No, I didn't hear them crack. But his dislocated ankle dangled unhinged long enough to traumatize my nine-year-old daughter and cause a woman to faint. (Not me.)

This was in 1997, way before Janet Marie Smith gussied up the place and way before I did the same thing to my ankle on a tennis court. I was at the net when the number-one player in the Philippines walloped a cross-court backhand at my décolletage. I should have ducked but turned instead to volley it forehand. My leg collapsed like a cheap folding chair.

It was my proudest moment: I didn't utter a single four-letter word. In my view, that made Robin and me soulmates. He returned to the lineup before the end of the season and played another seven years. I got back on the court and stayed just long enough to require two knee replacements.

It took Robin two and a half years to graduate. "My oldest daughter actually went here, so she's like, 'Oh, you're walking.'

"I said, 'Oh, yeah, I'll walk.'

"So, I actually went over, walked, and we had a game that afternoon, so I came over and threw a little BP in my gown."

* * *

Jordy Mercer returned to campus, two hours from where he grew up, in the fall of 2022. Basically, his wife kicked him out of the house. School was all online. He was only thirty-six years old.

Unlike Ventura, the all-American all-star, Jordy's career was like needlepoint, little things stitched together into a good baseball life. Always being in the right position, not making a mistake, not calling attention to himself. He is Oklahoma's retort to Wander Franco.

I asked him what surprised him most about working with the Cowboys. "The lack of baseball knowledge that these kids have now. When I was that age—was I the same way? They just don't know, Jane. They don't know. They can't process it."

Like what, for example? Say the opposing pitcher has thrown forty pitches in one inning, and you put on the take sign. "Our guys go up there and still swing at the first pitch," he said.

When Jordy assumed responsibility for infielders, drilling them and positioning them from the first base coaching box, Ventura was grandfathered into the role of wise but nonjudgmental uncle.

"The next couple weeks we have teams that like to bunt, like to move runners, like to manipulate the baseball in a bunch of different ways, so we are making sure we are touching on all of our fundamentals, our bunt plays. We did some drop-dead balls, getting live reads off the bat, so you're not just up there hitting a fungo from the same spot over and over and over. I love that drop-ball drill."

He worked with Riggio on double-play turns—making sure Roc had his glove and his feet in the right position. Not tagging blind, as Wash would say.

"And shortening up my feet in the infield, not having big movements that I shouldn't have," Roc said.

Equally important: He offered lessons in major-league cool. "You should see his shoe collection," Josh said.

"Jordy's the man," Roc said. "Robin helped more with the mental side of the game, how to handle certain situations, how to act like a big leaguer, how to control your emotions, how to handle yourself."

When the team hit a rough patch, Ventura knew just what to do. "I told 'em, 'If you have a losing streak, you do something goofy.' So, we lost like four or five games in a row. I said, 'Hey, Josh, can I just take 'em for thirty minutes?'

"'Whatever you want,' Josh said.

"So I told them all to stretch. I said, 'After BP we got a game tonight. Meet me in the classroom and wear something that you will not wear during the game. It can be shorts, T-shirt. Don't put shoes on. Just flip-flops.'

"So I get 'em in there. And I'm like, 'We are in the phase right now that we used to call "you are dipped in shit."'

"'Nothing's going right. You can't get any traction. No momentum. You're just dipped in shit. You can change it, but you're just dipped in shit and you gotta get it off.'

"So I'm like, 'We're gonna go into the jacuzzi room. You guys are gonna line up single file, and I'm gonna dunk you in the cold tank, and you're gonna come out, and it's all gonna be off you and you're gonna be rejuvenated.'

"I had Elvis blaring and they had a ball. And they're like, 'Where did you learn this?'

"Doesn't that say it all? I'm like, 'This is shit we used to just do. That was part of the game.'"

* * *

When I got home, Jordy texted the results of a poll he had taken at my request about Wander Franco's juggling act: "Zero percent of the coaches liked it. Fifteen percent of the pitchers liked it; and 90 percent of the position players liked it. They just thought it was really cool, position-player wise."

The Cowboys extricated themselves from that which they were dipped in long enough to win the Big 12 conference, which meant they got to host the NCAA Regional as the number-one seed, and the sixteenth-ranked team in the country. But suddenly, the stink was upon them again; no one could say why.

"It was not ideal," Jordy said. "Probably a combination of not pitching well and not hitting well to be honest with you."

Probably.

"Roc was pretty beat up," Jordy said. "It was like 0 and 2 and it was done."

Tournament. College. Childhood.

"You try to tell them," Robin said. "'This will be the last time you're on a team that everybody's really pulling for you. 'Cause you're gonna get on a minor-league team, and most of them aren't gonna want you to do well 'cause they want to be the guy that gets called up.'"

Six members of the team were drafted. Roc went to the Yankees in the fourth round, which he wasn't happy about, but they paid him more than their second rounder, he said, which made him feel better.

None have reached the majors yet. Wander Franco is out of baseball. In August 2023, he was charged with sexual abuse of a minor and exploitation in the Dominican Republic.

Robin's last season with the Cowboys was 2023. He remarried. Last I heard, he was traveling in Italy.

Jordy, who is now a broadcaster for the Pittsburgh Pirates and coaching his three boys, did not go to graduation. "I had a chance to walk but we had a game that night."

He was the last of the Cowboys' big-league student-assistant coaches—it's not easy to find guys who want to enroll full-time and the need became less urgent when the NCAA granted baseball programs an additional paid assistant coach. Which is too bad because you never know when you might need a few words of wisdom on your craft or how to make the game fun again even when it's dipping you in shit.

CHAPTER 13

JACKIE'S PLACE

Janie finds a man willing to talk about commitment

There were ghosts in the outfield. Ghosts where orange groves once grew beyond the right field fence. Ghosts on the basepaths at Holman Stadium where Jackie ran, Oisk threw, and the Duke connected. Ghosts in the gorgeous mint green, pen-and-ink spring training illustration hung in a hallway that the living hurry past in a place that used to be called Dodgertown.

It's a copy of artwork commissioned in the spring of 1955 by a new magazine called *Sports Illustrated* for the opening of the baseball season. Artist John Groth inscribed the original for Dodgers owner Walter O'Malley—"a typical day of Spring Training activities"—who kept it at the Dodgers offices on Montague Street until he hijacked the heart of Brooklyn.

Groth was a war correspondent who got himself into fixes involving live grenades with his pal Ernest Hemingway. Returning home intact, he sought safer action, employing a technique he called "speed line" drawing to sketch sporting subjects with streaks of black ink in rough, unperfected lines. Later he would fill them in with watercolors, in this case key lime green.

So here are the Brooklyn Dodgers of 1955 doing side bends, stretched across the page like the fronds of a palm tree catching the breeze on the horizon; players sliding in the sliding pit; hitters facing the "Iron Mike" pitching machine; an overdressed mother and son leaning against a batting cage in the days before climate change. Sportswriters with their Speed Graphic cameras trained on an anonymous fielder making a leaping catch, the pristine whiteness of the ball drawing your eye as it settles into the deep black pocket of his glove; and the string area where Branch Rickey's pitchers practiced hitting the corners.

It wasn't until I got home and looked more closely at my photos that I realized there were no Black faces among the Dodgers he'd sketched. No Jackie, no Newk, no Campy, no Joe Black or Junior Gilliam.

* * *

Tony Reagins was named baseball development officer in charge of getting kids to give a shit about baseball in 2015. "My job is to grow baseball," he said. "No matter what nationality, socioeconomic situation you're in, we want young people playing the game."

Young Black people in particular. "*Major League Baseball is not investing in Black players*. You hear that year over year. So, my job was to change that."

The lease on what was then called Historic Dodgertown was transferred to MLB in January 2019. "The commissioner came down in '15, and the facility wasn't being used very often," Tony said. "And he said, 'Well, what do you think about taking this over?'"

Indian River County, which owns the property, and MLB went halfsies in remaking the site into the Jackie Robinson Training Complex, a place for young Black players to learn Jackie's game. Reagins asked Dave Wallace, Sandy Koufax's pal from their time together as Dodgers pitching coaches, to call Sandy for permission to build on the site of the pitching mound Koufax used for private tutorials. "He goes, 'Are you fucking kidding me?'" Wally said. "'Go ahead and build it.'"

Once a World War II US Naval Air Station, leased by Branch Rickey and Walter O'Malley in 1948 so Jackie Robinson could live and train with his teammates, the place went to swamp rot after professional baseball left and before MLB took it over. An original welcome sign reading "DODGERTOWN WINTER HOME OF THE LOS ANGELES DODGERS OFFICES, GOLF COURSE, HOLMAN STADIUM" has been restored and stationed in front of the new administration building, its kitschy fifties lettering at odds with the generic hurricane-proof architecture seen in Florida malls and neighborhoods, all of which are named for lakes and shores and oceans, no matter how far they are from the water. "We thought we were gonna lose it because it was so old," Tony said. "And very, very heavy. I wanted it to have a presence here."

The old nine-hole golf course is gone. It's an open field now owned by the City of Vero Beach. Lennie's, a grungy bar that was walking distance through swamp and bog out beyond the batting cages, is also gone. That's where, one night in 1960, an old scout named Kenny Myers showed Koufax that his release point was too high and turned his career around.

Back then baseball was flush with talent, and Dodgertown had fields extending all the way to the horizon. There were so many players in camp in 1955, seven hundred or so, they had to be issued color-coded numbers: There were red, tan, yellow, and purple Dodgers.

* * *

By the time Marion and Julia Grissom were getting ready for the birth of the second to last of their fifteen children, they were running out of names. Marion worked thirty-nine years at the Ford plant in Atlanta, way better than picking cotton for ten years at seventy-five cents a day. Despite his place of employment, Marion wasn't a car guy. He gave his Ford pickup to his oldest son when he was of an age to drive. By 1967, he was driving a two-door, secondhand Mercury Marquis, canary yellow with brown wood trim.

That car was huge, as was Marion. Eight Grissoms could ride in it—a couple of his grown kids and a mess of nieces and nephews—and did until the brakes went out coming down a hill by their house. Pulling into the company lot one morning before Julia gave birth, Marion murmured to himself, "Marquis." He thought that sounded pretty good. Thus, the newest Grissom entered the world as a Marquis, a name befitting the noble man he became.

I told him: "If I had been named for my daddy's car, I would have been a Studebaker."

Raised on a dirt road in Red Oak, on the outskirts of Atlanta, in a house his father built with his own two hands, Marquis Grissom had enough siblings and cousins and neighbors to field three baseball teams. One day in June, before school was out, their street ball game was interrupted by a car moseying on down the road right through the middle of their makeshift field. "Hurry up, we're trying to play ball!" the kids yelled.

Marquis, who had an arm on him even at age seven, was practiced in the art of throwing rocks at intrusive automobiles. They all were. They called it "rockin' the car." But he was best, so he went last. Camouflaging his position behind a house at the corner, he grabbed a rock from the pile they kept for such occasions. Hurling it over the house, farther than he knew how, some 250 feet, he hit the top of the car as it was rolling up the hill. "Timed it perfect," he said. "Once we heard the sound, we all scattered."

Putting the car in reverse, the driver backed down the one way in, one way out road and chased down two kids who didn't run. They pointed to Marquis.

Turned out the man was a baseball coach, searching for a nearby ball field. He had so many kids on so many teams, he needed more space for practice. He knew an arm when he saw one. "I'll make you a deal," he told Marquis. "I won't tell your mom and dad you hit my car with a rock if you play on my baseball team."

Then he went inside to introduce himself to Mrs. Grissom and pulled out his badge. He was Officer T. J. Wilson of the Atlanta Police. "I damn near crapped in my pants, thinking I'm about to go to jail," Marquis said. "Later I got the worst ass whipping ever because my dad was six four, 280 pounds. Mom was under five feet tall."

Officer Wilson promised to fetch Marquis every day after school and bring him home every day after practice. He also would provide the equipment Marquis didn't have, the eighty-five-dollar registration fee, and stop on the way home for a McDonald's Happy Meal. For a boy who ate nothing from age "zero to twelve" except the vegetables the family grew and the pigs, cows, and chickens they raised, slaughtered, and salted away for the winter—half of which his father gave to neighbors and family—this was no small matter. "I'd have run through brick walls for him," Marquis said.

So began a baseball life that would span seventeen years in the major leagues and more than that in the service of kids who, like his younger self, need a safe place to play, equipment to play with, and coaches who recognize and nurture their ability.

Twice an all-star, he won four consecutive Gold Gloves for his play in center field; twice he led the National League in stolen bases. He won a World Series ring with the 1995 Braves and was named Most Valuable Player of the 1997 American League Championship Series. He spent his last season in uniform as first base coach for the 2009 Washington Nationals, the team that would draft his son, Marquis Jr., thirteen years later.

He earned $52 million playing baseball. "I made it to the league in 1989. In 1990, my second year, I made three hundred grand. I came home with all my money and built my mom and dad a house on two acres they had in Meriwether County. I had $119,000 and it cost me $115,000. I had about two thousand left in my pocket when I went to spring training.

"Next year, I signed for $1.5 million, and I started building my dream home. It took about a year and a half for that to get done. My third or fourth year, I made $3.5 million. That's when I started buying homes for all of my siblings."

After he retired in 2006, he put a million dollars of his own money into the creation of the Marquis Grissom Baseball Association (MGBA) to do for kids what had been done for him. He paid for the uniforms and the travel. He renovated and raked the fields. He cleaned up gently used equipment donated by rich folks at Buckhead Baseball—bats, helmets, gloves, cleats—and stored it in his barn, handing over the goods only when he found "a kid who's definitely gonna need it and appreciate it."

At that time, Major League Baseball had exactly one diversity outreach program—Reviving Baseball in Inner Cities (RBI), a community-based, grassroots plan for reseeding baseball in urban centers where it was all but dead. It started small in south central Los Angeles and grew into what is now a Nike-sponsored international campaign with programs in two hundred cities serving some one hundred thousand boys and girls.

That led to the creation, also in 2006, of MLB's first urban youth academy in Compton, California, where Jimmy Rollins, C. C. Sabathia, and J. P. Crawford honed their skills and found a way forward. "Changed my life," J. P. assured me.

Neither program interrupted the downward trajectory of baseball in the lives of African Americans. Marquis is one of a dedicated cohort of Black former major leaguers, minor leaguers, and coaches who grew tired of waiting for MLB to do something more and founded their own baseball academies.

By 2025, more than 1,326 young ballplayers had passed through MGBA's program, where they learned the fundamentals of baseball, math, and manners. Of them, some 400 have received college scholarships and 26 have been selected in the MLB draft, including Michael Harris Jr., the 2022 National League Rookie of the Year; Lawrence Butler, the Oakland A's right fielder and twice the American League Player of the Week in 2024; Cam Collier, the first-round draft choice of the Cincinnati Reds in 2022; Taj Bradley, starting pitcher for the Tampa Bay Rays; Termarr Johnson, the number-four pick in the 2022 draft; and Chandler Simpson lighting up the basepaths for the Rays in 2025.

Marquis was glum when we first spoke in 2021, tired of pleading for the "brick and mortar" needed to construct ballfields, batting cages, and classrooms. There were only so many fields he could build on his own. "Two reasons I started my organization: what it cost to play baseball, and African American players being undeveloped. My thought was: 'Why is Major League Baseball going to the Dominican Republic, Puerto Rico, Mexico, building these facilities around those countries, and stacking baseball players on top of baseball players and being able to pick and choose the ones they want? Why wouldn't they invest in what I'm doing? I'm doing it for all the right reasons.'"

MGBA started as a recreation league program before expanding into travel ball when Marquis saw the costs and benefits of the sprawling system of club sports and pay-to-play travel teams that have replaced Little League and other community avenues into organized ball.

He assumed management of the Atlanta Braves RBI program in 2021. The Braves foot the bill for uniforms, field rental, umpires, and coaches and charge only one hundred dollars. "There's no way you could play anywhere for a hundred dollars—fifteen games and then eight weeks of training for another hundred."

In 2024, he fielded eighteen senior RBI teams, four junior teams, and five softball teams. Little wonder he said he needed to hire more coaches and teachers. "Back in the day I would never have thought of an RBI kid to get a scholarship to go to college. Over the last four or five years, we probably had at least thirty to forty kids, maybe even more. And this year I'm pretty sure we'll have at least twenty-five."

We were sitting on crumbling concrete steps at a public park in College Park, Georgia, above Bill Evans Field, five miles down the road from his childhood home. The weather had not been kind to the baseball schedule. Just that morning Marquis had dragged the field and put down the lines, trying to get in a few RBI games before the rains returned.

The shape of his life is dictated by the rhythms of the baseball season and the overlapping schedules and demands of the many teams and programs he manages.

He trains his MGBA kids at another public park, Welcome All Park, in Fulton County, where he played for Officer Wilson. Today, Welcome All has three fields, and one designed for nine- and ten-year-olds has Marquis's name on it. He's not sure which is more jaw-dropping: the fact they named it for him or how far he hit the ball when he played there at starting at age seven.

"MGBA programs go ten months a year. We have a summer program where we do summer ball and fall ball. During the down time (October to February), we're doing speed and endurance training. Then we do an eight-week training program, twice a week, strictly development, no games.

"In November, December, January, we'll crank up doing speed, agility, light lifting with some of the elite kids because most of the kids can't afford that."

Tuition for the younger kids ranges from $1,100 to $2,500, including coaching fees and travel expenses.

He takes his elite travel teams to events at the Jackie Robinson Training Complex, and to Perfect Game tournaments like the annual fall mega WWBA World Championship in Jupiter, Florida, to which seventy-two elite teams were invited in 2024. "If we go out of town, we got hotels and travel. So, it'll probably cost you anywhere from eighteen to twenty grand 'cause you gotta stay three nights. You try to put three or four guys in the room together, and you end up getting ten rooms. You got fifteen or twenty players, and you gotta feed some of 'em. Some come with cash, and some of 'em don't come with anything and be gone for six days or five days."

He raises money through an annual celebrity golf tournament and an MGBA gala, where he first told the story he told me. One year at an Atlanta Braves Fantasy Camp, he got to talking with a man named Sidney Hinton, who happened to own a stake in a large power company. "We had a lot in common because he had a farm and I had a farm. He got a lake; I got a lake. He got a John Deere tractor; I got a John Deere tractor. We kind of hit it off."

"What's your budget?" Hinton asked.

"Thirty to forty thousand," Marquis replied.

Hinton cut him a check for $50,000, a down payment on continued largesse that added up to more than half a million dollars by mid-2024. "I started the financial literacy program, started the tutorial program, and started the career development program with that money," Marquis said. "We expanded it to a tutorial program focused on math and language arts, SAT and ACT prep. We do that right across the street in this building right here. That's the community center. It's free for all the kids in our program. You can come twice a week to get you some help.

"Teach 'em how to balance checkbooks, teach 'em what a dollar means and what banking is all about. And then we have a career-development program where we've been to Georgia Power, Coca-Cola. Chick-fil-A. They need to see what corporate America looks like. Of course, I didn't know how to write a check until I was eighteen.

"They need to put on a suit and pull their pants up and learn how to look people in the eye with a firm handshake, open the door for young ladies. It's all about presentation. It's all about attitude. It's all about character, and that's just as big as your talent. I harp on that fifty-fifty.

"We got to condition the cognitive side too, controlling your breath and staying under control. 'Don't get agitated when things don't go your way, and when they're poking at you, don't buy into it. Sometimes you experience racism, you can't let it get you off balance. So, when they do take a shot at you, you got that bulletproof armor where the bullet just bounces right back off.'"

During the pandemic, he created an outdoor program for his major leaguers on property he owns in the countryside in Fayetteville, Georgia. He calls them the Hill Boys. You can guess what they did. There were just three of them that first year: Cam Collier, son of Grissom's friend, former major leaguer Lou Collier, and Mike Harris, who brought along his friend Lawrence Butler. Marquis Jr. was the only pitcher allowed. His daddy built him an MLB-quality pitching mound.

Marquis admits he was trying to break them that first year. "I first played with him when I was about fourteen or fifteen," "Money" Mike said. "I played with him full-time. It put me in the position I'm in today and helped me become the man I have become."

Harris and Butler were two of just sixty Blacks on Opening Day rosters in 2025, three more than in 2024, and three less than the number of Venezuelans. That's just 6.3 percent, the lowest percentage since Jackie crashed the color barrier in 1947, and a precipitous decline from 1991 when close to 20 percent of major-league players were Black.

Like Grissom, Andrew McCutchen, now in his seventeenth major-league season, owes his career to happenstance. A coach who happened to see him play in the Dixie League happened to have a travel team. Another coach recommended him to the coach of an elite travel team, Team Florida USA in Panama City. Three brothers named Funk took him in for the summer. The club comped his fees. "If not for people like that I wouldn't be in the major leagues," Cutch said.

Here's the thing: Fortuity is not a strategy.

It caught up with MLB at the 2022 World Series when for the first time since 1950, not a single American-born Black player was on either World Series roster. That Astros Manager Dusty Baker and his third base coach Gary Pettis were the only Black people in uniform was a rebuke to MLB, which celebrates Jackie Robinson Day every April 15, claiming a high moral ground to which it is no longer entitled.

"It's Jackie Robinson Day?" Dusty said. "It's BS."

What would Hank say?

When I asked what my first move as commissioner should be, Dusty didn't mince words. "Get me some athletes. You know what I'm saying?"

* * *

By the time I met Marquis in Building 42, the indoor hitting facility constructed on the site of Sandy's mound, in June 2023, he was of another mind entirely about MLB. Within Building 42's 38,600 square feet of baseball were meeting rooms, classrooms, one state-of-the-art half field and four indoor batting cages to supplement nine outdoor fields, each named for one of "Jackie's Values"—Courage, Determination, Teamwork, Persistence, Integrity, Citizenship, Justice, Commitment, and Excellence.

MGBA's elite travel team was one of the sixteen teams invited to compete in the inaugural Breakthrough Series 17U championship. Bo Porter, now third base coach for Ron Washington's Angels, and Morris Madden, who did time with the Pirates and Tigers, had been invited to bring their teams too. Madden's Carolina Reds traveled from Charlotte, North Carolina, where baseball, he said quickly, is a vehicle to get kids into his academic program. "Our STEM program is based on a board game that uses the statistics of current major leaguers to teach arithmetic," he said.

Former Braves Brian Hunter and Marvin Freeman, members of that tight fraternity of Black men trying to raise up a new generation of African American baseball players, were hired as coaches, as was Marquis, there as an outfield and baserunning instructor.

The seven-year-old kid who got the policeman's car to back down the road is now helping MLB to turn MLB around. "You see my tone changed from last time I talked to you 'cause I really didn't know what MLB was doing," Marquis said. "Now I'm in the trenches with 'em. I love it."

* * *

Tony Reagins greeted me in his office in the administration building behind right field at Holman Stadium. It had the unlived-in look of an inhabitant who doesn't spend much time in one place. The PR guy had told him "ten minutes," but he didn't tell me, so I kept jabbering.

Reagins spent nearly twenty years working for the Los Angeles Angels, the last four as general manager, during which time they won two American League West titles. He was general manager of the American team in the 2023 World Baseball Classic, which ended with former Angel Shohei Ohtani striking out former teammate Mike Trout, who was drafted by Reagins in 2009.

I mentioned that Marquis had done an about-face after spending decades wandering in a baseball wilderness feeling like Ezekiel without MLB support.

"I thought that was Moses," Tony said.

There was plenty of wandering and lamenting to go around in the Old Testament. "I personally haven't done a good enough job letting folks know that this is out there, and this is what we're doing," he said. "Since I've been here, we've created twenty-seven programs that are intentionally, personally created for African Americans, males and females, to play baseball, softball, and girls' baseball."

Under the umbrella of "MLB Develops": the Breakthrough Series, amateur development camps for boys' baseball, girls' baseball, and softball; RBI; MLB Youth Academies; the Hank Aaron Invitational; the Elite Development Invitational for girls; the DREAM Series; the Andre Dawson Classic; and what's known simply as "The Program."

Then: the hallelujah draft of 2022 when four of the first players chosen were Black, all beneficiaries of MLB diversity programs, and one third of all first rounders were Black. Tony Reagins and everyone else at MLB crowed with pleasure, as my old friend Red Smith used to say.

When three years later, the 2025 Sports and Fitness Industry Association Topline Participation survey reported that 17.28 million Americans had played some kind of baseball in 2024, a nice increase of 11 percent over three years—though nothing like the 45 percent annual rise in pickle ball, America's fastest growing sport—MLB had reason to crow louder. The league cited the numbers as evidence of the success of Rob Manfred's "Play Ball" initiative which is what it sounds like: a concerted effort to make baseball relevant again.

You had to read the fine print to learn that 9.5 million of those who played were defined as "casual" participants, meaning anyone who played some kind of baseball between one and twelve times in the calendar year. So, if you picked up a bat at a company picnic and retired after pulling a muscle in your first at bat, that counted. Core participation, defined as anything more than 13 times a year, declined by 6 percent in the same three-year period.

Despite the investment in dollars and sweat equity, the number of Blacks on opening day rosters increased exactly .3 percent. Among them, seventeen had participated in MLB Develops programs and seven were developed by the Marquis Grissom Baseball Association. Eighteen others, including Marquis's son, Marquis Jr., and Dusty Baker's son, Darren, began the season in the minors but on major league 40-man rosters.

"The issues are deep," Reagins said.

And the turnaround is going to take longer than he expected. When he took the job, he thought he was looking at a five-year project. "Now I'm guessing maybe in the ten-to-twenty-year range."

Baseball economist Michael Haupert calculated that if Major League Baseball continued to lose Black players at the current rate, we'd be able to celebrate the first and last African American major leaguer on Jackie Robinson Day in 2079.

* * *

What did baseball lose when it lost its Blackness? Hank Aaron's dignity. Mr. October's Octobers. Ozzie Smith's aerodynamics. Rickey Henderson's Rickey-speak: "Rickey don't like it when Rickey can't find Rickey's limo."

Baseball lost its cool. Its style. It lost speed and daring. After squandering a half-century of African American talent while hiding behind the so-called color barrier, baseball had allowed the game to return to that ignoble condition, only worse because this time we knew what we were missing. It wasn't a white guy who stole home in Game One of the 1955 World Series. It was Jackie. It wasn't a white guy that got all of America to wear their ballcaps backward. It was Ken Griffey Jr., who set the style with unapologetic exuberance and athleticism.

Junior oozed cool. So much cool that fifteen years after he retired, *The Washington Post* devoted an entire column to the jaw-dropping news that the new coach of the Washington Commanders defied NFL convention by wearing his cap backward. "Whether it be the fashion, the style, the intangibles, whether it be Rickey Henderson's running, or Jeffrey Leonard with one flap down, and Dave Parker with one earring in the right ear—" Tony said.

"That earring is why I have a Dave Parker glove," I said, interrupting.

"—When African American young people and the African

American community don't see that presence in a sport, and particularly in baseball, the support dwindles," Tony continued. "That's the disconnect. When baseball was in its height, the connection with the Black church was music, fashion, and baseball. There's a reason most hip-hop stars wear baseball caps."

One decidedly unscientific data point of hope: white kids who think it's cool to be Black.

The only people who didn't seem to get it were the white guys running Major League Baseball. Maybe that's because they were too old and too white to realize what anyone with kids—or who remembers being a kid—knew. African Americans have a lock on cool. "There were so many Black stars in the '80s," said Tyler Kepner, baseball columnist for *The Athletic*. "Rickey Henderson, Dwight Gooden, Tony Gwynn, Ozzie Smith, and Kirby Puckett, on and on. They were cool and it felt cool as a suburban kid to root for them."

I know this because I am the mother of one of those kids. I hesitated to bring this to Tony's attention because that kid is now forty years old, and while he's trendy, he's hardly a trend. Tony's reaction gladdened my heart. "Your son thinking that everything Black is cool? I think *that's cool*. I'm getting goosebumps thinking about it."

* * *

Jackie Robinson Training Complex
Breakthrough Series Invitational 17U
Championship game of the Breakthrough Series Tournament

For the first couple of innings, I had the press box at Holman Stadium to myself. My only company was an unmanned streaming camera stationed over my shoulder. At my first visit to Holman Stadium, I met Carl Erskine, the impeccable Dodger, who was an even better father than he was a pitcher. He introduced me to his son, Jimmy, during Fantasy Camp in 2000. Jimmy lived much longer than most children with Down syndrome, thanks to parental pride and TLC. Carl always thanked me for asking after Jimmy; I guess most people didn't.

The last time we spoke before Carl's death in 2024, he tried to assuage my fears about the future of baseball. "Baseball has been played through so many cultures, so many decades, through depression years and war years," he said.

Not to mention Bowie Kuhn, George Steinbrenner, and Spider Tack.

"The game itself just has a magic of surviving," he assured me.

Scattered groups of parents with sons playing sought refuge from the sun in shaded seats and shadows, of which there were few. I was rooting for MVP/MGBA, a team made up of Marquis's players and others from the MVP program in Atlanta. The other team was sponsored by MLB scout Chip Lawrence, whose son was their shortstop. I didn't see Marquis anywhere.

The old stadium had had a complete makeover—6,478 new seats, new dirt, new mound, new warning track, new padding, new outfield fence. The dugouts and clubhouses were next on Tony Reagins's agenda.

In the third inning, a middle-aged Black gentleman in a Kansas City Royals jacket sat down in my row. It's hard to make a team windbreaker, any team windbreaker, look elegant, but he did. I lobbed my most penetrating question: "So you're a scout for the Royals?"

His name was Darwin Pennye. After four years as executive director of the Kansas City Urban Youth Academy, after decades of teaching and preaching the virtues of baseball as a high school coach, of hoping and giving up hope of becoming a major-league player, coach, manager, or front-office executive, he'd become an amateur scout, divining the talent among high schoolers lucky enough to get an invite to the Jackie Robinson Training Complex.

He was one of them once, a promising player drafted out of high school who chose to go to college instead because he knew he'd get a chance to play. Still, it was hard. "I grew up in the conservative game," he said. "I was very emotional. I had some style. To fit in, I had to lose a bit of myself." But never the wristbands modeled on the pair his mother gave him to celebrate the first time he put on a baseball uniform when he was eight. They were colorful, like him: red, white, and blue. "I never played a game but I didn't have the wristbands on. And I never wanted to play without."

He played five years in the minor leagues after being drafted by the Pittsburgh Pirates in the thirty-seventh round of the 1988 draft. When those dreams didn't work out, he had to consider other options.

"Who are you watching?"

"Everybody," he said.

At that precise moment, he had his stopwatch on Trey Lawrence, the skinny shortstop with what's called "a long, projectible frame," who was then moseying down the first base line. "I got him in 4.25. He needs work on his foot speed."

He scribbled his notes in a decidedly unofficial notebook with a sparkly pink cover and the words "Let's Advance God's Kingdom Together." "My pulpit has always been the ballfield," he said. "My congregation has always been the kids that I've coached."

He was athletic director and head baseball coach at Logos Preparatory Academy in Sugar Land, Texas, when Royals General Manager Dayton Moore asked him to run the team's new Urban Youth Academy. (Five teams, including the Royals, now have MLB-affiliated academies, plus Puerto Rico and New Orleans.)

More than one hundred thousand kids, both baseball and softball players, have passed through the Texas Rangers' academy since it opened in 2017, of whom more than 130 have received college scholarships, team historian John Blake said.

"Cincy has a $20 million state-of-the-art facility," Darwin said.

"We were still trying to figure out the scope of our program, how to give every kid an opportunity, not just the elite, to have a place in the game: broadcast journalism, groundskeeping, front office."

Moore's last season as general manager was also the first year that the MLB draft was cut to twenty rounds and when minor-league contraction cut the number of MLB-affiliated teams from 165 to 120.

Fewer teams meant fewer places to stash and develop talented but raw high school talents. Fewer rounds meant risk-averse scouts were more likely to draft polished college players. Of the 615 players drafted in 2024, five hundred came from NCAA programs.

"That first year, we kept an African American [draft] board," Moore said. "Once the draft had concluded, we had forty-six guys still on the board. According to our scouts, twenty-two to twenty-four of those players would have gotten an opportunity if minor-league contraction did not occur."

The question is: How many Lawrence Butlers and "Money Mikes" were left on that board?

"So, if the pathway to pro ball is through college, then we have to get more players in college," Reagins said. "And if you look at the African American numbers in D1 college, it's about 4 or 5 percent. And then if you look at the African American coaches in college, it's less than that, maybe 2 percent."

The NCAA hadn't made it easy on Black families, or college coaches, allotting only 11.7 scholarships for baseball. That increased to thirty-four full scholarships in 2025, which should allow a two-sport athlete to choose baseball over football, Darwin said. "But it didn't all of a sudden level the playing field, in my opinion."

Not if you're enrolled at an HBCU that can't fund the scholarships, and certainly not if you're a high school kid without showcase numbers to brag on.

The hallelujah draft in 2022, when five Black high schoolers were first round picks, feels like ancient history to Darwin. "There are none of those guys anymore. You better be Willie Mays coming out of high school if you want to get drafted."

* * *

I wanted to ask a question I wasn't sure how to frame. Instead, I repeated what Tony Reagins had told me about why he took the job. "What was really important to me was, this wasn't a one-off. It wasn't something that we were doing just to say, 'Hey, we were doing something right.'"

Is it a template for what should exist in every major league city, or more like a model house in a new development that gets lots of attention but nothing else ever gets built?

"That's a hard question," Darwin said. "I just want to see baseball get back in the neighborhood. This is great and it's symbolic, I just don't think that nine- and ten-year-olds should have to go to Atlanta to get better."

He was referring to the eight-field East Cobb Baseball Complex maintained by Perfect Game for travel-team competition. "I want a kid that has nothing to have the same opportunity as a kid who has everything. We don't have that. At one time, any boy or girl growing up could play this game and get better at it. The system from T-ball up, it's flawed. Our game has turned from what it was—a rite of passage—into a country club sport."

The annual Aspen Institute report on the "Project Play" in America 2025 showed how right he was. According to the report, the average American sports family spent 46 percent more on their child's primary sport than they did five years ago. Baseball is the most expensive of the three most popular sports, costing parents $1,113, 68 percent more than it did five years ago. White parents spent almost twice the amount on a primary sport as Black parents; twice as many white kids played high school baseball.

"Three areas have to change if the game is going to change," Darwin said. "One, you need some African American managers. Two, you need more African American scouts. Three, you have to flood the pool with talent. That's what the Negro Leagues did for Major League Baseball. The first decade after Jackie we had Roy, Joe Black, Mays, Aaron, and that's before you get to Frank."

Robinson, that is.

"Who's going to be the next Griffey? In the eighties, there were so many: the Doctor, Strawberry, Ozzie. Go back and look at the '89 All-Star Game: Bo, Bonds, Harold Reynolds, Dave Stewart on the mound, Lee Smith. A lot of guys besides Bonds and Bo, high school signs, got a chance to develop.

"When you think of today, who's the biggest Black star?"

"Mookie," I said.

"Who's next?

"Money Mike?"

Neither of us thought to mention biracial Aaron Judge.

Darwin nodded at Marquis's team coming off the field between innings. "You see those shoes they're wearing? You can't wear them to school. I put Jordans on, I can wear those to school, to church, and to the basketball court. It's fashion culture. Music culture. We didn't have that in our game. These are the people who are now breadwinners. Are those people going to baseball games?

"Baseball has always said, 'We're America's pastime, and we don't really need to market our product.' Until now. It's like, 'Oh, we lost everybody.' We took for granted that we would always have fans and kids who grew up playing Little League. And now it's like, 'Oh, no, I never had a bat in my hand.'"

What he said next surprised me. "I do think now is the time to recapture it. A lot of kids are dealing with effects of the concussion movie, especially those in the suburbs. What I always said, 'They had a chance to get some of those kids back.'"

Finally, I had found someone with the good sense to think like me.

"Look at the investment we've made in Latin America," Darwin said. "And look at the results today. Why can't we have the same development here? I wish every major-league team had an academy."

I told him I was in love. I would have kissed him but he's a pastor with a new degree in Christian Studies. I told him: When I'm commissioner, there will be a youth academy in every major-league city with facilities commensurate with the ones in Latin America.

"Amen," Darwin said.

In the ninth inning, I spotted Marquis in the dugout. He had been hiding from his players. "They play different when I'm there," he told me later. "I don't want that. I just want them to play the game."

They lost 3–2. He wasn't upset; quite the contrary. They need to know what good is. They need to measure themselves against the top competition from around the country. How else will they ever develop?

I wanted to know how he manages never to get discouraged. As part of the Atlanta Braves RBI Fall Development Program, the six-week fall camp he runs for local high school players, he and his coaches pick the top 44 kids who get to participate in the annual 44 Classic, so-named for Hank's uniform number. They visit the Civil Rights Museum and Martin Luther King Jr.'s home. They take batting practice at Truist Park and go through a pro-style workout in front of scouts and college coaches. "That kind of changed my outlook on what MLB was doing," he said. "And then you go to a Braves game, get introduced on the field, and play at the Braves' big-league stadium. That touches me, to be able to do that stuff, you know what I'm saying?"

CAPE COD PART II

Eldredge Park, July 29, 2023

Mouth stuffed with locally sourced rib eye, marinated in artisanal olive oil infused with locally grown black garlic, sliced thin and schmeared with my homemade aioli and plated on homemade bread, Dan Okrent was unable to speak when I told him he killed baseball.

The beef was raised on a farm down the road from where the Pilgrims pilfered corn buried by the Payomets in the sand at Corn Hill, a half mile from my home in Truro, Massachusetts, which is twenty miles from Eldredge Park, home of the Orleans Firebirds, where Dan Okrent was gagging. The garlic was grown inland in a valley where the Payomets took refuge in the winter. Only stupid white people think it's smart to plunk themselves down on the dunes and wait for their homes to crash into the sea.

I mention this only because I knew this was sure to be a historic picnic.

I had it on good authority from Tom Tango—not his real name, nor his first nom de plume, but definitely the real deal—who to blame for what happened to baseball. Tom is MLB's senior data architect for stats, author of the book *The Book: Playing the Percentages in Baseball*, and one of the first people I asked, "What happened to baseball?"

"Do you happen to know Dan Okrent?" he replied.

"Why, yes."

I know him well enough to know he prefers to be called Daniel, at least in print; that he makes the best martinis on the Outer Cape; that he never turns down red meat; and that he annually painted the big toe on his right foot robin's egg blue until one summer when he didn't.

Daniel Okrent invented Rotisserie League Baseball, which became fantasy baseball, which became a whole universe of fantasy sports from which he has earned not a *shekel*. He is the author of so many definitive books on so many important subjects that it is impossible to slavishly mention them all. He suggested *Last Call: The Rise and Fall of Prohibition*, but I can't omit *Nine Innings*, my idea of a perfect baseball book.

Also a playwright (*Old Jews Telling Jokes*) and the first Public Editor at *The New York Times* when the paper of record still went in for self-criticism, he discovered, promoted, and introduced the world (and me) to Bill James.

Tom said Daniel instigated the Great Upheaval. Such a *tummler*, this guy. "If you talk to general managers now, most of them grew up with some sort of fantasy or Rotisserie baseball," Tom said. "Those games are all about evaluating the stats of players to figure out how much you should be paying all these guys."

Imagine young Daryl Morey, now president of the Philadelphia 76ers, as a Strat-O-Matic whiz kid with a killer instinct. "To win, you needed to employ analytic concepts," he said at MIT. "I like to win more than anything else. So, if you're trying to win these games, you basically become like a GM."

Dan is also responsible for the so-called one-dollar player, the cup-of-coffee guy, against whom everyone is measured; the foundational value in analytics.

"So, it's Dan's fault," I said.

"Yes," Tom said.

* * *

Okrent was sitting in his favorite spot on the hillside at Eldredge Park, wearing his favorite Hawaiian shirt and choking on a piece of perfectly cooked beef, when I more or less said, *j'accuse*.

While he gagged, I reviewed the step-by-step chronology that led straight from Rotisserie to total analytic fuckery, the sequelae of events that brought us to this place and this moment. Start with the relentless human mind that seems to want to put itself out of business; add a good measure of serendipity; a technological revolution that produced a period of invention comparable to the Renaissance; and the mad genius of a cohort of new-age techies who saw things in the deluge of numbers they produced, numbers derived from the back of my baseball cards, waiting to be monetized, tokenized, and fetishized.

Gulping and swallowing, his gullet finally free of me, Dan lurched in my direction, reached for my neck with blood-stained fingers, and gasped, "You mean when I put my hands around its throat like this and said, 'Die, motherfucker!'"

* * *

"Welcome to Eldredge Field, where the stars of tomorrow shine tonight," Steve the PA announcer said, which is a Cape League tradition. The Firebirds had hauled themselves out of a season-long funk into maybe almost playoff contention. So there was reason for optimism as well as *schvitzing.* Even the bugs were moving slowly in the humid air. All of Barnstable County was under a severe storm watch.

I had spent two years assembling a bill of particulars leading straight from the Okrent Fenokees to the estimated 62.5 million North Americans who competed in daily fantasy sports (DFS) in 2022, 81 percent of whom also gambled on sports. Now that I had him where I wanted him, I wasn't inclined to let him get a word in edgewise.

The idea for Rotisserie came to him in 1979 somewhere above the great divide separating Red Sox and Yankee territory on a flight from Hartford, Connecticut, to Austin, Texas, en route to his monthly gig with *Texas Monthly*. He scribbled notes aloft and typed them up as soon as he landed. It was a long time ago.

He was learned in the childhood games of "All-Star Baseball" and "Strat-O-Matic" and had played in a rudimentary Rotisserie game in college organized by his professor at the University of Michigan, Robert Sklar.

The concept was not exactly new. The first documented fantasy baseball game took place in Brooklyn on December 8, 1866, when, according to the Hall of Fame, ten women and four men gathered to play a wooden tabletop game called "Sebring Parlor Base Ball."

In 1930, Clifford Van Beek created "National Pastime," one of the first games to attempt to accurately simulate the performance of actual major-league players. Bill James played "Ball Park Base Ball," a mathematical simulation of baseball. Jack Kerouac, the author of *On the Road*, was hip to baseball, creating in 1942 what he called "my solitaire card baseball game" with made-up teams, players, contract disputes, and transactions reported in broadsheets he drew himself. Fourteen years later, the game kept him company during a sixty-three-day stint as a fire lookout in the Cascade Mountains. Strat-O-Matic arrived in the midst of the Cold War and the golden era of baseball, just in time to accompany baby boomer boys to fallout shelters.

Okrent enlisted a group of like-minded wannabes—journalists and publishing types, ten men and one woman, not me—to join him in what was called Rotisserie League Baseball because they met at a bistro on the East Side of Manhattan called La Rotisserie Française. They conducted their first draft in April 1980, with each club owner constructing a roster with real-world players using their real-world stats and assigning real-world dollars to them in the annual spring auction. They all started with the same pot of money—$260. Unlike Major League Baseball owners, Okrent wanted a fair fight.

Standings were based on the cumulative statistics of each team's players in eight now-primitive categories: batting average, RBI, home runs and stolen bases for hitters, wins, saves, ERA, and Okrent's felicitously named pitching formula, IPRAT, short for "Innings Pitched Ratio," the ugliest constellation of consonants and vowels ever to appear under his name. Thus, it became WHIP (Walks plus Hits per Inning Pitched).

Online, computerized, or pencil-driven, fantasy games all have one thing in common. They animate the impulse lurking within Everyfan, especially short, (formerly) myopic, Jewish Everyfans, who know deep down in their smart, clumsy souls: *I can do better than that schmuck.*

While I was pontificating, my Birds scored four runs in the bottom of the first. To celebrate, I allowed Dan to join me in conversation.

"Worst trade ever?" I asked.

"How about Broglio-Brock?" Dan said.

An "engaged fan for over seventy years," Dan disengaged from the Detroit Tigers, the team of his boyhood, in favor of the Cubs in deference to his son's ferocious attachment to losers. Which explains why he thought giving up Lou Brock for Ernie Broglio was a disaster.

I countered with Nolan Ryan for Jim Fregosi, a trade my father bemoaned to his grave, when I buried him with a Mets Beanie Baby.

* * *

While Okrent was busy cooking up Rotisserie, Bill James was working in obscurity at that pork-and-beans factory in Lawrence, Kansas, writing and self-publishing his *Baseball Abstract*s. Bill advertised the mimeographed, hand-stapled 1977 edition in the back of *The Sporting News* for four dollars a copy.

Dan was an adherent way before the Okrent Fenokees were a glimmer in his eye. He would become Bill's Maxwell Perkins and Louella Parsons rolled into one, pitching a profile to *Sports Illustrated* and a book to Ballantine Books, both initially rejected. As his book-editor pal said, "You know, Danny, you and I, we love this kinda stuff, but you can't get people interested in that."

Undeterred, Okrent visited Bill at his home in Lawrence, where he remembered Dan yammering excitedly about his new game. Sabermetrics and Rotisserie were inextricably linked, and not just by Dan. Neither would have been possible without a silver-haired Brooklyn boy who had survived the Depression to become the chief economic advisor to the United Steelworkers. Marvin Miller, hired as executive director of the Major League Baseball Players Association in 1966, led the awakened proletariat out of financial slavery and into the promised land of free agency. The owners never knew what hit them.

Free agency was codified in the 1976 Collective Bargaining Agreement, the year after Catfish Hunter signed baseball's first multiyear, multimillion-dollar contract—$3.25 million of George M. Steinbrenner's Yankee dollars—a tantalizing demonstration of free-market economics.

The gaudy dollar signs diverted attention from another consequence of free agency that was already apparent to Dan, who had stopped chewing long enough to explain this watershed event. Human beings became fungible abstractions, assets, commodities. You didn't need a catcher who drove in eighty runs. You needed eighty RBI from the position that maybe you get cheaper from two catchers.

"After free agency, you can play at being GM, including making the financial decisions because dollar figures have been attached to human beings," Dan said. "Our auction put a value on a player relative to other players."

That's what made it so valuable to future front-office executives.

What free agency did for Rotisserie, arbitration did for sabermetrics, which the owners agreed to after the 1973 season in hopes of forestalling full economic emancipation. "Free agency was an option open to any schmuck who wanted to give Wayne Garland a ten-year-contract," Dan said. "But in arbitration you had to make a case. The sports agents, Randy and Alan Hendricks, hired Bill to prepare arbitration cases and he would overwhelm the other teams, and he did for several years. That was his first baseball paycheck that wasn't from writing the abstracts. Other teams saw this guy do this and that it was costing them money. That accelerated the interest in analytics. They had to have a way of arguing back."

Okrent's Jamesian opus was published in *Sports Illustrated* on May 25, 1981, the month before the fifty-one-day baseball strike began. Dan described Bill's foundational metrics as if they were moon rocks dropped from the night sky: Runs Created, the first attempt to capture a player's offensive value; Range Factor, the first measure of a player's fielding ability through total errorless chances per game; and Win Shares, his formula for gauging a player's contribution to each win, came in 2002.

The strike was a godsend for Rotisserie. In the absence of actual baseball, every baseball beat writer with white space to fill took the opportunity to brag on his Rotisserie team. Dan was the toast of morning television. His book-editor friend importuned him to importune Bill to have the next *Baseball Abstract* ready to publish in time for the next Rotisserie League draft.

During the strike, another first and little-known fact: Roy Eisenhardt, president of the Oakland A's, installed an Apple computer in the front office. "We took an Apple IIe and programmed it so that a guy could sit and record every pitch, ball, strike, foul ball, where it went, base hit, or out," Roy said.

Eisenhardt also installed a young attorney with no baseball experience as the team's general counsel. Like Bill James, Sandy Alderson was a quintessential outsider, a former marine—literally the poster boy for the United States Marine Corps—with degrees from Dartmouth and Harvard. He lacked the baked-in prejudices and bad suits of cigar-chomping, ash-dropping, old-time general managers, a title he received two years later when he was charged with the unpleasant chore of showing Billy Martin the door.

Alderson needed to hire expertise. He brought in baseball old-timer Bill Rigney and Jamesian disciple Eric Walker, whose five-minute radio segments on the local NPR station he admired.

"I didn't consider it to be groundbreaking or infallible, but I did feel what we were doing wasn't well understood or accepted by most teams," Alderson said. "So, I thought it gave us a competitive advantage."

The A's developed a metric they called TOP for total offensive production, a formula that took all the bases a player generated—including stolen bases, hit by pitch, walks—and divided by outs made, an early attempt, along with James's Win Shares, to quantify player value.

The end of the strike came early on the morning of July 31 with no givebacks. Free agency survived. When the settlement was announced, a hornet's nest of male reporters made for a bank of pay phones in the hall outside the conference room in the Doral Hotel, not one of Manhattan's swankiest addresses. They compared notes, pooled their information, and started dictating. I was not included in the conversation.

I reached Eisenhardt in California, and he gave me the story of the settlement just in time to make the *Post*'s final edition two minutes before the 2:30 a.m. deadline, a small print run delivered to Katharine Graham's zip code. It arrived on her doorstep four hours later, in time for her to see upon rising that the *Times* hadn't beat me on the story. It was maybe the worst lead I've ever written—it involved Mighty Casey—but I made the deadline by two minutes.

Roy rattled off the details of the settlement: free agency after six years of service and a compensatory player for teams losing a premium free agent. But there was no salary cap and no spending floor. Owners and players have been duking it out on this issue ever since. "Football eventually stabilized its economics by addressing the allocation of revenues directly," said Roy, who teaches sports law at the University of San Francisco. "Baseball has never really come to grips with that."

Not long after that conversation I began hearing whispers about the owners' intention to lock the players out at the end of the current collective bargaining agreement in 2026.

* * *

Meanwhile, the Birds scored four more runs in the bottom of the third inning, a very un-Birdlike offensive outburst, which gave two old sportswriters leave to yak more and watch less. Dan started musing about Vida Blue, the last player in his memory "so magnetic, so extraordinary that he pulled people back into the game. Not to compare him to Ohtani because nobody compares to Ohtani. The world was grabbed by that guy. You just felt baseball was more present."

"That's because baseball has no idea how to market its stars," I said. "Roy blames the 'Casey at the Bat' Syndrome. 'What does Casey do? Casey doesn't hit a home run. Casey strikes out. Baseball is essentially a failure sport. It is hard to make a celebrity out of Casey.'"

"They discourage personality because it gives the player more leverage in negotiations," Dan replied. "They think it's going to keep the price down."

* * *

In 1985, Bill James word-bombed the baseball-loving universe with a radical new theory. *Strikeouts? What's the big schmear?*

He went for the jugular when he wrote: "Strikeouts have a negligible effect on runs scored; the belief that a strikeout is a special negative out because it freezes base runners is essentially baseless."

It would take time for the idea to take hold, but it was a crucial, and to the old guard unthinkable, step in the march toward a previously unthinkable tradeoff: strikeouts for power.

An out is an out is an out.

This more than perhaps any other analytic discovery incensed guys like George Brett, who pinked with embarrassment when they struck out with men in scoring position. *Just another out? Just another out!?!*

"Baseball's mentality now is 'it coulda been worse,'" Brett muttered. "You coulda bounced into a double play."

Even a hardcore analytics guy like Clay Davenport, a founder at *Baseball Prospectus*, is surprised at how strikeouts are understood and accepted today. "*Strikeouts don't matter*," he said at the 2024 SABR Analytics Conference. "Boy, was that taken to heart."

This made Bill James persona non grata in the old school, a role he was happy to embrace. Onstage at MIT in 2023, Bill said, "Other people were trying to do things similar to what I was trying to do, but none of them had the package of things that was needed to sell it."

And part of that package, Bill declared, was his "aggressive attitude about telling other people they were full of shit."

* * *

In the era before personal computing—before ESPN went 24/7 in 1980; before James summoned an army of volunteers to create Project Scoresheet in 1984, collecting play-by-play accounts of major-league games; before John Dewan joined Project Scoresheet and then launched STATS Inc., the first company to provide advanced, play-by-play data to Major League Baseball; before John Thorn and Pete Palmer introduced On Base Plus Slugging (OPS+) in *The Hidden Game of Baseball: A Revolutionary Approach to Baseball and Its Statistics*; before Apple introduced the first Macintosh computer with a commercial aired during the 1984 Super Bowl; before Dave Smith and his cadre of dauntless Retrosheet volunteer historians took over where Project Scoresheet left off, gathering play-by-play accounts for 215,000 of the 240,000 games played since 1900; before *USA Today* began publishing *Baseball Weekly*, a compendium of weekly and fantasy statistics in April 1991; before Tim Berners-Lee, a British researcher at the European Organization for Nuclear Research, devised the system that would become the World Wide Web—before all that, managing a Rotisserie League team was a pain in the ass, a laborious chore requiring monomaniacal zealotry, some mathematical ability, a lot of free time, and a sharp pencil. I know this because I owned and managed Jayne's Fighting Ships in the inaugural season of *The Washington Post* Rotisserie League. I finished first because I drafted Fat Sid Fernandez of the Mets, mostly because I liked saying Fat Sid Fernandez, and retired unbeaten after the arrival of my son, the other notable event of 1985.

Rotisserie survived without me. Okrent and his band of merry obsessives published Rotisserie guidebooks, started a stats service, held spring training conventions, hired attorneys, and trademarked "Rotisserie League," but wordsmiths that they were, they failed to anticipate the World Wide Web and fantasy baseball. They were toast when ESPN and *Sports Illustrated* launched fantasy games in 1995, which had many advantages—especially their statistical services and a vast population of players. You didn't need friends to play their games.

"I remember *SI* was starting it, and Don Elliman was the publisher, a very good friend of mine," Dan said. "I said, 'Don, of course you can do it, but don't you think you should give me and my pals at least a small, tiny bit of it?'

"And he said, 'Nah.'"

Also, in 1995, baseball returned from the 1994 strike that killed the World Series and the first eighteen games of April 1995, a grievous, self-inflicted wound responsible for the enduring alienation of affection between the game and its fans that otherwise accomplished nothing.

"And the Three True Outcomes is '95," I said.

"That's also the year Dan Okrent stopped doing Rotisserie," Dan said.

He shut down the Okrent Fenokees without ever claiming a ring. Which was like "Hugh Hefner never getting laid," Jonathan Mahler wrote in the anthology *Jewish Jocks: An Unorthodox Hall of Fame.* Dan liked that so much he ordered me to mention it here.

"After Ken Burns's *Baseball* is broadcast in the fall of 1994, I became recognizable to baseball. People approached me in the ballpark or on the subway and said, 'Lemme tell ya I could have Rickey Henderson for eleven dollars.'

"Out of which came Okrent's Second Law: 'There's nothing more interesting than your own Rotisserie team and nothing less interesting than someone else's.'"

* * *

Rickey Henderson was Gary Huckabay's favorite player in high school. That did not make him unusual in the Bay Area, where he was the star center fielder at the Menlo School, an uncompromising Pete Reiser type who played for anyone who would have him. Rickey also was indirectly responsible for Gary's life's work and the birth of *Baseball Prospectus,* a snarky annual publication cum think tank that challenged every assumption about how baseball should be played. Huckabay had gotten sick of having to defend Henderson's offensive skills to morons who didn't understand ballpark factors.

While enrolled in an MBA program in marketing and technology management at the University of California, Davis, he held down a thirty-hour-a-week job running the Scantron machine at the university teaching center that took maybe forty-five minutes on a tough day. That left lots of time to log on to Rec.Sport.Baseball, a chat room hosted by Use.net, a precursor to the internet, where a cohort of like-minded insurgents gathered daily to argue, debate, and explode closely held baseball truths.

In the fall of 1995, Huckabay began to assemble a team: Clay Davenport, a numbers guy at the National Oceanic and Atmospheric Agency; Rany Jazayerli, a medical student en route to a practice in dermatology; Joe Sheehan, a journalism school student at USC; and Christina Kahrl, a graduate student in Chicago studying the Diet of Worms with a side gig at a publishing company that specialized in archeology. They called themselves "Stat Drunk Computer Nerds."

They bonded over Rob Deer, a slugger who hit more than twenty-five home runs seven consecutive years, walked more than fifty times eight straight years, and led the league in strikeouts four years. These were the Three True Outcomes in baseball, Kahrl declared, and Rob Deer specialized in all three of them.

They wrote odes to Rob Deer, formed a fan club for Rob Deer, established a webpage for Rob Deer, and stalked Rob Deer. Dave Pease, who created the *Baseball Prospectus* website, tracked him down in the parking lot outside the Lake Elsinore Diamond, home of the Lake Elsinore Storm. He came with a Rob Deer bat he purchased on eBay for fifty bucks, and the hope he'd be able to explain his admiration for Deer's all-or-nothing approach at the plate.

When Pease reported back that Deer signed the bat but sped off in a monster truck without making conversation, Huckabay was elated. A monster truck was so *Deer*.

Their mission was to democratize data while deconstructing the way baseball used it and understood it through the publication of a *Baseball Prospectus* annual. The first edition was missing the chapter on the St. Louis Cardinals. Another chapter was printed in Cyrillic. They were new to the publishing game. Savvy as they were about the future of data science, they were naïve enough to regard the website, which went live in October 1996, as secondary, a device for promoting their hardcover publications.

A sense of humor helped. Huckabay inserted jokes into copy, describing one infielder as having "all the mobility of Stonehenge." "It was data science meets *Saturday Night Live*," Kahrl said. "Gary's half Lorne Michaels and half John Belushi."

Rany Jazayerli introduced the world to the Three True Outcomes on the *Baseball Prospectus* website in 2000. "What are the Three True Outcomes, you ask?" he wrote. "Together, the Three True Outcomes distill the game to its essence, the battle of pitcher against hitter, free from the distractions of the defense, the distortion of foot speed or the corruption of managerial tactics like the bunt and his wicked brother, the hit-and-run."

VORP and DIPS arrived along with their creators, Keith Woolner and Voros McCracken, two guys who stumbled on what Kahrl calls "the pillars of modern analytics" while indulging their passion for fantasy baseball. Woolner, an MIT graduate, devised Value Over Replacement Player, the predicate to every iteration of WAR (bWAR, fWAR, rWAR) while collecting raw data for his team. VORP measured how much a hitter or pitcher contributed to a team compared to a replacement player—Okrent's one-dollar man.

The watershed moment came in 2001 with publication of McCracken's formula for DIPS, Defense Independent Pitching, successor to Okrent's WHIP, which holds a pitcher blameless for events beyond his control: errors, gales, midges, bad bounces, and assorted other fates of batted balls put in play like bad luck.

"The one true analytic discovery," Christina Kahrl calls it, amid a shitstorm of data. "It changed how we think about the game."

DIPS led to Tom Tango's FIP, which employs the old-timey ERA numeric scale, making it accessible to oldsters such as myself.

Both remove luck from the equation and in so doing highlight the stark difference between now and then. Then: teammates picked each other up after letting each other down. In Game Two of the 1966 World Series when Dodgers center fielder Willie Davis made three errors on two fly balls in Sandy Koufax's last game, Koufax hugged him in the dugout and Don Drysdale absolved him, pointing out how many runs he'd saved them.

A good FIP comes in handy during contract negotiations when your agent can demonstrate how your numbers were sabotaged by your shoddy teammates. It offers little insight into the value of being a teammate.

Baseball Prospectus grew crazy big, crazy fast as did its influence. Young Nate Silver, better known today for predicting electoral upheavals, arrived in 2003 with his PECOTA player prediction rating system, still a big seller for BP's fantasy subscribers.

Two former interns, James Click and Chaim Bloom, became big-league general managers. Fifty-some former *Prospectus* writers are currently employed by major-league teams. Among them: Joe Sheehan, assistant general manager of the Toronto Blue Jays; Mike Fast, senior vice president of baseball development for the Atlanta Braves; and Woolner, principal data scientist for the Cleveland Guardians.

* * *

The worst fifty-one days of my life were the best of Gary Huckabay's. His hero, Rickey Henderson, needed a place to work out during the 1981 strike and chose Gary's high school, where team members were attending a mandatory summer baseball camp. He was standing in the outfield one day when "an African American lady, maybe fifty or so, comes over and says, 'Have you seen my Rickey?'

"'No, ma'am.'

"'Oh, there he is!'

"And she looks over and there's Rickey Henderson and Dwayne Murphy. They were looking to talk to our skip. Rickey's like, 'Hey, we need a place to practice, and you guys have a batting cage. Is it okay with you guys if we just come down here to keep loose?'

"Skip is like, 'Well, it might be a distraction.'"

Gary let the coach know what's what. "It won't be a distraction, Coach," he promised. "But if we all quit, then it'll be a problem. And he's like, 'You can have as much space as you need.'"

Huckabay was as serious about playing baseball as he was about deconstructing it. One day while playing center field at UC Davis, the game pretty much deconstructed him. En route to a catch, he was clotheslined by a big galoot in left field, a tight end on the football team. Gary thinks it was 1990 or 1991. He got up, got married, got a graduate degree, had a son, and continued to play baseball as vociferously as he thought and wrote about baseball.

In 2004, he went to work for his beloved Oakland A's as a consultant to Billy Beane. He remembers trying to tell three players why analytics was a better methodology than the way the game had been run. "I can show you the numbers!"

"All three of them had exactly the same response: 'This will never ever work, period. Pitchers and their agents won't go for this because you're gonna end up with guys that normally could win fifteen to twenty games and make millions of dollars who under this set up might win six or seven and make $1 million.'"

His tenure was brief because he shot off his mouth about the stupidity of trading for thirty-year-old catcher Jason Kendall, who earned $34,922,077 during his tenure with the A's and hit a total of three home runs. *We can't afford to be that stupid!*

On Halloween 2016, fifteen years or so after he was upended in center field, Huckabay stepped onto his front porch and collapsed. His spine had turned to dust. Surgery stabilized what was left of his vertebrae and added some new ones made from cadavers and resin, returning a modicum of mobility. But a cascade of woe ensued. Diabetes wrecked his kidney function. Intercranial pressure, commonly called a "pseudo brain tumor," traced back to when he got clotheslined, took his sight. And then one day he lost 40 percent of his hearing.

But the guy who did stand-up comedy while teaching driving school in a Denny's at 6:00 a.m. never lost his sense of humor. He screened state-issued driver's ed snuff movies like *Red Asphalt* and went back to sleep.

In 2024, the founding members of *Baseball Prospectus* gathered at the annual SABR Analytics Conference in Scottsdale, Arizona, to honor him with the SABR Lifetime Achievement Award. Woolner, who introduced him, told me later: "Gary had the vision and was just arrogant enough to think, 'We can do it better than what we're seeing at actual front offices right now.'"

* * *

For ten days in the fraught fall of 2001, baseball was an afterthought. After the Twin Towers fell, Commissioner Bud Selig immediately canceled the games on 9/11 and for the following three days. Then, prodded by conscience and logistics, he canceled another three days of competition.

But the White House let it be known that it was "paramount for baseball to resume." The game still mattered to the country's sense of itself. Young, baseball-crazed Alex Bregman, all of seven years old, watched the 2001 playoffs with his Yankees-obsessed mother. He remembers how good it felt "to love something so much that brought people together."

They watched the Yankees lose the first two games of the American League Division Series in New York to the Oakland A's, which meant they had to win three games in Oakland. As it turned out, the final score was the least consequential result of the first game in Oakland.

The Yankees were ahead 1–0 when lumbering Jeremy Giambi singled in the bottom of the seventh inning, his second hit off New York's starter, Mike Mussina, and the A's third hit of the day. In the dugout, Yankees Manager Joe Torre did not so much as twitch.

A's Manager Art Howe turned to Eric Byrnes, the speedy pinch runner with the flowing blond locks that looked so good flying beneath his helmet, and said, "Are you ready?"

"I said, 'Absolutely,'" Byrnes said.

Then nothing happened. He still doesn't know why he was not sent in.

How unlike today it was: A right-handed starting pitcher was left in the game to face a left-handed slugger in the bottom of the seventh inning of a playoff game that could have ended the Yankees' season.

That was the situation when Terrence Long pulled Mussina's 2-2 pitch down the right field line, scooting between first base and Tino Martinez's glove. The bullpens were located on the field at Network Associates Coliseum. Visiting relievers got ready on two mounds in right field foul territory. But Torre didn't have anyone warming up, which meant that the ball was unimpeded. It skipped over the mound closer to the stands, caromed off the right field wall just on the fair side of the painted yellow foul line, and bounced back into the green corner where the outfield wall and the grandstand wall converged.

Shane Spencer, who had started only twenty-eight games in right field for the Yankees, was playing in place of Paul O'Neill, who had been injured in September and hurt more when facing left-handed pitching. Before Spencer launched his parabolic throw over the heads of not one but two cutoff men, shortstop Derek Jeter was on the move.

He had been stationed in the dirt perhaps fifteen feet from second base. "My job is to watch the runner," Jeter said in an interview prior to his Hall of Fame induction in 2021. "I saw the ball down the line. My job is to, one, see if there's going to be a play at third base, but once you see that Giambi is going to go home, my job is to be the third cutoff man to redirect the throw."

Because the cameras followed the path of the ball, then turned their attention to Spencer digging it out of foul territory, and then to Giambi, a runaway freight train of a man chugging around the bases, it seemed that Jeter came out of nowhere. Former Marlins General Manager Kim Ng, then working for the Yankees, said, "I've watched the replay a number of times to see what I missed. All of a sudden you just see him catching the ball and it's like, *What the fuck is going on?*"

In fact, he came from just inside second base, cutting across the grass behind the mound. He reached the first base line just as Spencer's throw arrived, his momentum carrying him into the vast swath of foul territory particular to the ballpark. He intercepted the throw with his bare right hand and flipped it backhand to catcher Jorge Posada staking out home plate.

Giambi did not slide, a decision that surprised and infuriated Oakland partisans and provoked one of baseball's most glorious and endless debates: *Was he safe? Would he have been safe?*

"Then I was just waiting to see what the umpire called," Ng said. "But it was just so fast. The trajectory was a little puffy. Shane does not crow hop. He just gets to it, turns, and fires. The ball looks like it's probably one foot off the ground. He throws it over Tino and it bounces before it gets to Derek."

Home plate umpire Kerwin Danley called Giambi out. There was no technology to second-guess him. Instant replay was still seven years away, allowing the delicious argument to ferment in perpetuity, a rebuke to the know-it-all present.

The Yankees won the game and eventually the pennant.

In the received wisdom, there was no imagining the play, much less preparing for it—though the next day Alex Bregman and God knows how many other seven-year-olds were out on the dirt preparing for that moment. It's the reason he wears uniform number 2.

He was crushed when I told him the Yankees had practiced the play in spring training.

"We practiced relays of the ball down the rightfield line," Torre said. "There's a man at first base. The batter hits a sure double. Where are you going to be? The first baseman is barely on the dirt behind the second baseman. So, there's a big gap between him and home plate. Your shortstop, he's the cutoff man to third base. Now the shortstop has to read the throw and where the play is going to be made. Derek read it."

* * *

On Monday morning, Cory Schwartz arrived at MLB headquarters in New York for a meeting with his colleagues in the office of MLB Advanced Media. The pitch-tracking system they had been working on, which wouldn't go live for another five years, was already out-of-date. "Our world had changed," Schwartz told a SABR conference in 2013. "We couldn't just do pitch tracking. It had to be full-field tracking of every player. We didn't want to just know what happened, we wanted to know how it happened, what enabled this unusual black-swan play to happen."

At the office, it was all anyone talked about. "We had a meeting with Bob Bowman, who was our CEO," Corey told me. "Bob was very upset. He said, 'None of you can tell me how the hell that happened and why the hell that happened.'

"He was borderline angry because we just didn't have access to the information we needed to deconstruct that play.

"Once we saw the backhand flip, the context of the entire play became the goal. Because in baseball, everything that happens on the field is relative to something else. The players are moving in concert to produce the outcome we see, whether it's the runners or the defensive players, how they position each other and pursue the ball and execute the play.

"You have to have all nine defensive players, you have to have the pitch, you have to have the base runners, and it could be argued all the way down to the coaches and the umpires. Was it really Shane Spencer's throw, or was it Tino Martinez being out of position to take a cutoff? Or should Soriano have gone out from second base and taken that cutoff? What happens if it's Paul O'Neill in right field instead of Shane Spencer?"

It would take fourteen years for that comprehensive system to be realized. When it was announced to an audience of techies at the 2014 MIT Sloan Sports Analytics Conference, it didn't have a name. When it went live on Opening Day 2015, baseball was split into eras—"the Statcast Era" and everything that came before, like the Christian calendar, AD and BC.

* * *

After succumbing to the Yankees in the 2001 Division Series, A's General Manager Billy Beane knew he was about to lose his two top run producers, as well as the closer and his thirty-four saves. It was time to put everything he had learned from Bill James and *Baseball Prospectus* into action.

It was a heady time to be a seamhead. In Beane, they found a lodestar. In Alderson and Bill James, and in Theo Epstein, who hired James the following year to work for the Red Sox, they had exemplars of outsiders who had burrowed their way inside.

Nine of the thirty head honchos running major-league teams in 2025 are Ivy Leaguers; two are former players. Three schlubs matriculated at Amherst, Haverford, and Tufts. Call it the revenge of the last-picked.

Looking back, Alderson, who left the A's after the 1997 season, saw how the drive to count and capture every bit of the action had led to "a more efficient, more probabilistic game" but also how "the drive for efficiency was based on probabilities that bled the game of its athleticism, and to some extent, emotion as well. That's a function of the people who are running the game today. I'm talking about general managers, managers. We've inbred to the point where everybody thinks the same way, looks the same way, approaches the game the same way, makes the same decisions, all of it with a view toward efficiency and risk aversion."

Forget the Oriole way or Cardinals baseball. There's only one way. The uniformity in baseball exists for the same reason pop songs sound alike and SUVs look the same: an algorithm has determined what works best rhythmically and aerodynamically.

But in baseball, uniformity had another consequence. Gone is the sense of anticipation that used to accompany every play. Gone is the drama that made it a joy to write and read about baseball. "Now anticipation is a function of execution, not of strategy or tactics," Alderson said. "You don't have to think along with the manager because everybody knows how the manager's thinking. It's a kind of one size fits all."

The problem with managing by probabilities is that they can only tell you what is most likely to happen, not what will happen at a specific moment in time. A reality Michael Lewis now concedes. "Sometimes the probabilities aren't the probabilities," he said on the twentieth anniversary of the publication of *Moneyball*. "I never meant to say that experience is completely irrelevant. I never meant to say that the person who's just got the numbers knows everything. And that there's no other form of knowing things, that someone who's actually done the thing might not have something really important to say to the person who's got the number. I never meant it to be that extreme."

* * *

Imagine toiling away at a computer for years with only a glowering blue screen with bleating numerals for company. The games on the field are an abstraction. The players are abstractions. Only the numbers on the screen are real.

That was stathead life in the burgeoning public research movement before 2006. Then, the pitch-tracking system Cory Schwartz was working on when he saw Jeter's Flip Play went live in the postseason. Called PITCHf/x, it enabled MLB to establish the speed, movement, spin, and location of every pitch in irrefutable detail. "Where was the pitch?" was no longer a theoretical question.

"It was kind of like finding the Rosetta Stone," Gary Huckabay said.

"The big event is data capture," said Sam Mondry-Cohen, who created the Nationals analytics department when he was still a young 'un.

And then the data got loose. Sam, who is now vice president for player personnel for the Miami Marlins, put it in English for me when he was still an underling with the Nats. "Essentially they made it so the data was findable without a password," he said.

Or "scrapable," in data-speak.

As Stewart Brand said at the first hackers' convention in 1984, "Information wants to be free."

"In 1980, Bill James was doing research in his basement and self-publishing a magazine you have to subscribe to," Sam said. "In 2008, these people are writing it and sharing it on the internet."

It was like the old playground argument—"Who's better, Mickey or Willie?"—only with data in cyberspace where the nerds waited for Major League Baseball to summon them.

FanGraphs, which started small as a fantasy site in 2005, burgeoned. Baseball Savant, which began in the public sphere, was acquired by MLB.

Woolner, who has been with the Guardians for eighteen years, says today most clubs have teams of fifteen to twenty in-house analysts, but it's hard to know. "Teams don't often like to talk to each other about that."

It's proprietary data.

Jim Palmer laughed when I told him that. "There's thirty-five in our analytics department," he said. "We've got one girl just to bring the infield in."

* * *

With the Firebirds safely ahead 10–2, I turned to Dan Okrent and said, "Okay, did Theo fix the game? What did they get right? What did they get wrong? What do we still have to do?"

"A lot and not much," Dan said. "You got the pitch clock right. And that's huge."

He'd been saying that since 2011 and produced an email to prove it.

Down on the field, Coach Nick called for an infield shift, which was disorienting as it had been banned in the majors. He has been a math teacher at Loyola High School of Los Angeles for more than forty years. He knows how to play the percentages. "I want to win," he said.

"I still think they need to work on the shift," Dan said. "The anti-shift stuff isn't working well enough. The lefties are still pulling. My solution to that is eighteen-foot fences in every ballpark to cut down on home runs, encourage doubles and triples—traffic on the bases—and place renewed value on speed and an outfield throwing arm."

"That was my idea," I protested.

"No, no, no, no, no. You said you could get your friend Peko to predict how many more extra base hits it would be worth. Whatever. The point is it does two things. It diminishes the sky-high Dave Kingman–pulled home run and encourages the most exciting plays in baseball."

Dave Kingman was Rob Deer before Rob Deer was Rob Deer. "He'd be an all-star now," my friend Dave Smith told me. "Back then he was John the Baptist in the wilderness."

The new rule limiting "disengagements," an awkward way to describe pickoffs and step offs, was okay with Dan. "The throws to first, I kind of like," he said. "I think that it's not fully comprehended. You're not really allowed two throws. You're allowed one throw because if you use the second throw and you don't get 'em, the guy can take a twenty-foot lead. But it does help speed the game up. And I like that. The larger bases I think are trivial. Strikeouts are down, right?"

"Nope."

MLB fans have been subjected to forty thousand strikeouts every year since 2017 (except for the 2020 COVID-19 season). More than 8.2 percent of all at bats ended in walks during the same period. In 2024, 4.4 percent of 5,453 pitches thrown were hit for home runs.

All of which explains why one-third of all at bats since 2017 have ended in one of the dreaded Three True Outcomes. And that explains why despite the changes imposed in 2023, baseball feels so static.

"So, basically, it's a faster version of the same game," I said. "Or as Buck Showalter put it, 'It's just boring faster.'"

"And the ghost runner?"

"A disgrace," Dan said. "That they don't do it in the World Series shows it's a disgrace."

"Also," he said, "I hate the thirteen-man pitching staff. That leaves only four bench players! Jesus. Four!"

Dan favors a return to a nine-man staff last seen during the Iron Age, when pitchers were pitchers and men were men, and some of them went nine innings.

Ain't happening. Theo Epstein pines for the days of the eleven-man pitching staff. "Then the workhorse starting pitcher who can throw you 230 innings will now get rewarded very handsomely, whether through arbitration or free agency," he said wistfully.

In which case, I pointed out, the great firemen of yore—Ryne Duren, Tug McGraw, Mariano—might make a comeback. "Bring back the heroes."

Dan shook his head

"Not if we have a fourteen- or even fifteen-man pitching staff," I said.

"Too many," Dan tutted.

"Not if you can only use eleven of them in a game," I said. "The other guys, the previous day's starter, who you're not going to use anyway, and the deadest-bullpen arms become healthy scratches. Like in hockey. So the pitching staff becomes fluid. You give arm-starved managers two or three fresh arms every day. It might even cut down on Tommy John surgeries."

This was my grand plan. Before Dan could object, I told him, "Rizzo doesn't think it's nuts."

I quoted Riz verbatim. "Oooh, a taxi squad. So the next day you could bring in two more pitchers and then take two out. Yeah, that'd be fine. We're using five pitchers a game. That's why this eleven-pitcher thing is tough. But the taxi squad fixes that."

I mentioned that Bill James had sent a letter with a long list of fixes to the pitching crisis, and at the top of the list was: "Make a rule that no pitcher may pitch on consecutive days."

"Ridiculous," Dan said. "Teams would have to have sixteen pitchers on the roster."

Something like that.

I continued down Bill's list. "Make a rule that any starting pitcher who is removed from the game before pitching six innings or before allowing four runs to score is ineligible to appear in a game for ten days after that."

"Maybe if you hate the bullpen start."

Which I do.

"I'm not sure that I do. And maybe five instead of ten?"

This is the one we liked best. "No pitcher who appears in a game may be removed from that game during an inning unless or until he has been charged with a run allowed in that inning."

"As an aside, active tanking began in Rotisserie," Dan said suddenly. "We were doing that in Rotisserie back in the early '80s when we introduced anti-tanking rules."

"If you solved it then, you should be able to solve it now."

"It had to do with the following season's draft," he said. "I can't remember exactly what."

Tanking is an abrogation of the implicit contract between a team and its fans that you're actually going to try to win. "Theo perfected it in Chicago," Dan said. "If you knew you didn't have a competitive team, you would overpay for a couple of stars, so you would have trading chips. The other thing that would help anti-tanking would be to go back to the June 15 trade deadline where a team would have to admit to its fans, 'We're not going anywhere this year.'"

There's tanking and there's tanking. Just like there's sucking on purpose and just plain sucking. "The ones that just plain suck should be punished too," Dan said. "It's bad management."

Fielding a Triple-A team capable of losing one hundred games for three consecutive seasons, as did the Houston Astros in 2011–2013 in order to corral high draft choices, worked so well it was abolished by the 2022 Collective Bargaining Agreement. Now the eighteen suckiest teams go into a lottery. Of course, that didn't prevent the Miami Marlins from selling off everything that moved after the 2024 season, including seventy staffers.

A third truly nefarious strategy involves purloined "luxury tax" money, officially the Competitive Balance Tax, which redistributes the wealth by taxing the rich and giving to the poor. It was adopted at the urging of the union to level the economic playing field after the 1994–1995 strike when owners unilaterally tried to shove a salary cap down the players' throats. "The deal was we're gonna have substantial revenue sharing and we're gonna preserve free agency," said Don Fehr, who succeeded Marvin Miller as executive director of the Players Association.

Under this part of the CBA signed in 1996, have-nots are required to have a payroll equal to one and a half times the loot they receive on top of what they had budgeted to spend of their own money.

What happened? "Teams basically decided, 'I'll take the money,'" said Fehr. "'I don't have to do anything. I just have to perform at a minimum level sufficient so the fans don't string me up.'"

According to *The New York Times*, some grievances filed by the union in 2018–2019 against the Pirates, the Rays, the Marlins, and the A's, which were not resolved in collective bargaining in 2022, are still pending. (One reason the A's got busy spending on free agents last winter.)

Fehr says there's an easy fix. "If you're a revenue-sharing recipient and you tank, however you define it, your revenue sharing gets shut off."

"You have to pay a price for finishing last," Dan said. "For instance, they can only have a thirty-five-man roster for the next season instead of the forty-man roster. Something that really hurts."

"No draft picks," I said. "Or relegation? If you field a Triple-A team, go play a Triple-A schedule in a Triple-A ballpark with Triple-A salaries and Triple-A food."

Which is basically what the Philadelphia-Kansas City-Oakland A's are doing now, playing in a Triple-A ballpark, before Triple-A crowds in Sacramento, where they are known as the just-plain A's.

"It works fine in English soccer," I said. "And on *Ted Lasso*."

Dan grunted. He thinks the idea is beneath me. He wants his pound of flesh.

* * *

In the top of the fifth, I noticed that the Whitecaps had loaded the bases. The Birds brought in a new reliever—new to the team, I mean. Roster churn became a fact of life on the Cape when MLB moved the draft from June to mid-July. The Birds had lost nineteen of their original players, which was nothing compared to the Cotuit Kettleers, who lost forty-one. The new guy struck out the side. With the score 10–3 going into the sixth, I went back to pestering Dan.

"About the commercials," I said.

"When I wrote *Nine Innings*, it was ninety seconds," Dan said.

"So let's go back to that and add two longer breaks between the third and the fourth innings and the sixth and seventh innings, which will cut down on mound visits and give everybody else a chance to go to the bathroom."

"Oh, I think that's kind of a good idea," he said.

"Six minutes," I said.

"Four," he replied.

The fortieth anniversary of Rotisserie League offered an irresistible opportunity for reasoned reappraisal and giving Dan shit. Author Michael Weinreb called his essay "Okrent's Deadly Toy."

It wasn't exactly an appreciation.

Christina Kahrl, then a senior editor for ESPN, wrote a piece titled "Fantasy Baseball's Lasting Legacy," the first in-depth look at what Dan had wrought.

"A world where the game is not just a distraction, but almost an unfortunately necessary byproduct of moneymaking activities," Kahrl said. "That's the guilty thing not just about sabermetrics but about fantasy sports. There's an argument to be made, the real game is being played on the spreadsheet and not on the field.

"We turned human beings into commodities and then we applied a value judgment to them, about whether they're good or bad commodities, whether they're overpaid or underpaid, all according to a metric."

* * *

If Statcast existed in 2001 for Game Three of the 2001 American League Division Series, the Flip Play wouldn't have happened. Joe Torre would have replaced Mike Mussina with a left-handed reliever. The A's would have pinch-hit for Terrence Long. If not, Torre would have employed an unbalanced defensive shift cluttering right field with infielders, and Jeter would have been stationed in short center field with his back to home plate.

The only way Jeter makes the play is from his shortstop position, shaded toward second base, where he had a panoramic view of the ball's trajectory and Spencer's hurried throw, setting the improbable in motion.

"So, what's the value of Statcast allowing you to do this?" I asked Tom Tango.

"You mean can I put a number on it?"

"No, a value."

Tom seemed bolloxed by the question. Numbers are always the answer in his line of work. "A sure run was turned into an out," he said, finally. "That's big value. At every point that the ball is handed off from one player to the other, the question is, 'What's the chance of this team winning? What's the chance of a team scoring?'

"So, if we had enough data, we could create a chart saying, 'As the ball is moving second by second, we could say the chance of a player scoring a run or getting thrown out.'

"Then you might see, as Jeter's coming in, suddenly the chance of him being thrown out would jump up. That's the whole premise of Statcast. Right now, we're tracking, frame by frame, three hundred frames per second, the location of every player, and of the ball. So, we're in the position now to be able to explain everything that's going on."

But, really, they can't. Because the animating forces behind the Flip Play were Jeter's knowledge of his own body, his instinctive mastery of spatial relations, the trust of his manager, and the freedom to do what years of practice, training, and experience had prepared him to do.

Ironic, isn't it? The Flip Play gave birth to a system dedicated to digitally quantifying every millisecond of every play, but it can't measure or acknowledge what made the play possible.

"Analytic people have trouble seeing the unexplained parts," analytics pioneer Ari Kaplan said.

* * *

Quite suddenly the game demanded my attention. The Whitecaps had loaded the bases again in the eighth inning. I saw Sean Matson warming up in the Firebirds bullpen under the watchful eye of Bullpen

Coach "Cookie" Cook, a fifth-round draft choice in 2010, who walked away from baseball after reaching Triple-A to become a sculptor and spiritual guide to young relievers.

Cookie threw 92 to 96 mph, which was considered a plus fastball back then. He was six feet, six inches tall, 230 pounds, and got a $299,000 bonus from the Cleveland Indians. "No way if I'm in this year's draft I'm going in the fifth round. I couldn't run with those wild horses."

Now, he's a skinny lefty with red hair down to his ass. He told me: "You want to know what's changed? This is what's changed. We've gotten so much better at this. We're nasty at this now. We're gross at this now.'"

The Whitecaps scored three runs. It was almost a game. Steve, the public address announcer, interrupted the rally with a plea that became more urgent with a not-too-distant rumble of thunder. "If you came here with a Jeep, you may not be leaving with a Jeep unless you stop up here in the booth first because I have your keys."

"That's cute," Dan said.

* * *

Not so cute—the financial fissure dividing baseball into haves and have-nots, an issue Dan and I debate annually at his favorite clam dive where he always orders fried scallops. Since our last lunch, four players, led by Aaron Judge, had signed free agent contracts each worth in excess of $300 million. And that was *before* Shohei Ohtani became a free agent.

The financial imbalance was acute, but the league was thriving. I consulted my troika of wisemen, Don Fehr, Roy Eisenhardt, and Michael Haupert, about what baseball should do.

Mike and Dan came up with almost identical proposals, requiring half of all team revenue (not including stadium value and MLB brand dollars) to be allocated to the players and split equally between the thirty teams. "That's your cap," Mike said. "My proposal is that players get 50 percent of total revenue.

"And here's the beauty part. Any unspent salary allowance is turned over to the Players Association at the end of the season."

According to his calculations, payroll in 2023 was only 42 percent of total MLB revenues. "This would likely lower salaries at the very top end but raise them at the bottom and middle. Under my plan, you could institute a minimum salary at whatever level the players want. The higher the minimum, the less available to shower on Shohei Ohtani and Juan Soto.

"Benefits: The owners get fixed cost certainty. The players get a fixed cut of total revenues. Collective bargaining becomes much easier. Drawbacks: The Mets can no longer spend five times more on players than the A's in Steve Cohen's quest to get a World Series trophy. And the players are adamantly opposed to a salary cap."

"I like mine better," Dan said.

His counter: "MLB appoints an independent appraiser to assess the current market value of every team. Once that is determined each team is awarded proportionate shares in a common pot, based on their market value. So if the Yankees are worth ten bazillion dollars and the Mariners are worth five bazillion, the Yankees get twice as many shares as the Mariners and so on.

"Each year, total revenue from all sources—broadcast, streaming, tickets, hot dogs, Motorola patches on the Cubs' sleeve—is thrown into a common pot and divided in half. The first half—call it the Franchise Pool—is distributed to each team according to the number of shares it has, thus providing ample reward for the most valuable franchises and owners who've invested the most in their teams. But the other half—the Player Pool—is divided by thirty, an equal amount to each team, that MUST be spent on player salaries. In other words, a level playing field at free agent time."

He liked Mike's idea about returning unspent money to the Players Association so much that he stole it. He also agreed to my demand that "the sleazy money teams make from gambling kingpins" be used to build my urban academies.

* * *

Forty-five years ago, Dan Okrent's Rotisserie League Baseball created a revolutionary way to "consume" baseball. "Consume" is a new baseball idiom. As in, some people consume baseball on the radio, some on TV; some consume baseball cards; some consume fantasy sports. "Betting is another way of consuming the game," Sandy Alderson told me.

It is a term of art just fatuous enough to leech the sting from the reality of baseball's abhorrent about-face on gambling, which Manfred called "a massive opportunity for fan engagement."

Rotisserie begat fantasy games sponsored by ESPN and *Sports Illustrated*, CBS, and Yahoo, which begat the mega fantasy site DraftKings, which became the "Official Daily Fantasy Game" of Major League Baseball in 2013, which led to what is now known as the Daily Fantasy Sports (DFS) industry.

Also that year, the lawsuit challenging the illegality of sports betting, *Murphy v. National Collegiate Athletic Association*, began wending its way to the Supreme Court.

In 2017, the year before the Supreme Court issued its decision, ruling that betting was a states' rights issue, industry lobbyists met with MLB executives, cajoling them into joining forces with DraftKings and FanDuel. The train was about to leave the station, they argued. Might as well get on board while they could exert some control.

MLB considered its options and concluded it would be swell if betting companies were required to use the leagues' proprietary data to set betting lines.

Judge Kenesaw Mountain Landis doesn't scare the shit out of anyone anymore.

I'm the granddaughter of a bookie and rumrunner who used my dad, then a towheaded two-year-old toddler, as a decoy in the Model T when he crossed the border with Canadian hooch. For me, gambling is not a temptation, and banning it is not a moralistic imperative. But it is wrong for baseball. Wrong because it attracts fans of the *action* not the action. Wrong because exchanging sanctimony for sleaze isn't a good look or a good trade-off.

Wrong because it tempts players to do what the sign posted above the clubhouse door forbids. Five players were suspended in 2024 for violating those rules. A Caesar's Palace exec told me that the night Ohio joined the confederation of states allowing legalized sports gambling—thirty-eight of them by the spring of 2025—"Banned-for-Life" Pete Rose made the first bet, plunking down twenty large on the Reds to win the World Series.

It's also wrong, Sean Doolittle said, because it undermines the relationship between players and fans. He began receiving Venmo demands for money from indignant bettors in the months before he retired. "You blew the game and cost them a chance of winning five hundred bucks," Doo said. "If you thought players were starting to be commodified from fantasy baseball, Rotisserie leagues, like, it's next-level with the sports betting."

Dan agreed. "This is a really bad idea," he said. "Teams in the league should not have any financial interest in gambling. They have no choice but to allow it, but they should not benefit financially."

No one really knows how much MLB can or will earn, explained Eric Ramsey, market analyst for *Legal Sports Report*. It's not like they get a cut of every bet. MLB profits through sponsorships, by leveraging intellectual property, and by selling its data to Sportradar, which, according to the company website, disseminates "real time game statistics around the globe to eight hundred sportsbooks and nine hundred media companies."

"MLB now owns a stake in Sportradar," Ramsey said, which means they make money on both ends of the transaction.

He calculated that baseball is responsible for 10–15 percent of total annual sports betting revenue. "So as an extremely rough estimate: Total sports betting revenue from baseball in 2024 nationwide was around $1.5 billion or so."

Not a single one of those profiteers ever so much as thanked Dan Okrent or brought him a steak sandwich.

* * *

The intermittent heat lightning flashing above the band shell beyond center field had turned insistent. The wind picked up. Some folks on a nearby blanket were listening to the Firebirds play-by-play guys, who mentioned "rumoring of a tornado warning."

I checked my phone. A tornado had touched down in Foxborough, eighty miles to the west of Eldredge Park. Three inches of rain had closed Logan Airport across Cape Cod Bay in Boston. Paper wrappers began dive-bombing the field. Dan's sensible wife, Becky, began packing up their things. But I wasn't done with Dan. "But you do accept responsibility?"

"Yeah, I accept my responsibility. We all have the responsibility to fix what analytics have fucked up because analytics is the game. But I don't feel guilty because you should always want more information."

"Because that's the nature of human progress?"

"You can quote me on that."

He was trying to extricate himself from the hillside, and no doubt from me, but the still-damp slope didn't make escape easy. Closer to home plate the terrain is terraced for blankets and chairs, with railroad-tie steps carved into the slope, but not in Dan's preferred location. There's no graceful way off this end of the hill.

"I'm doing my bit," I said, blocking his path. "What about you?"

"We have to figure out what can we do that will restore the game to its glory—" Dan said, to a rumble of not-so-distant thunder "—or even part of its glory."

Finally upright, Dan said, "When people say, 'How do you feel, having invented this?' I say, 'I feel the way that J. Robert Oppenheimer felt having invented the atomic bomb.'"

That sounded familiar, so I checked in with my new pal ChatGPT when I got to the car, which informed me that his first public usage of these pithy bon mots was during a 2004 appearance on *PBS NewsHour*, which didn't sound right.

ChatGPT was wrong. "I used it in *The Wall Street Journal* sometime in the nineties," Dan insisted.

Also in a 1985 *New York Times* interview about Rotisserie; on ESPN in 2012; on *NPR* in 2013; and in *The New Yorker*, *The Boston Globe*, and the *Times*, again, in 2015.

The lesson for baseball is clear. When you stumble on perfection, don't fuck it up.

CHAPTER 14

THE PROBLEM WITH PERFECTION

Why isn't good enough good enough?

I was late for my date with the robo-ump. Traffic was hell getting off the Cape, as it is every Sunday.

By the time I got to the park in Worcester, Massachusetts, the last collaboration between Janet Marie Smith and Larry Lucchino, play had resumed in the second inning of the game suspended the previous evening in the downpour that chased me from Eldredge Park.

The WooSox were trailing 1–0.

Polar Park is an aspirational ballpark, built with civic hopes and $160 million in taxpayer money. Expectations were high for the new abode constructed for the transplanted PawSox, Boston's longtime Triple-A affiliate, who played in a dump in Pawtucket, Rhode Island. Hope was it would reinvigorate a degraded industrial neighborhood called the Canal District whose factories once sent plaster, grindstones, and molasses down the now-fetid Blackstone Canal to Narragansett Bay. Always a heavy lift for a ballpark.

I met Bill Wanless, WooSox vice president of communications, under a futuristic light fixture in the lobby that called to mind the rings of Saturn. He had invited me to come watch the robo-ump in action. I brought a copy of his email in case bona fides were required. "I will definitely bring you into the control room where the ABS person is." That's automated ball-strike, in case you didn't know. "Nice young man named Josue."

On weekends human umpires still called balls and strikes, but each team got three chances to tell him he was full of shit. These challenges could be initiated only by the pitcher, the batter, or the catcher. You can tell because the player asking for said challenge pats himself on the head. Also, it's posted on the scoreboard and announced by the ballpark announcer.

Weekday games go full robo, turning the home plate ump into Charlie McCarthy, the wise-ass tuxedoed dummy who was ventriloquist Edgar Bergen's better half. True, umpires have been called dummies and worse forever. It's part of the job description.

Fact is, according to FanGraphs, umpires have improved every season since the arrival of pitch tracking in 2008 as measured against the Statcast strike zone. Mike Rizzo says they are the best arbiters in professional sports.

Bill escorted me upstairs, stopping at an aquamarine door marked "Taj Mahal," Lucchino's coy name for the supersecret cell where MLB was testing its supersecret technology.

Bill threw open the door: "One million dollars of equipment," he said proudly.

In the far-right corner of the room, in the first row, hovering just above home plate, headphones glued to his ears, Josue was monitoring each pitch on two screens: one a laptop in front of him showing the trajectory, spin, and location of the pitch as it crossed the elusive territory of the strike zone. Territory that has been defined, redefined; expanded and contracted; oriented and reoriented, squeezed and unsqueezed over the course of baseball time.

Rendered in Polar Park blue and olive green, the strike zone was definitely not the Statcast image burned into my frontal lobe. I ventured a mild inquiry about the display on the screen. "I'm not allowed to say," Josue said. "Still testing ones out."

I stood at his left shoulder, which conveniently blocked my view of the desktop computer screen he consulted between pitches. To see that screen, I would have had to climb over the arm of his chair, kneel between his feet, put my head in his lap, and crane my neck so violently to the right that no chiropractor would ever see me again. Also, that would have been highly unprofessional and anatomically impossible. Major League Baseball's secrets, such as they were, were safe from me.

I essayed another question, one so banal I figured even Josue, a quality engineer, not a baseball guy, couldn't fail to answer. "Which is more fun?"

"I like this because I have to focus on every pitch," he said while tapping away on his cell phone. "With ABS, it's just..." He pointed to his headphones. With ABS, also known as the full robo, all he had to do was listen as the computer called every pitch. With the challenge system he had to pay attention.

The Taj Mahal is also home to the WooSox broadcast team and its public address announcer. "The previous pitch has been challenged," the PA announcer said.

Based on Morgan Sword's description at the MIT Sloan Sports Analytics Conference, I was expecting hoots and hollers of fan engagement: "The way we've been doing it is actually put it up on the video board so nobody knows until you see the animation of the pitch, kind of like tennis used to do, and the crowd cheers. It's fun."

Not so much at Polar Park where the announcer, adopting the demeanor of a stentorian robot, rendered the decision so briskly that I am unable to report who asked for it or what the decision was. It was no fun at all.

I resolved to pay more attention. Josue continued tapping away on his handheld. In the bottom of the fifth inning, Trevor Story, the Red Sox shortstop who had been more or less on the injured list since signing a six-year, $140 million free agent contract in 2022, challenged a called strike on a 3-1 count.

"MLB says no interviews," Josue said suddenly, looking up from his phone. "We're not talking to the media."

"But I was invited!" I protested.

I was prepared to be dazzled. That human beings are capable of creating a virtual, three-dimensional strike zone hovering in cyberspace is inconceivable to me. The only thing harder is being a human being and making those calls.

I stood my ground. I would not leave. I refused to be a good girl. I wanted my real reporter pals to be proud of me. I also didn't ask any more questions.

Soon enough, kind Bill returned to escort me into the sunshine.

I found myself a seat on a patio behind Section 204. Dusty Baker's son, Darren, just back from a groin injury, was playing second base for the Red Wings, the Triple-A affiliate of the Washington Nationals. "Big City" Matt Adams, last seen at a Savannah Bananas weigh-in, was trying to resuscitate his big-league career with the WooSox.

A train rattled past the left field wall. It was nice to be outside on a perfect day for baseball. All the seats atop the mini version of Fenway's Green Monster were full. Bright red Adirondack chairs stationed on the outfield berm beckoned.

Which led me to consider baseball's obsession with perfection. Not the good kind, the human kind, twenty-seven outs and an unblemished scorecard. I'm talking about the technocratic kind, the bitch goddess that creates the expectation of a more perfect perfection, of never being wrong. Author Rebecca Solnit calls it "a stick with which to beat the possible." And technology is its cudgel.

By the end of the 2023 season, MLB had gone mum, mumm-er than mum, on the subject of the robo-ump. Then in May 2024 came an announcement from the commissioner's office saying the system, which they had been testing since 2019, would not be major-league ready until earliest 2026.

A month later, MLB quietly allowed that henceforth Triple-A games would use only the challenge system I briefly observed, noting, as if everyone knew this to be true, "It has become the preferred system over full ABS among both in-uniform personnel and fans."

In July, the commissioner declared the technology is "good to a 100th of an inch" and "pluperfect" in documenting the path of the ball but allowed there were technical issues still to be resolved. Seems they were still having trouble perfecting a perfectible strike zone.

"They're worried about the system being hacked," a former MLB honcho told me.

"Posh," a current honcho said. "It's about perfection. Going all-in fully automated means there's no safety net. Logically that makes no sense. The challenge system was inevitable."

Former Seattle Mariners Manager Scott Servais raised a different question. "ABS will change how pitching is developed. You will pitch to the square," he said. "You don't think the guys at Driveline will come up with a fucking formula that every pitcher will fly over there to learn? 'Okay, teach me this pitch I can get in the zone, but the hitter can't actually hit, and ABS will register it as a strike.' They'll come up with that in two weeks."

Former umpire Jim Joyce weighed in: "I get so upset reading about how people cannot wait until the robo umpire comes. I don't get it. It's not gonna perfect the game of baseball. God forbid, there would be a malfunction happen in the World Series. What do you do? A do-over?

And, by chance, it happens to the Yankees in the World Series? People's heads are going to explode."

* * *

I went back to Morgan Sword for an update on the update he gave at MIT. MLB was still futzing around with the shape of an automated strike zone then. Should it be two-dimensional or three-dimensional? A rectangle or an oval? How far back on the plate should it sit?

MLB had settled on its preferred geometry: a two-dimensional rectangle set halfway back on home plate with the left and right edges lined up with the edges of the plate—seventeen inches wide. They settled on a formula using each player's height, as measured in spring training, to determine the top and bottom of his strike zone: 53.5 percent at the top and 27 percent at bottom, having increased the top by 2.5 percent to placate cranky pitchers who missed their high strikes. "It avoids all the technological complexity of identifying where somebody's knee is or adjusting things for their stance," Morgan said. "The downside is it treats all six-foot-one hitters exactly the same even if their stances are different. The question is whether that's a trade-off that people are willing to make to get consistency."

I'd be happy to be treated like any six-footer.

The strike zone has changed repeatedly through time. If you ask the players, they'll tell you it can change from pitch to pitch and game to game and always umpire to umpire. In the Koufax era, it was an east-west strike zone. Pitchers pitched up and in, down and away. With pinpoint control, they claimed their territory, expanding the zone, changing speeds, exploiting the corners, and hitting the black. Statcast eliminated any ambiguity about what was or wasn't on the black.

Today the strike zone is a rectangle like a wall mirror hanging in a ladies' dressing room at Bloomingdale's. It's hard for an ump to see both ends, especially with catchers having abandoned the traditional hamstring-aching squat in favor of a lowered tuchus and an extended chorus girl leg aimed at stealing low strikes.

A Greek chorus of baseball old-timers—Mike Rizzo, Tom Glavine, Leo Mazzone, the late Whitey Herzog, and new guy Sam Mondry-Cohen—are of one mind on this subject. *Take the mirror off the wall.*

"Instead of that Bloomingdale's mirror, I would increase the east-west part of the strike zone and lower it from the top," Rizzo said. "I would keep the bottom and make it a little wider. With the launch angle swings and the pitchers pitching higher, four-seamers up in the strike zone, it really adds to the strikeout total. You lower the strike zone, there's less incentive for pitchers to pitch up. Guys that have a good feel for the strike zone won't swing at them, the ball will be down a little more, and easier to put into play."

Today's pitching mantra is: Prevent contact. As opposed to the outré notion: "Let 'em hit the fuckin' ball." Which produced more action on the bases, more opportunities for bloopers and web gems, more of the chaos of the ball in play that made Roger Angell's heart glad.

Technology has played its part in reorienting or disorienting the zone. "With ball tracking, the outer edge of the strike zone is well defined with home plate so you can really measure what is and isn't a strike," said Mondry-Cohen. "The top and bottom is more subjective, so it's harder to say an umpire missed a call high or low. But in or out, very clear. That's one of the consequences of technology in the game."

Hall of Famer Tom Glavine is not a fan. East-west appeals not just because it worked so well for him, but because he says it's easier to adjudicate. It has to do with the movement of the catcher's mitt. "Movement in the glove generally is going to trigger a reaction. East and west eliminates more of that because if my catcher's set up on the outside corner and the umpire sees glove movement away from the corner, that pitch is probably off the plate. He sees glove movement toward the plate, that ball has gotta be *on* the plate. The movement becomes less of a factor when a catcher's moving his glove up and down because it's harder for an umpire to judge where actually is that pitch."

Sword sighed when I relayed these conversations. "Baseball's having its reckoning right now of 'it's another intrusion of technology into a game that is being weighed down by technology.' We need to find a way to deploy technology so that it improves the game, and it makes it more entertaining and more charming and creates emotional connections for people."

He found it interesting that people reacted so negatively to the fulsome robo; I found it inevitable and reassuring.

Years into the effort to devise a more perfect perfection, MLB realized nobody wanted it. Maybe because the pursuit of perfection in life and baseball is not only unattainable but maybe even boring?

"One of the things that I think was frustrating for the players and coaches about using the full ABS is that there's no target for all of that aggression and adrenaline," Morgan said. "So we actually had a player in the Arizona Fall League turn around and start screaming at this camera behind the plate. And I get it. If you keep removing these places for humanity to show itself on the baseball field... it's got to go somewhere."

The player was Jacob Heyward, Jason Heyward's younger brother and a career minor leaguer now trying to make his way in baseball as a manager in the San Francisco Giants system. In the fall of 2019, in Arizona in an early test of ABS, he became the first and, praise Jesus, the last player to be thrown out of a game by a robot.

The pitch that caused the ruckus was a curveball that broke down and in on him for strike three. To my eyes, it was a ball. He thought so too and protested vehemently but not violently. The human ump, the vehicle for delivering a call he didn't make, took up for the robot and threw Jacob out of the game for arguing balls and strikes. "I wasn't even talking to you," Jacob protested.

* * *

Variability is baked into umpiring just as it is into hand-sewn baseballs because decisions and stitches are made by human beings. "The ability to adjust to nonuniformity is what great players can do," my smart friend Peko said. "It is well-known that umpires make different decisions depending on the count," she continued, invoking what's known as "The Compassionate Umpire Theory." "An 0-2 count increases the size of the strike zone while a 3-0 count shrinks it. Because the calls are biased, they are changing the outcome of the game maybe in a way that makes it more interesting. The robot wouldn't be making the same mistake and would maybe make it less interesting."

This led to a prolonged etymological disquisition on the differences between perfection, precision, and accuracy, and which is preferable. "The robo-umps are not more perfect," Peko said. "I think they are more accurate."

Joe Maddon wonders how much the current zeal for accuracy is about gambling. "If you're betting a lot of money, you want accuracy." When major leaguers got their first taste of Robo Life in spring training 2025, not everyone was thrilled. Turned out there was wiggle room in this more perfect world, a margin of error close to half an inch, pitcher Corbin Burnes told *The Athletic*, raising exactly the question Peko posed.

"We have to decide if it is more valuable to have human umpires who make mistakes 10 percent of the time than robotic umpires that make mistakes 1 percent of the time, in which case there's something that we're valuing more than accuracy. And that's fine. I think we just have to be honest with ourselves about what we're trying to achieve.

Because the more random you make the game, the more useless the analytics are."

Say that again.

"Accuracy is not the only quality in a referee. One of the other qualities is that people can yell at them. That's a nonnegligible thing. I think that the way you should be using technology in sports is to make people better at their job. We have to think more creatively about how to deploy this technology."

"So, the less perfect result may just make for a better game?"

"Yes," she replied.

I repeated this to Morgan. "Your opinion on that issue depends a lot on your job title."

"And your age?" I asked.

"Yep. If your career and your livelihood depend upon what happens on the baseball field, it's understandably aggravating when it's not called perfectly because the stakes are so high, and people get paid and lose their jobs over what happens on the field.

"But if you're the dad and his son in the second deck at Citi Field, screaming at the umpire is part of the tradition of the game. The fact that it's imperfect and human and you're watching somebody do their best and not always succeed is an important element of the entertainment."

"I just think the pursuit of that kind of perfection, and I don't mean just in baseball, is gonna kill the human race," I told Morgan. "Like dinosaurs and Twi-Night doubleheaders."

"Yeah, right," he said. "It's even broader than baseball. People are just less forgiving and understanding about that than they would be about the fallibility of a human umpire."

I don't object to perfection on principle. A perfect game, for example. So I called my old friend Rich Hill, who knows a thing or two about the fickleness of perfection. At first, he was inclined toward the full robo but then wavered. "I just think it would take away from the human element of the game," he said finally.

"Okay, enough," I yelped.

"We're not an element! We're the humans! The data is an element of us."

Rich considered that for maybe two seconds, which is as long as a player gets to trigger a challenge, and said, "That's perfect."

* * *

I cruised by the Taj Mahal to say goodbye to Josue on my way out of the park and to get the challenge totals for the afternoon. "There were five," he said. "Three challenges the umps were correct. One the ump was incorrect. The last time the player tried to challenge, it was disallowed because time expired."

Three for four is okay by me.

CHAPTER 15

HE IS SO THAT GUY

What's luck got to do with it?

So, here's the deal: bottom of the ninth, Classic Auto Group Park, home of the Class-A Lake County Captains, eighteen miles from the big time, where at Progressive Field the 2023 Cleveland Guardians were in the process of losing to the Minnesota Twins.

There was nothing Chase DeLauter, the Guardians' 2022 first-round draft pick—perchance the slugging corner outfielder of their dreams—could do about that. Thanks to a broken bone in his left foot, the dainty fifth metatarsal that was having a hard time supporting his six-foot-four, 235-pound self, he had barely played since turning professional the year before.

Finally whole, he had begun his 2023 season with a thirteen-game hitting streak, which had ended the night before I arrived. He embarked on a new nine-game streak the next evening with a first-inning single. He was beginning to show why the MLB Network had called him "the best hitter in the entire draft."

His mother, Melissa, had driven from their home in Martinsburg, West Virginia, for the weekend. Riding shotgun: her mother, Lisa, and her stepmother, Jane, recently divorced from Melissa's father. "They get on fine," she assured me. "They divorced the same guy."

Chase stepped to the plate in the bottom of the ninth inning with the Captains behind 3–1. The lights still glowed beyond the left field fence where the new team owner had installed a nine-hole miniature golf course. But the picnic tables and red Adirondack chairs stationed on the grass berm beyond the right field fence—just like the ones at Polar Park in Worcester—were empty. The triple chin on the flaccid mug of special guest Sir C. C., pallid mascot of the Cleveland Cavaliers, had collapsed on his sternum. "Not the first string," a Captains staffer confided.

The Peoria Chiefs reliever went into his windup.

* * *

I met Chase outside the clubhouse a couple of hours before the first pitch. He looked bigger and shaggier than last I saw him in 2021 at Eldredge Park, his hair newly organized by a headband, a Cleveland hoodie pulled down over his eyes, a hint of the reserve coaches had observed in him. God gave him all five baseball tools but not the gift of gab.

I wanted to see his idiosyncratic scissor swing, about which classicists like *The Athletic*'s Keith Law are dubious, up close. It is a swing of nontraditional beauty like, say, Lauren Bacall. (Did I mention that Bette the Dog is named after her because they have the same long legs?) Nobody had ever told him you're not supposed to hit this way.

"My bats are in the dugout," he protested.

"Doesn't need to be your bat."

He trudged off to the clubhouse to find something to swing. I thought back to that first meeting on a dusty baseball field behind the Nauset Middle School in Orleans, Massachusetts. He was a big, gangly kid surrounded by a scrum of littler kids, some of whom maybe reached his knees. It was the last day of the Firebirds' baseball camp, and drills were decidedly informal. It was basically just a whole bunch of boys chasing each other around in the dirt, many in Aaron Judge jerseys—Yankees outliers in a waning New England summer.

"You all want to be Aaron Judge?" I asked.

"Yes, yes, yes!" they said. All except one kid from Manhattan's Upper West Side, who said, "I want to be a physicist."

Chase spent a lot of time with the kids that summer. Cape Leaguers get paid twenty-five dollars an hour for working at team-sponsored clinics, which is the only paying job allowed. It came in handy. He doesn't come from money. There wasn't any for the private coaches, the travel ball teams, and showcases that are de rigueur today. Which is why the Cape League season, his first chance to be seen by major-league scouts, mattered so much.

He was an unknown from James Madison University, a mid-major Division 1 school not exactly known as a baseball powerhouse. Yes, he was a three-sport star in high school, West Virginia High School Player of the Year, a member of the National Honor Society, but he had offers from exactly two schools. He wasn't interested in West Virginia University because they offered him academic money, and he wanted a school that wanted him for baseball, a school that would let him pitch and hit.

On his first visit to JMU, he didn't exactly dazzle. "He didn't hit all that well," said Jimmy Jackson, who recruited him as a pitcher. "He was very thin, a little weak. The head coach wasn't interested in him as a hitter."

But Jackson, now pitching coach at the University of Maryland, saw in his left-handed delivery an echo of Chris Sale, only slower. He figured his fastball would improve and it did. Chase was throwing 93 mph when they shut him down to protect his arm from an injury that would interfere with his hitting.

When he called Kelly Nicholson to recommend Chase for the 2021 Firebirds, DeLauter had played in exactly sixteen collegiate games. "I said, 'I know nobody knows this kid yet but I'm telling you, he's the best hitter I've ever been around in my whole life. I'm not kidding. I've never seen anything like this.'"

The Guardians had two scouts on Cape Cod. They started following him his sophomore year at JMU. They saw what Jimmy Jackson saw. At the end of the Cape season, Chase was tied for the league lead in home runs (nine) while striking out only eighteen times. He batted .298 with a .986 OPS and was named Outstanding Pro Prospect.

Coach Nick prepared a predraft profile for the scouts he knew would be calling. "I comped him against 150 guys who were left-left, and the closest comp was Jason Heyward," Nicholson said. "That's a pretty lofty comp."

In the spring of his draft year, his junior year in college, he began to attract national attention. J. P. Morosi, MLB Network announcer and columnist, tweeted:

"Great story for baseball parents and aspiring players: Chase DeLauter never attended a national showcase while playing at Hedgesville [WV] High School."

"To be honest I really couldn't afford it," Chase told Morosi. "I mean obviously where I'm from, it's a smaller town, there's not really teams close that I could go to that would go to Perfect Game."

He was batting .437 with eight home runs and thirty-five RBI a couple of weeks later when he rounded first base in the top of the ninth inning of what would be his last collegiate game. Somewhere between first and second, he broke the fifth metatarsal on his left foot.

Shortly after the July MLB draft, he broke it again. The same bone, in the same foot, that had cost him most of his last college season would cost him his first year in professional baseball. His first surgery had not worked. The Guardians sent him to the Green Bay Packers' team orthopedist for a second surgery, requiring a bone graft.

His foot was still in a boot when he showed up at a Firebirds reunion that spring in Scottsdale. When he reported late to the Captains in

June 2023, he had played in only six minor-league games. "It's been over a year since I've even hit a ball off a pitcher," he said when he returned with a bat.

Turns out it's hard to swing a bat, much less scissor, in shower shoes. "I've been scissoring since I was five years old," Chase said. "There's a bunch of big leaguers that hit like it. Yordan Alvarez scissors. Bobby Witt Jr. scissors. Mike Trout's done it a couple times."

I saw enough in his embarrassed swings to understand Jimmy Jackson's explanation. "When his right foot strides forward and it stops in the ground and he goes to swing, his left foot will kick back toward the first base dugout. If you watch a hockey player make a slapshot, you'll see the same identical move, the back foot will go behind their butt."

"That thing went in and out of style more times than the mullet," said Bob Keyes, owner of Bio-Kinetics Research and Development in Utah. "The first people that come to mind are Willie Mays and Roberto Clemente because it was so exaggerated on those two."

It's not so much an advantage as it is the way his body is supposed to move, Jackson said, the way it's always moved. "All this shit gets taught out of these kids when really most of what they do as a kid is correct. Luckily, he wasn't coached by many people, and they left him alone because he was good."

DeLauter was one of four players drafted in the first round in 2022 who never played travel ball. "He is an outlier," Jackson said. "Maybe there's one a year in every state that could come close to Chase, a kid that has gone unseen. But there aren't a lot of Chase DeLauters. He's the 1 percent of the 1 percent. I think by him staying away from the private coaching and training and travel ball, that helped him to excel."

"Do you think your swing would have survived travel ball?" I asked.

"If somebody would've tried to change it when I was young enough, I don't think so," Chase said. "Only because at the end of the day, when you're young your body just moves the way it's supposed to move. Whatever way my body lets me do it, that is the way it does it."

Before I left him in peace, I took a picture for his mom. "Me and my mom don't talk baseball ever," he said. "She's just my mom. You know what I mean?"

Good thing, too, because Melissa said, when I found Chase's cheering section behind the first base dugout, "I don't even like baseball. I only like it because of Chase. It's soooooooo boring."

* * *

Chase's girlfriend, Bella, joined us in the stands. She was beautiful and blonde and tan like a college girlfriend should be. Though in point of actual fact, they didn't become an item until he was ready to leave Harrisonburg. She was still enrolled, working toward a degree in nursing with an eye on neonatal care. Melissa was rhapsodizing about visiting Chase in Arizona after the 2022 draft. "I'd love to live in Arizona or Florida," Melissa said. "Chase said, 'Why don't we get a house big enough for everybody?'"

"We'll see," Bella said tentatively.

"I'd love to be a wife living in Florida going for manicures while someone else looks after the kids," Melissa continued.

Ex-step-grandmother Jane Usavage raised her hand to volunteer. Grandmother Lisa signaled she would do the housekeeping. "Chase is a homebody," Melissa said. "He wants to be at home with his game in his own bed."

I pointed out that major leaguers sleep in a lot of different beds. Bella said Chase wouldn't allow her to go out by herself in the Cleveland neighborhood where the team had housed him. Urbanity was new to him.

"There was no money, none," ex-step-grandmother Jane said. "Melissa would scrimp and save. Melissa put herself through college while raising four kids and operating a day care center. Their father was in the military, and then they got divorced and he moved next door. They're just a local yokel family that hunts and fishes.

"I made sure they had a vacation every summer," she said. "I took them to Ocean City or Bethany Beach. His grandfather, my ex-husband, was very supportive. We did a lot of gloves and cleats and sneakers and shoes, and camps."

They all pitched in, taking him to baseball camps in Pittsburgh, Ohio, and Virginia; some tournaments gave him a break on registration fees. She had never heard of Perfect Game.

He didn't have a favorite team growing up because they were all so far away. He did remember seeing Derek Jeter get his 3,000th hit on TV when he was ten years old. "I think that's when I became a hitter fanatic."

We had been texting and talking off and on for two years. I thought I was beginning to get a sense of him. "He just doesn't open up about a lot," ex-step-grandmother Jane said. "Melissa is not verbose. For her to start talking, and smiling, she's gotta have a couple of beers."

Which she had. "He's like a piece of meat," Melissa declared. "He's not allowed to have sex. He is a baseball slut. Wherever they want him, that's okay."

Meanwhile her son had scored the first run of the game in the bottom of the first inning and walked in the fifth. "A lot of these guys are making nothing," she said. "They're working at Taco Bell."

As the sixteenth pick in the 2022 draft, DeLauter received a $3.75 million signing bonus, $400,000 under the amount allotted for that slot because, he said, he was the last first-round draft pick to sign. The first chosen, Jackson Holliday, received a bonus in excess of $8 million from the Baltimore Orioles.

Ex-step-grandmother Jane was a comptroller in the accounting department of a large corporation. Melissa is an accountant. They tried to tell him hard financial truths. "Don't pay off your school loans now. Money isn't everything. It disappears a lot faster than you think."

"He said, 'Jane, you'll take care of my money and Mom will be my manager.'

"I said, 'Oh, dude. You need a financial advisor you can sue.'

"Melissa is like, 'Janie, he's not gonna listen to us. You can only say certain things up to a certain point.'"

* * *

Norman Rockwell and his umpires wouldn't recognize this American childhood. It's as structured and professionalized as it is expensive, the province of training camps and club teams and tournaments promoted by proliferating corporations promoting themselves as scouting services. In this world, "to showcase" is a verb.

And it's not just true in baseball. It's true in cheerleading, soccer, seven-on-seven football, and girls' volleyball. The first thing Melissa DeLauter told me was that it cost more to send her daughter to volleyball tournaments than it would have cost for Chase to play travel ball. There wasn't money to do both. "People say Chase is an outlier," she said. "And he wouldn't have to be if parents with less talented kids stopped spending so much money..."

She didn't finish the sentence, nor did she have to. I had heard the same from Darwin Pennye and Marquis Grissom. "Parents gotta stop drinking the Kool-Aid," Marquis said. "Everybody is not a travel-ball ballplayer."

"PG is for the elite," Darwin said. "They get all the others who think they're elite."

And parents invested in making their kids elite. Leo Mazzone, who coached the Braves pitching staff from 1990 through 2005, encountered parental ambition at one such tournament. "A mother comes up to me and says, 'My husband and I are working on my son's mental game.'

"I said, 'Yeah? How old is he?'

"She said, 'Ten.'

"I looked at her and said, 'Do you know, ma'am, that he doesn't have a clue what the hell you're talking about?'

"Then I stopped myself because what I wanted to say was, 'You and your husband need to work on *your* mental game.'"

Perfect Game is the biggest, baddest brand name in modern America's pay-to-play childhood, a vast sports industrial complex of competing organizations, and private coaches, vying to attract the best young athletes to its camps and competitions with the promise that "your son or daughter will be seen," meaning by college recruiters and pro scouts.

Perfect Game was birthed in Cedar Rapids, Iowa, in 1997, the aspirational dream of baseball scout and father Jerry Ford. The facility he created for his son, a place to train year-round like California and Florida prospects and be seen by the scouts he attracted, morphed into a virulent strain of youth baseball.

By September 2024, the PG website claimed that 876,492 young ballplayers had been perfected or not, as the case may be. By the spring of 2025, they boasted that 15,134 PG players had been drafted—2,240 major leaguers! Bryce Harper! Manny Machado! Gerrit Cole! Mike Trout! Alex Bregman! Freddie Freeman! Francisco Lindor!

I did the math. "Guess what percentage of PG players have made it to the bigs?" I asked Rich Hill, whose twelve-year-old son did not have a Perfect Game profile.

"Maybe one-half of 1 percent," he said.

"Try one-quarter of 1 percent."

"We tolerate Perfect Game," said Chuck Ricci, amateur scouting director for the Tampa Bay Rays. "It isn't just PG. It's travel baseball in general. It has really brought down how kids value high school baseball, and that's a shame because they've played with those kids sometimes since Little League."

Today, Little League is the province of losers and also-rans like me, consigned to mop-up duty at age ten. "If you're not playing travel ball by ten or eleven years old, could you still make it?" said Eric Byrnes, ex-big leaguer, ex-Banana, current manager of his sons' travel ball teams. "You could. You're a long shot."

J. P. Fasone, a hitting trainer I met at Driveline, said, "You'll have a twelve-year-old come in and he's got his travel ball coach, his spring coach, and a hitting coach and a pitching coach. In the past you played on your Little League team, and if you're good at it you succeed."

It's easy to understand Perfect Game's appeal to coaches like Josh Holliday and Marquis Grissom. "Where else are you going to see the top two thousand kids in the country in one place?" Marquis asked.

Two thousand? How about the 11,658 players that showed up for PG's 2024 Houston Super Regional NIT tournament for teams 6U to 14U, requiring 350 umpires and 150 baseball fields at 32 different baseball complexes.

Perfect Game's innovation was to operate like an NFL combine for babies. "You get to see 250 players run a sixty-yard dash, throw the ball, and take batting practice," Josh said. "We are gathering fifteen- to sixteen-year-old data on international prospects. They hit the market at sixteen. So, if I got a sixteen-year-old catcher in the Dominican Republic with elite physical skills that I'm gonna sign for $2 million, how does the sixteen-year-old in Florida match up? Where it gets tough for me is when we start extending that down to eleven-year-olds and twelve-year-olds."

But why would you need that kind of data on a twelve-year-old?

"Well, that is because there's money to be made," he said.

Welcome to the burgeoning $40 billion "global youth sports market," a segment of the disposable income economy driven by success-seeking parents and private equity investors detailed in the Aspen Institute's annual report on America's State of Play. Twice the amount of cash flowing through the NFL, the Aspen Institute says.

Among the investors: Washington Commanders owner Josh Harris and his partner David Blitzer, whose portfolio of fifteen properties includes 80 percent of Cooperstown All Star Village, and a majority stake in Ripken Sports. They're also big in flag football.

The 2025 report documented the paradoxes and realities of this "youth sports space" in which kids are playing less (boys especially) but specializing earlier, subsidized by parents who spent 46 percent more than they did in 2019—on average $1000 large. All in the belief that investing early will lead to high school success, which, as the borscht belt joke goes "could lead to dancing."

Perfect Game is to Little League what a megachurch is to a one-room chapel on the prairie. Jeff Passan, senior MLB insider at ESPN and author of *The Arm*, calls it an "industry Leviathan." Its sphere of influence has grown from six states to forty-one states plus Japan. Korea is next.

There's always a tournament or a showcase somewhere, if not sponsored by Perfect Game, then by Prep Baseball Report, Prospect Wire, Prospect Select, or Area Code Baseball. Wherever there's a showcase, there's a congregation of scouts in golf carts. "That's all it takes to get the kids to go," Holliday said.

Rankings and glitzy personal profile pages linked to highlight reels courtesy of the company that bills itself as "the world's biggest scouting service" are a potent lure. Also, there's merch. "I think the model that Perfect Game uses is to get you coming back," Tony Reagins said. "A lot of families think that if I continue to come back, that my ranking will go up and thus I'm a better player and I have a better chance to get drafted."

Then he laughed.

USA Baseball's Pitch Smart program, sanctioned by MLB, offers age-appropriate guidelines, but they are only suggestions. There are no training requirements for coaches, no mandatory shut-down periods for players or blackout periods for scouts. No governing body with any authority.

"It's the fucking Wild West," said Deven Morgan, director of youth baseball at Driveline, who has petitioned MLB to establish universal pitch limits and a centralized reporting system to count and share the actual number of pitches and innings kids throw.

He solicits, collects, and posts what orthopedist Jeff Dugas calls "child abuse" stories on social media. Like a ten-year-old he'd just heard about who threw 102 pitches in two and two-thirds innings and gave up twenty earned runs.

"Then we get surprised when kids get hurt because some hard-on coach was desperate to win a fall ball game," Deven said.

A decade-long study of pitchers chosen in the first five rounds of the MLB draft published in *The American Journal of Sports Medicine* in 2023 asked, "Do High School Showcase Exposures Predict Injury?"

Yes, yes, a thousand times yes.

In that decade, the mean age of Tommy John surgery declined by three and a half years; the mean age of showcase debuts declined by about a year, while showcase appearances doubled. The likelihood of needing surgery increased 19 percent with each additional mile per hour.

"Higher HS showcase volume in elite pitchers was associated with a lower likelihood of achieving at the MLB level," the authors wrote. They recommended a minimum age requirement of sixteen. Currently, the minimum age is thirteen. MLB is on record saying it wants to regulate the showcase calendar and establish blackout periods when kids may not be scouted.

At the Andrews Sports Medicine and Orthopedic Center, where Dugas repairs some two hundred elbows each year, 60 percent of all Tommy John surgeries performed in 2015 were on young ballplayers.

Read that again.

That shocking number decreased to a somewhat less shocking 42 percent in 2023. But the number of Perfect Game fireballers throwing 95 mph in showcases increased from three in 2018 to thirty-six in 2024.

What is to be done?

"Go out and play catch in the backyard," said Keith Meister, the Texas Rangers team physician.

"You can limit how many games you can play and travel teams you can play on," said biomechanist Glenn Fleisig. "And penalize violators by banning them from entering the MLB draft with their age group," I replied, "and limit the number of showcases to five."

I suggested five, thinking I was being restrictive. Deven blanched. "Uh, I'd say two," he replied.

Dead arms aren't the only problem. They're also dead tired. "Kids who play travel ball have less time off than major leaguers," Kelly Nicholson said.

But the zeal for specialization and professionalization goes on unchecked. A player like Chase DeLauter, who insisted upon being more than one thing, could only be hatched outside the system in a hollow in West Virginia. "When I see a bio that is travel ball, baseball only, it's a red flag," Buck Showalter said. "Let him see other things and make a decision that he wants to do baseball instead of having it crammed down his throat from a parent."

What the kids see is PG big leaguers and the rankings, especially the rankings. "It's, 'Oh, he's ranked such and such.'" Pennye said. "Kids look at those guys, 'You know who that is? He's got a cannon for an arm.' Because he's ranked. The rankings don't mean crap."

Joe Torre saw the trickle-down on major-league diamonds. "This conditioning started when they were teenagers and going place to place playing with people they didn't even know, auditioning, instead of learning team concepts of trying to win the game. I don't think enough players understand when they go to the plate what situation is at hand. They're just up there with one thing in mind. They're going to hit the ball as far as they can."

And if you can't do that, Chase DeLauter said, "then you're not worth anything to teams."

* * *

At 10:34 p.m. on Friday, August 18, 2023, with two out and two on in the bottom of the ninth inning, the count on Chase DeLauter was one ball and one strike.

The runners took their leads. The Chiefs' pitcher went into the stretch. Amped up, mic'd up on-field host Andy, who'd been screaming and beseeching everyone else to scream with prompts from a scoreboard decibel meter for eight and a half straight innings, went briefly silent.

Despite the promise of postgame fireworks, the ballpark was at least half empty, so the sound carried when Melissa DeLauter's voice rang out, piercing the lakeside humidity with an airmail delivery to her son: "Hit the Fucking Ball!"

His swing was short and compact, the fastball high and a bit outside. He waited for it to come to him. When he planted his front right leg, his left leg kicked back just like a hockey player about to unleash a slapshot.

The Guardians had not messed with his swing. "Scissoring is how Chase DeLauter's body self-organizes to accomplish that task," said Rick Cerfolio, who was the Guardians' director of player personnel when DeLauter was drafted. "We've allowed him to swing in the way that's most efficient for him."

He didn't just hit the fucking ball. He clobbered it so hard it clanged off the base of the left field wall. The left fielder stunk up the throw, which took an unseemly flight path, crossing the diamond and trickling down the first base line, allowing the tying runs to score. Emboldened, Chase turned on the speed Jimmy Jackson bragged about, the long locks flying, absent the helmet that had abandoned his head.

Holy shit, how he ran. When he reached home plate, he didn't even bother to slide.

"HE IS HIM," hoarse host Andy shrieked, which sounded sacrilegious to me. "HE IS SO THAT GUY!"

God knows he had waited long enough to be that guy. For that exquisite moment, nothing hurt. Nothing broke. He didn't drown when his teammates doused him in Gatorade. Little kids pressed their noses against the chain-link fence calling his name, which is what everyone in uniform dreams of, unless you're a flaccid team mascot looking to call it a night.

Every game tells a story, Cerfolio says, and this one game, this one at bat, told what Chase DeLauter can be if his body allows it. "A lot of times nowadays you see guys getting out of the box slowly, and he was sprinting," Cerfolio said. "He showed his power, he showed his speed, his mentality for wanting to get around the bases as quickly as he could, right off the bat, versus standing there and watching. He showed off all of his tools in one play."

The Captains flickered the stadium lights in appreciation, the best curtain call Classic Auto Group Park could muster. The team blasted the news on all its social media platforms: "TELL A FRIEND TO TELL A FRIEND. CHASE. DELAUTER. WALKED. IT. OFF."

"I told you he'd hit a home run!" Melissa crowed as she and the two grandmothers bolted through a field gate.

"Well, sort of," Chase said, between hugs.

He looked at Jane and said, "You're driving. She's been into the beer."

* * *

Arriving at training camp whole in 2024, DeLauter had a head-turning spring like the one that prompted Casey Stengel to pluck Mickey Mantle out of Class C ball in 1951 and bring him to New York to make Joe DiMaggio miserable. Giddy Cleveland scribes wove pretty spring fantasies writing his name into the Guardians' Opening Day lineup. The sort of stories that got Red Smith in trouble with his editors at the *New York Herald Tribune*, ordering him to quit godding up those ballplayers.

If anybody deserves godding up, it's a kid who made it all the way through the system without being part of the system. "Black, white, zebra, green, blue, if you're good enough, they'll find you," Chase said. "I played Legion ball in high school, went to a mid-major D1 school. I mean, I was good enough. I got bigger, faster, and stronger on my own."

* * *

The Guardians sent him back to Double-A in the spring of 2024, and on April 25 he reported pain in his left foot while running the bases. The same foot and the same bone he had broken at JMU and again after the draft.

There was good medical news this time, though. The diagnosis: "Your Feet's Too Big," as Fats Waller might have said. Or at least too wide for your cleats.

This was something they could fix.

In his first game back with the Akron RubberDucks, he ran into the outfield wall in pursuit of a ball and went back on the IL. Bloggers and tweeters appended the dreaded appellation to his name: "the Injury Prone..."

After more rest and more rehab, he took a brief, tantalizing star turn, homering in three straight games, and was promoted to the Guardians' Triple-A team, one elusive step from the big time. Then, in the ninth inning of his seventh game, he tried to beat out a ground ball and felt something in his hamstring.

It reminded me, in an awful way, of the night I saw The Mick do the same, trying to beat out a meaningless ground ball to short, in a meaningless May game on a raw night in the Bronx in 1962. He tore the adductor muscle off the bone, another in a succession of fluke injuries that meant he never fully became who he might have been.

This time Chase was spared. "Hamstring tweak," Cerfolio texted, though the attached emoji looked aghast.

It's impossible to know what lies before him: a swing that "doesn't play," as Keith Law of *The Athletic* put it. A body that can't support his core ambition? Or the success he craves.

I keep waiting for a nice ending for Chase.

This much I know: This is the kid you root for. The kid who feels about baseball the way lots of American kids, including me, used to feel.

Just one more, please.

CHAPTER 16

OTHER WAYS OF KNOWING

Looking at the data with 20/20 vision

Dusty Baker, manager of the 2022 World Champion Houston Astros, was sitting in the visitor's dugout at Camden Yards thinking about Joe Biden. At one end of the dugout, a cluster of bloggers, tweeters, podcasters, and a couple of reporters awaited his daily pregame briefing. On the dirt behind home plate, a crowd of well-wishers pressed against a rope line, waiting for a fist pump, a hug, or a handshake from the man who had lent his good name to the Astros when their name was dirt.

Two days earlier at the White House, the Astros celebrated their championship with the president, presenting him with a "Biden 46" jersey and accepting his plaudits. It's one of the classier perks of athletic exceptionalism. Except when Donald Trump is president, in which case boxed Chick-fil-A and McDonald's are served. The Astros feasted on heavy hors d'oeuvres, lots of steak, lemonade, and chocolate pastries, a team gourmand confided.

The oldest president saluted baseball's oldest manager as "the legendary Dusty Baker." Baker grinned his boyish, gap-toothed smile, though "legendary" might not have been his choice of words, conjuring as it does thoughts of old bones in permafrost.

He was in the midst of a rugged American League West race in which the Astros trailed the Texas Rangers by three games and would do so until the last day of the season. And at age seventy-four, every decision he made of whom to play where and when and how much was criticized as sclerotic by thirty-year-old bloggers and tweeters whose questions were becoming tiresome.

"Dusty, it wasn't easy," Biden said. "People counted you out, saying you were past your prime. Hell, I know something about that."

Baker stood at Biden's shoulder, resplendent in a black-on-black checked suit with a cobalt-blue thread running through the weave, a crisp white shirt, and a kaleidoscopic day-at-the-races tie featuring swells in electric blue fedoras and dames in magenta cloche hats urging on a jockey on a neon-green horse. "He looked presidential as fuck," said former Astros hitting coach Jason Kanzler.

For the record, he also has Carhartt work shirts and Duluth jeans in his wardrobe, though he is best known for wristbands adorned with his likeness. In Houston's colors they looked like an advertisement for the Rainbow Coalition. He calls himself "a man of many faces."

It was early August hot in Baltimore in what used to be called the heat of the pennant race. That was before MLB subscribed to a "bigger-is-always-better" playoff money grab that rendered regular season games meaningless. "So what's this thing with the human element I keep hearing about?"

I ticked off a list of human-element guys: Scott Hatteberg, Rich Hill, Mike Rizzo; Dayton Moore, Charlie Manuel, and Buck Showalter.

Linguistically speaking, it doesn't have the ring of *worm burners*, but it raised a question that Dusty Baker, maybe the game's most fully human human, was well-qualified to answer.

"What happened to empiricism on the diamond?"

"It means nothing, Jane. It's unbelievable. They try to sell me some bullshit, and I'm saying, 'That ain't what my eyes tell me.' Their next comment was: 'Your eyes will lie to you.'"

A smart guy named William Shakespeare once said, "The eyes are the window to the soul."

A cartoon-sized college football coach known as Coach Bo, winner of 194 games at the University of Michigan, explained it to Baker at the banquet celebrating his first National League Manager of the Year award in 1993. "I said, 'Mr. Schembechler, when you're down to picking the twenty-fifth player and they're both equal, how do you make that decision?'

"He said, 'Call me Bo.'

"I said, 'Mr. Schembechler, what do you look for?'"

Schembechler answered, "Nuts and guts."

"He says, 'Dusty, it's in the fucking face, it's in the *fucking* face.'

"I said, 'What do you mean it's in the face?'

"He said, 'You look him in his eyes, and you can see to his soul. You could tell who the bullshitter is. You could tell who's scared. You could tell who has nuts and guts.'

"So, I never ever forgot that. And when I got one of these little punk boys upstairs that's telling me 'Your eyes are lying to you,' that's because all they see are the numbers. They can't even see the soul. They don't believe in feelings. They don't believe in no kind of anything other than the fucking numbers. That is so dangerous."

He's seen some things. He saw Jimi Hendrix torch his guitar at the Monterey Pop Festival in 1967 and Hank Aaron circle the bases after breaking Babe Ruth's home run record. He was in the on-deck circle for that. He was a party to the game's first high five occasioned as it was by his thirtieth home run in 1977. He was in uniform for 2,039 regular season major-league games, plus forty more during the postseason, six of which earned him a World Series ring with the 1981 Dodgers. He coached 810 games for the San Francisco Giants and managed 4,046 more as the skipper of five playoff teams, two of which reached the World Series. That's 7,448 games in uniform, give or take, not including 557 games in the minors, those he played in high school and Little League games his father threw him out of because he was a hothead. And you're gonna tell him he doesn't know what he's looking at?

"He is a master at believing in his eyes and having amazing confidence in what he saw," said his third baseman Alex Bregman.

The first time we spoke, Dusty told me about taking his son, Darren, to Vancouver when he was a boy of twelve or thirteen. The top was down on their rented convertible, and it was a beautiful day. Darren, now a second baseman in the Washington Nationals minor-league system, was doing what kids do—staring at his phone. "Put down the machine!" Dusty barked, with what I imagine was the same tone my mother reserved for the idiot box.

Darren put down his phone just as an eagle swooped low over their heads. "Look, Dad!"

"Hell, yeah. Look out the window, Son, what we got?"

Darren said, "Dad, I wouldn't have seen that if I was looking down."

"That was a godsend," Dusty told me that afternoon in the dugout.

"You need to survey the land," he told players in San Francisco. "Look where the center fielder is playing. Look where the left fielder is standing. That's how they're going to pitch you."

He bellowed at devout denizens of the Washington Nationals video room: "All I hear y'all talking about is launch angle and tendencies and exit velocity. Fuckin' exit velocity! Motherfucking exit velocity! How about motherfucking *exit* hits?"

He never changed pitchers without looking in their eyes first. "Sometimes I know I want to take 'em out. Sometimes I haven't decided. One time I went out and the guy handed me the ball. I handed it back to him."

When he went to the mound to speak with Max Scherzer one day in New York early in their relationship, he inquired which eye Max wished him to check.

Scherzer has a rare condition called heterochromia iridis, which is why he has one brown eye and one blue eye. It's integral to his Mad Max MO and the reason the Nationals mounted a huge, intimidating photo above the right field bleachers, black-and-white except for Scherzer's eyes, glaring at home plate.

"Which eye do I look in?" Dusty asked. "He said, 'The brown one. That's my pitching eye.' Then he got dogs with the same eyes: one blue, one brown."

Oriole Ryan Mountcastle stepped into the batting cage. "I ain't figured this kid Mountcastle out yet," Dusty said. "Is he a good player?"

I had no idea, but I had to say something. "I think he's awkward. I mean, he gets the big hits."

I must have seen him get one or two.

"Yes, he does," Dusty said kindly.

Ignorance wasn't the only reason for my blathered stammer, and there was no way to explain it without embarrassing myself further. To have been asked my opinion meant that Dusty trusted my eyes too.

* * *

He was the 504th selection in the twenty-sixth round of the 1967 draft, picked by the team he least wanted to join. The Atlanta Braves were newly relocated from Milwaukee. The South was not a welcoming place for a young Black man during the summer of love.

Ten days later, on his eighteenth birthday, his mother gave him two tickets to see Jimi Hendrix at the Monterey Pop Festival, twenty dollars, and the family Rambler for the weekend.

Jimi's ecstatic guitar—"scary and majestic," Dusty wrote later—changed the way he saw the world and himself, a baseball man who heard music in the game and its rhythms, encouraging players to listen to music when they lost the cadence in their swings.

Music suffused his life. His mother played Lou Rawls to rouse the five Baker children for school. He took piano lessons and dreamed of becoming Little Richard. "One day she came in and saw me with my feet up on the piano. She said, 'Have you lost your mind?'

"I said, 'Momma, I saw Jerry Lee Lewis on TV.'

"She wanted me to be Liberace, see. She had me playing the 'Hungarian Rhapsody' on Sunday in church."

His father, Johnnie B. Baker Sr., was a blues man. Guitars autographed by B. B. King, Elvin Bishop, Carlos Santana, and John Lee Hooker now grace his son's walls.

When he was fourteen, his father lost his job and moved the family from Riverside, where Dusty was born, to Sacramento, where he and his brother were the only two Black kids in their high school. His parents divorced when he was a senior. He played basketball and football in addition to baseball. He was good at all of them, but only football channeled his anger, something his father understood. When Dusty signed with the Braves without Johnnie B. Baker Sr.'s permission, he took his son to court, got his salary put in a conservatorship, and didn't talk to him for three years.

But Hank Aaron had promised Christine Baker he would look after her son, and Dusty promised his mother he would continue his studies. He saw that his $15,000 bonus would pay tuition at American River Junior College for himself, his mother, and four siblings. For a brief time, he thought he would go into journalism.

Hank Aaron introduced Baker to jazz, to Atlanta's Black political elite, and to the peanut-farmer governor, Jimmy Carter. But he couldn't protect Dusty from the redneck hate that spewed out of the left field stands as he made his way through the Braves minor-league system: Austin, Shreveport, Greensboro, Palm Beach, and finally Richmond, where he played Triple-A in 1969.

That fall, the Braves sent him to the Arizona Fall League, where he saw Janis Joplin play a gig in their home ballpark in Tempe. In the raw caw of her voice, he heard the strain of upheaval and rage that filled that American season. He hung out with the hippies. He liked them because even though they had stormed the fence to get in, they were peaceful about it. The next day, the outfield was strewn with discarded roaches. None of the coaches could figure out why everyone was playing out of position.

When the Braves told him he had to give up his student deferment and report to spring training earlier, he joined the Marine Corps Reserve rather than the State or National Guard. The way he saw it, marines were not likely to be called upon to fire on hippies and student protesters. It was 1970. He saw what the Ohio National Guard did at Kent State.

When the game was done with him in 1986, after nineteen major-league seasons, a couple of Silver Slugger Awards, a Gold Glove, and an all-star selection, he worked briefly as a stockbroker. "Then the stock market crashed," he said.

So he went back to baseball, initially as a coach and then as manager of the San Francisco Giants. He was sitting on the bench in the home dugout when the Loma Prieta earthquake turned the ballfield into a rolling wave of turf and dirt during the 1989 World Series.

Yep, he's seen some things.

He became the Giants' manager in 1993 and won three Manager of the Year awards. He did not hesitate to remind churlish Barry Bonds that he had held him as a newborn, before he left the hospital. Barry's mother had been Dusty's babysitter.

He had surgery for prostate cancer in December 2001, which rendered him incontinent for a time. He allowed his players to see him in the diapers he wore for two years. *Are these yours?* they'd ask upon seeing the boxes stacked in his office. "I wasn't hiding but I wasn't teaching either," he said.

Not intentionally, perhaps. But he's been outspoken ever since, reminding men about screening and gratefully extolling the virtues of the little blue pill.

The Giants were nine outs from winning the 2002 World Series, their first on the West Coast, and leading the Anaheim Angels three games to two and 5–0 in Game Six, when they imploded. His father, who cut him from his Little League team three times, said, "Son, if you didn't win that one, I don't know if you will win one."

He was fired after that season, criticized as a prima donna for having Robin Williams in his office and young Darren in uniform and on the field, where he almost got run over at home plate. Dusty saw things differently. He didn't know if he'd live to see the boy grow up, and he wasn't about to let him out of his sight.

He managed from 2003 to 2006 in Chicago, where Steve Bartman leaned out of the left field stands during the 2003 National League Championship Series and swiped the ball from Moises Alou and deliverance from Dusty and the Cubs. In Chicago, he left tickets for Obama and Buddy Guy.

In Cincinnati, he managed the Reds from 2008 through 2013, taking them to the playoffs three times. He also made sure his players saw the National Underground Railroad Freedom Center located just outside the Great American Ball Park. He showed them the vestiges of the tunnels that paved the way to freedom for runaway slaves who made it across the Ohio River.

When his rookie slugger, Joey Votto, was treated for depression and panic attacks after the death of his father, Dusty showed up at the hospital with the best of all gifts. "He kissed me on the forehead," Votto said.

Out of a job, and out of baseball in 2014 and 2015, he planted collard greens and roses and grapes that became the stock for Baker Family Wines until the Nationals came calling in 2016. Twice they won the National League East, and twice they lost in their first-round series. General

Manager Mike Rizzo had prepared a new contract for his signature. Ownership had second thoughts and allowed Baker to dangle for days not knowing whether he had a job.

"He's one of the smartest baseball guys there is," Rizzo said. "We should have kept him here."

Unemployed again, he saw baseball devolve into an unrecognizable facsimile of itself. The apotheosis came on a minor-league ballfield during a game between the Class A San Jose Giants and the San Bernadino Dodgers in which one team struck out fifteen times and the other eighteen times.

"Not a single ball was put in play for the first three innings," he told me. "And the only run scored was on a ninth-inning home run. It was just horrible."

The Astros came for him on bended knee in the winter of their comeuppance. Former Astros pitcher Mike Fiers had confirmed details of a high-tech (video), low-tech (upside-down garbage pail) sign-stealing scheme the team employed throughout 2017 when they beat the Dodgers in the World Series.

In January 2020, Commissioner Manfred meted out the punishment such as it was: General Manager Jeff Luhnow and Manager A. J. Hinch were suspended for a year and fired by the Astros. None of the players involved were fined. In spring training, Jose Altuve and Alex Bregman apologized on behalf of themselves and the team. Dusty had just signed the first of four one-year contracts, allowing the sullied franchise to exploit the reputation of the most righteous man in baseball.

* * *

So, imagine how galling it must have been to find in the forty-fifth year of his major-league life that experience, judgment, the accumulation of baseball wisdom, everything he'd seen counted for so little with the people who count. "The people running the game are running the people who played the game out of it," he told me one day.

Dusty saw what they didn't. He saged the clubhouse when it needed saging. He fed players in need of feeding. On the Jewish High Holidays he brought lox and bagels for Bregman, and then, realizing he should have brought enough for the whole team, he went back to the deli. "I was sick one day, and he brought me matzo ball soup," Bregman said. "I swear to God, I got two hits the next day and felt better."

It wasn't unusual for him to make five stops at five restaurants to pick up a taste of home for players of the many nationalities in the clubhouse. "It's not only that he goes out of his way to do it for you, but there's always a meaning behind it," Bregman said.

The meaning is: *I see you.*

I'm not sure what to make of the Christmas ham he sent every year to Rizzo's former administrative assistant in Washington, who happens to be Jewish. But I can tell you how much his Happy Valentine's Day text meant to me.

* * *

One day on the field at Nats Park, he ran into pitching guru Dave Wallace. "We were talking about what he does and how he's jovial and the guys joke with him," Wally remembered. "He says, 'You know what we do.'

"I said, 'What's that?'

"He goes, 'We do all this stuff. We also know when to call bullshit on these guys, and they know it.'"

Criticism of Dusty coalesced in 2023 over his use of his old catcher, Martín Maldonado, while young "hitterish" backup Yainer Diaz languished on the bench. "I like when he's in the lineup," General Manager Dana Brown said pointedly in mid-season.

The way Dusty saw it, nuts and guts were chief among the assets that Maldonado brought to the lineup. To date there is no known metric for them, though Peko Hosoi is working on it. "Maldonado is a God-fearing man that's also borderline gangster," Baker told reporters.

"Yainer right now is at West Point learning war strategy, whereas Maldy's already been at war."

He knew the defensive metrics, internal, external, and advanced, documenting the decline in Maldonado's "pop time," "caught stealing percentage," and "blocks above average." And that his "pitch framing" ability, never good, had plummeted. Not to mention the fact that Maldy was striking out more than a third of the time.

But he also had a pitching staff without two stalwarts, Luis Garcia and Lance McCullers Jr., forcing him to rely on greenhorns J. P. France and Hunter Brown. When I offered my expert opinion that Maldonado was the right catcher for the young 'uns, he replied, "Yes, he is, but always trying to convince the brass that just sees Diaz's bat. Very young to catching. Someday he will be very good."

After Houston beat the Minnesota Twins in the 2023 American League Division Series, reporters went to former Astro Carlos Correa for a debriefing. "I don't want to give credit to Maldonado, 'cause he'll bring it up at some point when I talk to him during the offseason. He knows every hitter's weaknesses, and he's going to exploit it. He pitches against the expected slug, and we knew it, and still it was hard to make the adjustments the way he was pitching."

"Maldonado-ed," *Sports Illustrated* proclaimed in its recap of the series.

Dusty was not mentioned in the story.

* * *

When Dusty excused himself, I introduced myself to Jason Kanzler, who was lingering by the nearby bat rack. I think he had overheard some of our conversation. "I tend to value and appreciate heuristics just as much as I appreciate data and objectivity," he said. "Because the human brain is an incredible supercomputer that is really good at understanding certain things that we cannot yet explain with objective information."

"Heuristics" is another word you hear around the batting cage these days. It's shorthand for problem-solving methods based on practical experience and knowledge as opposed to data. You might call it the human element.

"I wish people would just recognize that we can't live our lives only by numbers," Kanzler said. "It's not possible yet. And I don't think it ever will be unless we can replicate a human brain. It's not like Dusty didn't understand analytics or know analytics. He was definitely very open especially to our platoon situations. That's a mind that's seen a lot of things."

Dusty had a surfeit of what Bill James called "soft knowledge." In Washington, they'd say he knows how to read a room.

Bill says soft knowledge gets pushed aside by hard knowledge, meaning stats. "So, the biggest thing we still have to figure out is how to define and measure team positive behavior and team negative behavior."

That's what everybody wants from Peko and her Sports Analytics Lab. "Is that something that we can measure?" she said. "And the answer is: Sure there are things we can measure.

"It's also an example about the temptation to use the data that you have rather than the data that you need."

* * *

Batting practice was almost over when Dusty returned to the bench. I had saved the toughest question for last as reporters are taught to do.

"Is baseball all better?"

"Shit," he said. "It ain't all fixed. It's not like they want a pitcher that knows how to pitch."

The pitch clock accomplished what MLB wanted: speeding up and shortening the game. But fifteen seconds isn't a lot of time to recover when you're throwing every pitch max heave. "I've had some guys out of breath," Dusty said. "You know, it's like, 'Dang, I wish I could give that guy a breather.' Baseball's become an aerobic act."

The first study on the pitch clock, published in June 2024 in the *Journal of Orthopaedics*, concluded the clock was not a factor in increased pitching injuries. Max Scherzer be damned. The authors offered the obvious caveat—the study was based on one year of data.

Causes and solutions seem both elusive and obvious. Cause: They're throwing too hard. Solution: Quit throwing so hard. But they won't quit.

You could have knocked me over with a feather—or an Eepheus pitch—when I heard Kyle Bobby tell those British baseball podcasters that Driveline is investigating what Betty Friedan called a paradigm shift. Deven Morgan and Jason Ochart explained it to me. "Current biomechanical research is based on inverse dynamics, which begins with a motion—and capturing the data generated by a swing or a throw—and works backward to figure out the forces that caused it," Jason said.

The load on the elbow joint, for instance. "The problem is that inverse dynamics intentionally ignores everything about muscles, and tendons, in the production of force," Deven said.

They left out the muscles? Huh?

"What Kyle is trying to do now is to use forward dynamics research to understand what the muscles of the arm are doing in the pitcher," Jason said. "Current biomechanics only measures what the body is doing in space."

In other words, it measures what *is*. "Forward dynamics is the process of *predicting* the motion of a body based on known forces or muscle activations. Kyle thinks it's the key to solving the UCL issue. Or at least understanding it more."

Meanwhile in Alabama, Glenn Fleisig was investigating a different kind of paradigm shift. Having found in earlier studies that throwing heavier baseballs actually lessened force on the elbow, he asked MLB to fund what seemed like a counterintuitive proposal. Would increasing the weight of the official Rob Manfred baseball from five to six ounces and increasing its size by 5 percent lessen the torque on the elbow?

He and his team conducted a blind-ball test with twenty-four college and minor-league pitchers who threw at least 87 mph. Four balls were tested: one standard, one the same size but an ounce heavier, one the same weight but 5 percent larger, and one larger and heavier. The heavier, larger ball lessened shoulder rotation and elbow torque, as well as the break on the ball and the velocity.

No matter how hard pitchers try, Fleisig said, that ball won't allow them to max out their elbow stress on max heave.

"Maybe we got something here," Glenn said.

Scientists never say that. Kyle Boddy did his best not to act surprised: "heavier balls = lower elbow torque, larger baseballs = lower torque." *The Orthopaedic Journal of Sports Medicine* will publish the study.

But in the here and now, Dusty was left to find nine outs from exhausted relievers. That's if he got any length from his starting pitcher. Forget matchups. Late-inning baseball was survival of the fittest and the freshest.

* * *

Bregman was in the cage, taking a last harried round of batting practice. "What's with Bregman?"

He'd been struggling. Dusty replied with a story about when he was in the marines and had to leave spring training camp for two weeks to report for duty. It took three days to be able to see again. "It's like how did I ever hit this? It looked like they were throwing 1,000 mph. I was like, 'Goodness.' Because your eyes..."

Again, with the eyes. He was telling me how hard it is to do what hitters are called upon to do in the era of stuff and speed.

"He's played a lot," Dusty said. "He doesn't know it, and don't tell him, he's off tomorrow. And he hates to be off. He wants to play every day, every inning he can. I love the guy. He is a gamer and he's a throwback. And he plays some of the best third base I've seen.

"He's tinkering. He'll find it. And plus, you know, he's had some bad luck. Luke Appling told me when I was a kid, 'If you want to be lucky you gotta think lucky.' And I believe that. The good hitters think lucky."

I met Luke Appling, the good old boy Hall of Fame shortstop, during my first reportorial trip to spring training. He was sitting with a bat propped in the crack of his ass—as ballplayers are wont to do. I could see him ogling my very un-tan ankle. "Like that white skin?" I said stupidly.

"I *always* liked white skin," Luke replied.

"That sounds like him too," Dusty said.

* * *

As the Astros boarded their bus outside 1600 Pennsylvania Avenue, second baseman Jose Altuve ordered forty pizzas to be delivered en route to the team hotel in Baltimore. The guys at Kanzler's table, who'd ordered platter after platter of steak from obliging White House staff, had bogarted all the good stuff. "Never saw any of it," Bregman said.

Dusty removed his tie and handed it to his third baseman, the proud owner of "Bregman Family Racing," a stable of eight thoroughbreds. "He told me to wear it to a race for good luck," Bregman said.

Instead, he wore it to the big party the night before the Breeders' Cup at Santa Anita, where his two-year-old colt, No Nay Mets, went to the post as the favorite and finished fourth in the Juvenile Turf Sprint.

"I should have listened to Dusty," Bregman said.

CHAPTER 17

BOYCHIK

Breggy lets the writer in on the hitter's conundrum

Boychik called from the team bus en route to the airport. It was getaway day, and the Astros were heading home after beating the winningest team in baseball in two out of three games.

"What did Dusty say?" he asked immediately.

He had seen me chatting up his manager in the dugout. He took extra swings in the cage because for the first time in God knows how long, the ball was jumping off his bat as if jumping off a trampoline, which is how it feels when everything is right. "He's the best," Alex Bregman said. "We gotta get him his ring."

When I first asked Dusty who would be the best guy to talk to about the reinvention of hitting, he said Bregman. So began a conversation that continued through three baseball seasons, and offseasons, through the arrival of baseball's new rules, a World Series championship that got Dusty that ring, and the waxing and waning of Alex's swing, which seemed to come and go with the regularity of the phases of the moon.

Bregman is an old soul in a young man's body, whose old-soul swing, honed in another era, reasserts itself at the worst possible times.

Formed by the past, perfected in the present, he is in a constant battle for control; constantly trying to balance the prerogatives of old and new, which may be why Dusty wanted me to talk to him and why I found his conundrum so compelling.

"Is he wrong? About the tinkering?"

"No, he's right. I am. Because I know that it's not right."

The contraction needed no antecedent. With hitters, it's always the swing. Despite being ranked seventh in baseball in wins above replacement (WAR) from 2017 to 2023 (behind Mike Trout and ahead of Juan Soto), Bregman's swing seemed to have acquired a disconcerting life of its own.

In the first game of the three-game series in Baltimore, one swing made him hopeful. *There it is.* He went three for four in the second game with a single and a double, both on 0-2 counts, a walk, and two RBI. More to the point, the ball went where it was supposed to go when things are right, both opposite-field line drives.

"You looked squared up."

"The ball was flying off the bat in the last round of batting practice," he replied.

"Yeah, I saw that, and you also wiggled your tush more."

"I need to do that."

"To hit or to be yourself?"

"I just need a little bit of rhythm."

Which is why old-school Dusty went all empirical and kept him in the lineup. He looked like Bregman circa 2019 when he was one of the best young hitters in the game, an all-star, winner of the Silver Slugger Award for American League third basemen, with forty-one home runs, 112 RBI, and 119 walks, most in the American League, and finished second to Mike Trout for the Most Valuable Player award.

It didn't last. The following seasons, though punctuated by moments of brilliance, never measured up. A body wants to do what a body wants to do, which is what it first learned to do, which is what feels normal even if it's not the best thing to do.

Which is a mindfuck.

To be a major-league hitter, you have to be a philosopher. You have to accept you'll fail two-thirds of the time, that you are now and will always be a work in progress. You have to be prepared to live inside this conundrum: The swing is yours, it's *of* you, *part* of you, but also *outside* you. A physical act but also a feeling; a mechanical process that demands repetitive precision from parts that aren't built that way. "And you have to do it in open space, which is crazy," Alex said.

Infinite space means there are infinite ways to fuck up. It's what Soviet physiologist Nikolai Bernstein called "the degrees of freedom problem" in 1922 when the Kremlin asked him to do a study on the efficiency of manual labor.

Imagine losing all sense of proprioception—the sublime gift from your brain that tells you where you and your parts are in space. It comes from the Latin *proprius*, meaning one's own, individual, and *capio*, *capere*, meaning to take or to grasp. I once saw my friend Bob, who was dying of AIDS, try to put out a cigarette in the palm of his hand because he had no proprioception. Only his laughter made the moment tolerable.

Now imagine you're a major-league hitter and you lose the ability to know where your bat needs to be in order to connect with a ball.

I'm not exactly a world-class athlete. A sports orthopedist once told me I have the heart of an athlete and the soul of an athlete in the worst possible body for an athlete. So, my frame of reference is limited. But I really wanted to understand and blurted out the only analogy that came to mind. When I traveled with the Baltimore Orioles for *The Washington Post*, I walked into a lot of hotel walls in the middle of the night looking for the bathroom in the place it had been in my hotel room three cities ago. The disorientation was complete and stupefying.

"Is that what it's like?" I asked Alex.

"One hundred percent," he said. "You're so used to doing something, and then all of a sudden, it's just like, '*Whoa.*' I feel like I lost that feel in 2020 and have been fighting to get it back ever since."

* * *

Bregman was born on the cusp of upheaval. He is not just a witness to the analytics revolution, he's a product of it, and ambivalent about it too. As a boy he was inspired by Jeter's Flip Play, but by the time he came of age as a major leaguer, analytics dictated defensive positioning that ate into instinct. That troubles him.

"When you lose instinct and when you lose creativity, you lose people talking about the game and people continuing to grow ideas in their minds, the instinctual things that they could do to win a game."

When the Astros chose Bregman second in the 2015 draft, he was a slick-fielding shortstop at LSU who, like his contemporary, Mariners shortstop J. P. Crawford, had been taught to hit down on the ball. "To hit the ball on the ground or on a line pole to pole."

Statcast arrived that year, generating granular data on every swing, every pitch, every throw, every batted ball. Guessing became a thing of the past. The game was turned upside down. And so was he. "As soon as I get into professional baseball, like the first month, it's, 'Hey, you need to get the ball in the air and stop hitting ground balls at all.'"

The charts and the equations were irrefutable. "They said, 'You don't swing and miss a lot. So, if you swing, it needs to be at a pitch that you can drive in the air. If it's not a pitch you can drive, don't swing.'"

Bottom line: When he learned to get the ball in the air, he became a star. His mastery of the strike zone and his refusal to swing at bad pitches elevated his OPS into elite territory. Analytics made him a better hitter even as it made the game worse.

Welcome to the bigs, Boychik.

* * *

We met at 8:00 a.m. outside the clubhouse on the day the World Champion Houston Astros reported for spring training in 2023. He ushered me into an interview room, just beyond the front door where scruffy print reporters, TV cameramen, and pretty on-screen talent had congregated.

He looked particularly fetching in his fresh-out-of-the-box matching shorts and mock turtleneck top sent by a company he endorses. It was like he was dressing up for the first day of school. I did not wear my Mary Janes.

The room was maybe twelve by fourteen and cluttered with photo cables, camera bags, and tripods. An open parabolic photo umbrella extended almost half the width of the room. "When I was growing up, they taught if you want to hit the ball in the air you need to hit down on it to backspin it," Alex said. "But in reality, you just want to get on the plane with the pitch and stay on the plane of the pitch as long as possible. If you're hitting down on the ball, there's only one point of intersection."

That point of intersection is the width of a ball measuring 2.86 to 2.94 inches in diameter.

He grabbed three balls from a cardboard box and held them in a line extending from the palm of his hand, which was hard because his hands aren't that big. "If there are three balls stacked like this—"

I caught the third before it hit the floor and held it up next to the other two. "If I have a swing that can only hit one baseball, I'm in and out of the zone. But if I have a bat path that gets in the zone early and stays in the zone—*through, through, through*, that's where I want to be."

But that's not where he was. He was where he used to be. His body goes back to what it knew before he had to teach it a new way to swing. "I know that naturally I open up too soon. My body reverts to opening early. That's been my number-one miss my whole life."

Ducking beneath the photo umbrella, he assumed his batting stance and showed me the difference in posture and rotation that is both subtle and essential. Hips open: imagine a dejected hitchhiker walking down the side of the road, sticking a thumb out at the sound of a car coming up from behind, and turning his left hip out to see if the driver has slowed.

Hips closed: Now imagine standing with flashlights attached to your hips, knees, shoulders, ankles, all parallel and in alignment, facing home plate.

"See," he said, shimmying his hips. "Open, closed, open, closed."

"Yeah, that's just how I do it."

He was nice enough to laugh. "When I hit the ball to the opposite field on a line, I know that I'm in there square. As soon as I start hitting the ball in the air to the opposite field, I know that I'm coming off the ball. It's one of those things where the ball's flight tells you if you did it right or not. When it's bad, I hit ground balls to the pull side to short, and I pop balls up to right field. When the ball stays low to right field, on a line, it's really good. And when I hit the ball high to left field, it's really good."

"That's when you say let it eat," I said.

J. P. taught me that. Alex laughed.

Ben McDonald, who pitched for LSU before he was selected with the first pick in the 1989 draft, got to know Bregman on campus when he broadcast Tigers games. "The shit happens too fast. It's too violent, too quick of a thing to do it right every time."

Bregman could do it until he couldn't. "There's people who make adjustments at bat to at bat," he said. "And there's people who make adjustments game to game. The best players are the ones that can make adjustments pitch to pitch. Once I feel it, once I get it, I have the ability to repeat it often."

But the feeling was gone.

"So, for two years, I'm thinking, *stay closed, stay closed, stay closed*, and it's not working, and I'm just like, *I don't know what I'm doing wrong, and I do not know how to fix it.*"

Recovering his swing was complicated by repeated injuries. A strained right hamstring in 2020 put him on the Injured List for three weeks. A strained quadriceps in 2021 kept him out of the lineup for two months, preventing him from doing his customary regimen of one thousand swings and one thousand hip loads each day. The muscles healed but the apprehension survived. One offseason he had elbow surgery; the following year he broke his finger in the World Series.

Like most ballplayers, Bregman organizes his playing life around repetition, training his body to repeat a motion in space over and over. That's fine for the good times. But when things go awry, the only fix is "repetitive obsession."

"You constantly work to get back to the field to get to feel it again," former manager Scott Servais said. "The only way that your mind knows is 'I have to take more swings. I have to talk to more people.'"

In moments of duress, Dusty Baker offered moral support and tips he got from Stan the Man when he was young and in the throes. "Stay out of center field in the air." "Stay on top of the ball up the middle."

He worked with Astros batting coach Troy Snitker to develop drills that forced him to stay square. One required him to hit with a resistance band wrapped around his knees to keep the spacing between them consistent. "Brutal," Bregman said.

I know. I tried it once.

They tried new swing thoughts. *Get the knob of the bat in front of the pitcher. Don't let the pitcher see your belt buckle.* Then, during the 2022 American League Championship Series against the Yankees: *Stay tall, land closed.*

After he hit his fifteenth playoff home run in Game Two of the World Series against the Phillies, tying Babe Ruth, who didn't have the benefit of all those extra playoff games, it began to slip away again.

Damn that leaking hip.

By the time we met that first morning of spring training, he had no idea what was good anymore. "It's just show up and go."

I wondered if he had considered trying the weighted bats that Jason Ochart designed for Driveline, the ones J. P. used. I wanted to be helpful.

"I haven't seen them," he said.

* * *

Dusty called a meeting in mid-September 2023 to tell his team he wouldn't be back in 2024. Bregman, who had gotten off to a predictably slow start, had been at his best in August, batting .318 with thirty-five hits, four homers, twenty-one RBI, and twenty-one runs scored. Then he disappeared in September. The Astros needed Seattle to beat the Texas Rangers in the last game of the regular season to clinch their sixth American League West Division in seven years.

After dismissing the Minnesota Twins from the Division Series, the Astros faced the Rangers in the American League Championship Series. His most consequential at bat of the series was not one you want to remember, but he did. He knew the moment I was thinking of without prompting. Game Two, fifth inning, two outs: the miss returned. "Grounded to short. It was a 1-0 cutter from [Nathan] Eovaldi. I got a little ahead. I flew open. If I waited those three ticks..."

Baseball is a world of what-ifs. If his hip hadn't leaked, maybe the Astros win a game at home and tie the series at 1-1. But it did, and they didn't.

Back home after winning all three games in Texas, Dusty was thrown out of Game Six, officially for throwing his hat. He staged a twelve-minute sit-down strike in the dugout, and retreated to his office, where, later, he listened to angry music. "Probably Tupac. Maybe Biggie. Maybe Too Short."

After losing Game Seven, his last game in uniform, he addressed the team in the clubhouse. "I told them after the last out it was the best four consecutive years ever. I told them thank you and that I loved them—I think.

"Bregman would remember."

Bregman is a nice Jewish boy. After the Astros won the 2017 World Series, his father, Sam, declared: "It's the fulfillment of four generations of short Jewish Bregmans who dreamed of playing in the major leagues..."

Alex told me, almost shyly, about taking his young son to synagogue for the first time. During the 2023 playoffs he wore a cap with a hand-drawn Star of David to honor the lives lost in the October 7 massacre in Israel.

When I asked him about Dusty's farewell, he thought about how much he and his prayerful, seventy-four-year-old Black manager shared. He had become a husband and a father on Dusty's watch. He had resurrected his high school Spanish and gotten fluent enough to record "White Dude Spanish Lessons" for YouTube so that, like Dusty, he could be a leader in the clubhouse.

"We had so much in common, not only on the field. We're just kind of baseball lifers, and then, off the field, we both love to have a good time. One of the things I love about Dusty is he let his guys go out and play and he listened to the players too. He was like, 'You're my guy. I believe in you.'"

When the regular season ended, Bregman had played in all but one game.

* * *

I know a little about hitting. My last competitive at bat dates back to a college-era softball game on the Connecticut lawn of the prominent Manhattan financier for whom I worked as a Gal Friday. Yup, that long ago.

I pulled a ball in the hole between short and third and busted ass down the line. My boss, the venture capitalist, was playing first base.

I don't remember if I was safe or out or whether the game continued, but I know neither of us was safe from me. In the collision, I broke his ankle and gave myself an emergency room–grade concussion.

Like Breggy, I'm a gamer, but I have no idea how he—or anyone else—can do what he does.

In 1990, when Yale physics professor Robert Adair published *The Physics of Baseball*, the average major-league fastball was 90 mph. He explained what was involved in hitting it by dividing the swing into segments—Looking, Thinking, Deciding, Acting, and Contact—and assigned each a portion of the 424 milliseconds it took the ball to make its way from hand to plate, concluding, "Hitting a 90-mph baseball is a superhuman feat that is clearly impossible."

For this, Bart Giamatti anointed him "Physicist of the National League." Adair's formula was big news. *The New York Times* published a splashy graphic that took up much of the first page of the sports section back when the paper of record had one. His equation is still quoted in certain baseball precincts as if a 90-mph fastball remains the gold standard.

I asked Alan Nathan—professor emeritus of physics at the University of Illinois Urbana-Champaign, better known these days in baseball as "The Physics Guy"—to update Adair's calculations. "At 90 mph a hitter has 124 milliseconds to look at the ball before proceeding to the other segments," the Physics Guy said. "At 95 mph he has 101 milliseconds or 20 percent less looking time."

Not surprisingly, looking is the most crucial part of the process. As in: See the ball, hit the ball. "At 100 mph, the total flight time from release to home plate is 377 milliseconds," Alan said.

Of which a hitter has just 77 milliseconds—that's half of a blink of an eye—to look at the damn thing.

Not only are fastballs faster, they look faster than they are, a perceptual "fuck you" made patent by Statcast technology that measures exactly where a guy actually lets go of the ball, which is not sixty feet, six inches.

This is called Release Extension (RE), which is the key to Perceived Velocity (PV). Six-foot-eight Tyler Glasnow releases the ball seven feet, five inches in front of the pitching rubber. That's why his 96.3-mph fastball appears to be traveling at the speed of light.

Can you imagine standing fifty feet away from that, reacting to that? "I don't know how anyone could hit anything anymore," Gray said.

Breggy shrugged.

* * *

After the 2023 ALCS loss to the Rangers, Bregman headed to the Arizona desert with his wife, Reaganelizabeth, and son, Knox, to spend the winter training at the Exos gym outside Phoenix.

The way he saw it, 2023 was good enough for someone else: .262 batting average, twenty-five home runs, ninety-eight RBI, 103 runs scored, and an OPS of .804. He was the only player with ninety-plus walks and fewer than ninety strikeouts and was ranked sixth in flyball percentage (46.9 percent). But he was turning thirty and would be a free agent at the end of the 2024 season. So, no, it wasn't good enough.

The language of hitting is less lovely now. No more "stepping in the bucket" or "squishing the bug." His load was a mess and he was dumping his pelvis, and none of the old cues worked. That's when "you have to be willing to go out on a limb to make an adjustment," Alex told me.

So, he did. "We started introducing some overload and underload speed training. I got our hitting coach to write me up a program. He had an exact model of my bat made as an underload."

Just like the speed-training bats Jason Ochart designed for Driveline, with added weight in the handle to help speed up your swing. "We've seen some shocking increases in bat speed. It's very similar to the stuff J. P. was doing."

I thought for sure his swing thought for 2024 was going to be: "I shoulda listened to Jane sooner."

Then the season started.

The offseason regimen had given him a sense of physical invincibility but messed up his mechanics, leading to the worst two months of his career. He walked half as much as he had in 2023 and his OPS dropped below .800, not the statistics he wanted before free agency. He was batting .219 at the end of May.

"The old still wants to kind of creep back in where I shift my body toward the pitch as opposed to controlling my forward move and swinging from my rear leg," he explained.

Again, I asked myself, "What must that feel like?" I picked up an old, cracked Harmon Killebrew bat salvaged at a garage sale for ten dollars, thinking somehow I'd find the answer in the grain of splintered wood. I lifted it over my shoulder, spread my feet wide, hips facing an imaginary home plate, flashlights attached, and peered into the distance. The uncertainty of the immediate future—what was coming?

A sweeper or a split? Would I see it? And would reflex allow me to do so in time to make the needed adjustments? To go out on a limb, if necessary, so I could finally say, "Let it eat"?

I already knew what Alex was feeling. It's what I feel, what every writer feels, when you just can't find the right word.

CHAPTER 18

INFIDELS AT THE GATE

Crazy gets inducted but the old radical reminds us what matters most

The infidels arrived early for their 5:00 p.m. appointment with destiny. Owner, founder, promoter, and Chief Banana Jesse Cole paced nervously in the vestibule of the library wing of the Hall of Fame in one of his seven yellow tuxedos, a matching bowler perched on his brow. Over his shoulder on the south lawn, a bronze Roy Campanella, catcher's mask not quite lowered over his face, squatted behind home plate sixty feet, six inches from a bronze Johnny Podres awaiting the last pitch of the 1955 World Series, an event that engendered almost as much anticipation in Brooklyn as this one did for the Savannah Bananas.

"We're in here and we're not even major-league players," said "Mr. Electric" Christian Dearman, who was verging on hyperventilation.

His Banana teammates and their pink Party Animal foils had come to Cooperstown to be enshrined in a new Hall of Fame exhibit. Actually, they were being enshrined in a hallway connecting the Hall of Fame Library and the Hall of Fame Plaque Gallery. Having arrived before everyone else, I didn't realize I was in the right place until I found myself squished between a stationary wooden bench bisecting the space and eighty iridescent men who quickly turned the gallery, such as it was, into a mosh pit.

But where was Bill "The Spaceman" Lee?

"Probably in the bar," Jesse had told me in the vestibule.

I was worried about him, especially after listening to the message on his answering machine: "Now I carry money in my pocket when I pitch. I only live to pitch. You never know when you're going to have to tip the paramedics."

Catcher Eric Jones was concerned too. "There's nobody that wants to be at the ballpark more than Bill."

He was the reason I came. I drove five-and-a-half hours to see baseball's last radical on the slab in Cooperstown, baseball's mound of consecration.

But Banana authorities were adamant, Jonesy said. "Somebody, maybe Jesse, told him, 'We understand but you can't die on our mound.'"

There would be no return until he was cleared to pitch, and no one was going to clear him to pitch, which doesn't mean he wasn't available. Bill Lee is always available.

"I'm on the DL," the Spaceman announced as he entered the hall.

"You mean the IL," I said, relieved.

"No, the DL," Bill said. "The dead list."

Turned out he had had more than a little electrical problem in his heart, as had been diagnosed in Savannah in August 2022. He collapsed again on the mound in Indianapolis ten months later. Went into the stretch and the lights went out. His Medtronic device fired up, and he popped up like a jack-in-the-box, worrying that he would be charged with an earned run if they took him out of the game. He strolled off the mound and climbed into the stands, giving high fives, until he was corralled by medical personnel and taken to the hospital.

Unhappy at being held captive, he removed his IV the next morning and discharged himself, walking to the ballpark in his uniform and a pair of yellow nonslip Methodist Hospital socks. He told me, "I'm gonna sue Medtronic for preventing me from dying on the mound."

There was another incident two months later on a hot August afternoon at Polar Park in Worcester while he was having a catch in the outfield before throwing out a ceremonial first pitch.

Doctors at UMass Worcester discovered a 95 percent blockage in the circumflex artery behind his heart, which, like everything else about the Spaceman, did not adhere to the straight and narrow. This artery made a hairpin turn, defying the ability of two male, right-handed surgeons to make the sharp right. "I need a lefty," Bill said.

That diagnosis did not deter him a week later from playing in the last game of the season for the Burlington Cardinals of the Vermont Men's Senior Baseball League, thirty-five and over, one of many teams for whom he's played since 1989. He pitched the last three innings, retiring nine straight.

Spaceman seemed spacier than usual and had forgotten his underwear as well as a case of "Spaceman Red" he had intended to sell in a bar on Main Street.

He looked like he could have used some of the "bone medicine" comedian/activist Dick Gregory brought to his home in 1976 after Graig Nettles tried to separate him from his shoulder. "The problem," Gregory told the Spaceman, "is you have too much soap suds in your body."

He perked up when folks armed with notebooks and tape recorders materialized, as they do when he enters a room. They wanted to know how he was and what was on the other side of the red "Jesus Church of Baseball" T-shirt under his jersey.

Soon enough he was in prime Spaceman mode bragging that his Hall of Fame archive is bigger than Cy Young's because "they only had one paper when he was pitching" and telling everyone who would listen how he played right field for Bob Feller during his last outing on the mound in June 2009 at Doubleday Field.

I had been thinking about Feller since I left Cleveland, where I saw the bat Babe Ruth used during his last appearance at the Stadium not two months before his death in 1948. Eddie Robinson, who was in the dugout with him that day, grabbed Feller's and gave it to The Babe to steady himself climbing the dugout steps. He shuffled to the microphone for his last words to New York, dragging the bat behind him. That's when Nat Fein took the Pulitzer Prize–winning photo that you see everywhere with the big number 3 on The Babe's wasted back.

Eddie displayed the bat in his restaurant in Baltimore and finally sold it for ten thousand dollars, which seemed big at the time. Eventually, it made its way back to Feller, who wanted it for his museum in Van Meter, Iowa, and was pissed enough to pay "something less than $100,000" to display it. After his death, it was moved to Progressive Stadium in Cleveland and placed in a round glass vault outside the swells' dining room with a life-size blowup of Nat Fein's photo. The bat rests against the crack of The Babe's butt. Ain't baseball grand?

The annual Hall of Fame game, discontinued after sixty-eight years because modern major leaguers found it inconvenient to travel to a very out-of-the-way ballpark for a benefit game, was replaced by the Hall of Fame Classic, an intramural tussle between old-timers. In the first inning, Feller faced Hall of Famer Paul Molitor and recently retired Steve Finley, who was half his age.

Spaceman had warned Molitor: "Don't hit the ball up the middle. The guy's old."

"So, what does he do? First pitch he hits a line drive by Feller's ear. It wouldn't have killed him, but it would have hurt. I'm playing right field. I'm shaking my head. Next guy's Finley. He hits the ball over my head. I play it on one hop off the wall and hold him to a single. Now Feller's pissed. So, he goes and gets a ground ball to short. They force the runner at second and a run scores, and they take Feller out of the game. He gets one-third of an inning and a standing O.

"He's standing on the dugout step when I come in. He goes, 'Lee, you've got to catch that fucking ball.'

"I said, 'Bob, I held him to a single. No way I'm catching that ball. I'm fifty-three. You're ninety.'"

(The Hall of Fame account credited Molitor with a bloop single and Finley with a hard single to center.)

"Then in the fifth inning I hit a double off my nemesis, Steve Rogers. I drove in the tying run and scored the go-ahead run. Puts us up two to one. Now Feller's hugging me in the dugout. He wants to have my children."

Finally, a young scribe got a word in edgewise about the Bananas.

"Here's what it is," Spaceman said. "We play real baseball within the confines of absurdity. It's all spontaneous, but with a little rehearsing in between. It's P. T. Barnum meets the Harlem Globetrotters. It's a fantasy. It's Shakespeare. It's *A Midsummer Night's Dream*. It's Euripides of the underworld. Don't forget I danced in Euripides—"

Bill paused to remind me that he had danced with the Wicked Witch of the West, Margaret Hamilton, at an homage to opera queen Sarah Caldwell in his Red Sox uniform in 1978. "I've seen the girl eat the pomegranate seeds—wait, who was that girl?"

Bill shrugged. "I've crossed the river Styx, and I'm not afraid to swim it naked."

"But what's the point?" a reporter asked.

"What it means is: We are having fun; the major leagues are not. We are the future. They're the past."

No one was surprised that when it came time to take the team picture, Bill plunked himself down, front and center, on a swath of newly installed Bananas wall-to-wall carpet. "Like Miss Peggy Lee," Bill said, stretching his legs and propping himself up on an elbow. "So sultry."

* * *

As a comic setup it's hard to do better than this: two faux baseball teams, playing with faux rules, come to the locus of baseball tradition to decide a faux championship on a field named for the faux inventor of the game, legendary fraud Abner Doubleday.

It was a beautiful day, that moment when the seasons hang in the balance, and summer is not quite ready to yield to fall. The blue of the sky, the green of the grass, the yellow of Bill's jersey when he arrived late but in uniform were saturated with sunlight.

Recent inductees Lee Smith and Ted Simmons, dressed in official red, white, and blue Hall of Fame jerseys and Savannah Banana caps, wandered the infield mingling with cast members and schmoozing with Very Important Bananas and their Very Important Guests trying to take it all in. Only the New York State troopers stationed along the foul lines weren't smiling.

Smith was standing in a crowd by the first base line, admiring the scene. "They're really getting the fans back in it because I think they've been overlooked."

Baseball infrastructure, physical and psychological, separating players from fans, has grown in size and durability since Smith's playing days. "When I played all the bullpens was right on the sidelines. So, we got a chance to talk to the fans during the game. Now all the bullpens are down under—the fans can't talk to the players. I got friends that are still friends to this day that I met sitting in that bullpen."

He liked my idea of a designated signer after every game, though Cal Ripken Jr. drove him nuts. "We would leave his ass at the ballpark because he'd be still out there signing autographs."

On the other side of the diamond, Ted Simmons was reveling in Banana-dom. His wife, Maryanne, had gotten hooked on Banana-TV. She wasn't alone: Seven million others watched the streamed games in 2023. "She's been berserk about them for two and a half years."

When she heard the Hall of Fame was looking for volunteers to attend the weekend extravaganza, she told him, "We're going to Cooperstown."

He arrived with ample skepticism born of twenty-one years of squatting behind home plate, but was reassured by infield practice. "It was first-rate," he said. "I realized they were athletes. Actually, it was better than Major League Baseball because they were also doing tricks."

The Spaceman showed up during warm-ups carrying a Bobby Doerr glove, a ball snug in its pocket. The superfluous glove represented a hope, a prayer, a statement of purpose and self. Without a game to play, or an inning to warm up for, he seemed unsure what to do. He made conversation with Smith and Simmons, who like everyone else were milling around in the small grassy area behind home plate, clogged with Banana props.

The squat, brick dugouts, built for a ballyard that opened in 1920, could in no way accommodate the Bananas' traveling party, much less all their equipment.

Bill went looking for someone with whom to have a catch. Finding no takers, he began tossing the ball against the brick wall between the dugouts. Like me throwing at a garage door attached to a vibrating pink house.

Simba understood. "Back in the day when Bill Lee was the Spaceman, everyone in baseball felt kind of connected to him. He told me, 'God, I just want to be out there.'"

"He told me he wants to die on the mound," I said.

"He's not kidding," Simmons replied.

Some people really can't live without baseball. Bill Lee is one of them.

* * *

Simmons, known as Simba in his playing days for his long, flowing hair, was summoned to the plate to lead the Bananas in their opening ritual: the revelation of the Baby Banana, a takeoff on the *Lion King* salute to Baby Simba.

Upstairs in the TV booth, Biko Skalla, whose official title is "broadcast entertainer," invoked the "hollowed" ground of Doubleday Field.

The Banana formula isn't complicated. They alternate trick plays with kitschy crowd-sourced games in which spectators are invited down to the field to humiliate themselves. Lots of people get "pie-ed." Lots of fat jiggles. Fat jiggling is very big with the Bananas. All to a pounding, nonstop soundtrack that has something for everyone. On the playlist: "Can't Stop the Feeling!" (Justin Timberlake circa 2006); "Jellyfish Jam" from *SpongeBob SquarePants*; "Gonna Make You Sweat (Everybody Dance Now)"; "Thank God I'm a Country Boy"; "Hey, Baby (Uhh, Ahh)"; and of course, Coldplay's "Yellow."

Despite catching 2,456 major league games, Simmons was feeling spry and grooving to the music. Solicitous young female producers in shorts and headsets kept offering to escort him to a seat in the Pavilion, where Lee Smith had taken refuge from the sun. "Heck no," he said. "Too much is happening on the ground. This music, ever-present, every greatest hit, it brings the past five generations to the dance floor. That's transformative. Used to be the old pipe organ. We've come a long way from the organ."

That was the point, Simba said.

Lee Smith, with his 487 major-league saves, was coaxed out of the stands to make a cameo appearance in the top of the ninth. He didn't go to the rubber and bounced the ball in the dirt, just as I did at Yankee Stadium, which made me feel a whole lot better about myself. Umpire Vince gave Lee a mulligan. He threw a perfect strike on the inside corner, and it counted.

For the record, the Party Animals won their ninth straight game to claim the Banana World Championship. "One of the absolutely mind-boggling comebacks in the history of sports itself!" Biko declared.

Fans swarmed the field. Players armed with ballpoint pens asked little kids to sign their jerseys. This small piece of business, this reversal of roles, a way of making fans feel important—of making fans—is why Banana Ball works.

In 1925, when *The New Yorker* was new and The Babe's Ruthian home runs were getting a lot of ink, the magazine published an essay explaining what made his clouts radical, transgressive even. They were so big they fundamentally altered the relationship between clouter and observer. "The Babe's home run is an effort on the part of the machine to *connect* with the crowd. When the ball reaches the bleachers, contact is made. The game and the watchers of the game for that instant have the ball in common."

Now home runs are ubiquitous, and another strategy for connection has become necessary. Human contact might be the way to go.

Soon after the Bananas quit Cooperstown, they announced that their 2024 schedule would include a cruise to the Bahamas and games at six major-league ballparks, among them Fenway, the Spaceman's ancestral home. He was determined to throw out the first pitch. If necessary his teammates would carry him to the mound on a wooden plank or maybe in a palanquin. If he croaked, he croaked. "In that case, I suggest they just put a little tarp over me behind the mound and deal with me after the game is over."

Coach Viro told me about Jesse's grand plans for franchises in four, maybe six, cities, with leagues and league play and trades, which would require objective criteria for establishing player value.

I knew what was coming.

Please, God, no.

"Banana analytics," he said.

Viro created a metric he calls "Juice Factor," the Banana version of wins above replacement. "You get a point for almost every offensive stat that exists in Major League Baseball plus extra for Banana-specific feats," he said. "I actually gave a higher point total for stealing first than for a home run. I do not deduct points if you miss a trick."

Bill's abbreviated season yielded no juice. In fact, his numbers showed negative juice, which is the problem with numbers.

Spaceman was unimpressed. "The Bananas are about spontaneity and potassium replacement. That's fuckin' Casey Stengel doubletalk."

In mid-November, while waiting for an appointment with yet another heart surgeon, one who could negotiate the funky turn in his circumflex artery, the Spaceman showed up at a charity softball game in Lewiston, Maine, in a cold, late fall rain to raise money for the survivors of the mass shooting in which eighteen members of the community died. The other big attraction was Lewiston native Patrick Dempsey, McDreamy of *Grey's Anatomy* fame, newly ordained *People* magazine's Sexiest Man Alive.

The Spaceman went to the plate in logging boots, a cowboy hat, and his Savannah Bananas jersey. He went one for two, drove in a run, and pulled a groin muscle while running the bases. "I think I retired," he told me later, "but I have no short-term memory."

On December 1, 2023, at Dartmouth Hitchcock Medical Center in Hanover, New Hampshire, Dr. Hannah Chaudry—"a little lefty from Lahore," Bill calls her—saved the life of a man who loves to play ball more than he should.

And then she thanked him for the opportunity.

CAPE COD PART III

Eldredge Park, August 12, 2023

"Hey, Skip, look who's here!"

Miss Sue, general manager of the Orleans Firebirds, opened the field gate at Eldredge Park when I showed up two hours early for the last game of the season. Hard to say which was more shocking: me being early or the Firebirds being one win away from becoming the 2023 champions of the Cape Cod Baseball League.

Manager Kelly Nicholson turned at the sound of her voice, and I waved my reporter's notebook.

From back home in Washington, DC, and from Eastlake, Ohio, where former Firebird Chase DeLauter was trying to stay in one piece, I had watched the Birds clamber up the Eastern Division standings to win the division, soar through the first two rounds of the playoffs, and face their archrivals, the defending champion Bourne Braves, in a best-of-three championship series. I told myself if there was a Game Three at Eldredge Park, I'd be there.

On Saturday night, August 12, I booked a plane ticket and rented a car. I decided not to bring Bette the Dog, even though she was their part-time mascot and full-time good luck charm.

Having made my grand entrance, I made my way over to Coach Nick. "Do you have a comment for the foreign press?"

"I'm so damn excited . . . you're here."

He looked around for Bette. The Firebirds have never lost when Bette's in the house.

Two hours before the first pitch, the hillside behind the home dugout had filled in like a newly planted garden after a week of spring rain. A profusion of variegated colors: bright red coolers, army-olive blankets, coral bedspreads, and towels featuring smiling baby blue sharks, wading pink flamingos, and art deco *New Yorker* covers awaited their occupants, all vying for space on the slippery hillside amid a tumult of folded beach chairs, stripes akimbo.

Not a blade of grass nor a human being was to be seen except Miss Sue. "It's been so damn long coming," she said.

The last time the Birds played for the championship, in 2013, they were swept by the Cotuit Kettleers. Their last championship, one of eleven since the league resumed play after World War II, was in 2005, Coach Nick's first year as manager. They beat the Bourne Braves.

I inquired about a postgame party, angling for an invite. "Skip has gotta go home tomorrow," Miss Sue said. "School starts on Tuesday."

Days were growing short on Cape Cod. The traffic on Route 6 had ebbed to a tolerable stop 'n' go.

A half hour before the first pitch the sound system came to life, filling the hollow with Toby Keith's rallying cry, "How Do You Like Me Now?"

A gaggle of Firebird moms and dads assembled at the mound for ceremonial heaves in the direction of their sons. The square-jawed home plate umpire, a Norman Rockwell wannabe, bent over to sweep the plate. Miss Sue said he was new.

Just prior to the first pitch, five seagulls flying in formation circled the mound in an aviary salute to the home team before heading out into the sunset behind the band shell in deep center field.

"Infinitely preferable to F-16s," I pointed out.

Miss Sue shrugged. "Every morning a flock of Canada geese visits the field and leaves quite a mess. A guy who lives across the street, Steve, arrives with his Australian shepherd and lets him loose. 'Buddy, go get the turkeys.'"

We took our places on the second row of Miss Sue's bench because we're too short to see over the knee wall if we sit any lower. She always sits at the end of the bench, hailing distance from Coach Nick.

"They look bigger," I said.

"They may be," she replied. "They may have grown in stature the last couple of weeks."

"Miss Sue!" Coach Nick called midway through the first inning. "Lights!"

I was glad to see that the Stalker gun still wasn't talking to the scoreboard so the miles per hour on every pitch would not distract from actual pitches. Better yet, the pitch clock equipment, which was supposed to be tested in 2023, had never arrived. Watching the game with only my eyes would be a relief.

On the hillside extending down the first base line to the outfield fence, people were stepping on people and their trampled beach towels. A couple of kids had taken refuge in the branches of a tree shading a life-size bronze sculpture of a boy with a glove reaching high above his head for an unseen ball.

It was a huge crowd. "How many?" I asked Miss Sue.

She surveyed the hillside, the band shell where people had gathered on the lip of the stage, and the school parking lot where rows and rows of beach chairs clogged the right of way to the porta potties and the hamburgers. "We count the 50-50 raffle tickets and multiply by two," she said. "We used to pass the hat times four, but we don't pass the hat much anymore."

She looked across the diamond to the Bourne fans congregated by the visiting dugout. "Seventy-two hundred."

She was off by 123.

Among them were Eli and his dad from Needham, Massachusetts, who appeared at Miss Sue's elbow waiting to be noticed. We scooted over to make room for them. "Who do you think will win?" I asked nine-year-old Eli.

"Whoever's better," Eli said, with a level of dispassion that spoke to reason and stubborn disinterest.

Eli is a football guy.

He did have a couple of baseball questions. Why were the initials "BK" on the jerseys of two boys sitting on upside-down buckets just on the other side of the fence? "For Bat Kid," Miss Sue said. "We're gender-neutral."

"Do they all chew bubblegum?" Eli wanted to know, admiring the aggressive bubbles emanating from players in the on-deck circle. He was almost close enough to pop them.

"Yes," Miss Sue said, cheerfully seizing a teachable moment, "and it's a wonderful thing because they're no longer chewing tobacco."

The best baseball is improbable baseball. It's Derek Jeter's Flip Play. It's Rajai Davis, who had twelve regular season home runs, hitting the big one off young Aroldis Chapman. And it's the 2023 Orleans Firebirds, who started their season with two wins and seven losses, playing for the championship on their home field.

So, I wasn't really surprised when the Birds' diminutive Japanese second baseman, Jo Oyama, who had been hitting in quicksand, led off in the bottom of the first with a home run over the right field fence. Or that he did it again leading off in the third. Horns honked in solidarity on Route 28 behind home plate.

The improbable seemed if not probable then at least imaginable until the Birds' starting pitcher allowed four straight singles in the fourth inning, one of which was booted by Oyama. The Birds' preening nemesis Derek Bender drove in a run and advanced to second base.

"Everyone's available," Miss Sue crowed. "If he needs Matson, he's ready."

Coach Nick went to the bullpen but not for Sean Matson, the unscored-upon Harvard reliever. The score remained 2–1 until the top of the sixth inning when two of Coach Nick's other relievers conspired to load the bases and allowed the go-ahead run to score on a Bender double. He stood on the bag, yanking on the corners of the Braves logo, turning it into a bullet bra for the benefit of his titillated teammates, one of the uglier trends in self-pimping I've seen lately.

"C'mon, Birds, bear down!" Miss Sue bellowed. "Don't let them get away with it!"

With two outs, Coach Nick relented and summoned Matson, the closer who had inherited the job from another Harvard guy who quit the team in June. "They were like, 'Screw it, let's just throw the other Harvard guy into the closing role,'" Matson told me.

It was his fourth playoff appearance; he had saved two of those games, including the Birds' come-from-behind 4–3 win the night before. But his arm didn't feel good in the bullpen, and he was worried when Coach Nick said, "We may just ride you as long as possible."

Sean's concern was misplaced. "The legs go first," Red Smith always said, including the last time we spoke two days before his death. It's equally true of exhausted relievers and writers. Having conked out in my rented car for an hour before heading to the field to find Miss Sue, I was beginning to wonder how much I had left in mine.

"I could feel my legs start giving out a little under me," Sean said later. "But there were so many people there and I had so much adrenaline going that every time Coach said, 'Can you give me one more?' I was like, 'I got one more inning. There's only one more this summer.'"

The two-strike fastball he threw to Bender—him again!—in the top of the seventh inning was supposed to be up and in. But he threw it up and away and above those preening letters. "Honestly, I don't know how he made contact with it," Sean said.

Bender watched the ball hook around the left field foul pole and into the visiting bullpen, ogling it like it was an underdressed coed. It was the first earned run Matson had allowed all year.

Bender flipped his bat and leaped into an airborne pirouette, bleached curls akimbo, bringing him face-to-face with catcher Henry Hunter. Bender screamed at him in elation. Miss Sue screamed in anguish. "You're full of crap. That's bush-league."

Coach Nick rushed to the plate to separate the players, then stood aside, arms folded resolutely across his blue Orleans chest. In the lull, Eli allowed that he might sign up for Little League in the spring. Turned out he had been practicing a bit with a foam bat and ball during the annual family Cape vacation. He wanted a pink glove like Ronald Acuña Jr's.

I asked what would make baseball more interesting to him.

"Tackling," he said.

I wanted to say: "Are you watching this?"

Two home runs from a five-foot-six, 165-pound Japanese second baseman who taught himself English by watching movies like *Home Alone*. A runner thrown out at the plate on a perfect throw by the Birds right fielder. Another baserunner—Bender!—caught trying to steal third on a strike-'em-out-throw-'em play by Bender's adversary, Henry Hunter. And, three innings of relief, which was two innings too many, from Sean Matson, who was named the league's Most Outstanding Relief Pitcher of the season with seven wins, seven saves, and no losses in 29.2 innings of exquisite work.

But Eli was nine years old, so I bit my lip.

Eli is a problem. Major League Baseball needs Eli. Lots of Elis.

While the umpires conferred, I called my smart friend Peko with an idea. Could she and her students at the MIT Sports Analytics Lab create a new way for kids to consume the game? A game they could play on their phones at the ballpark and only at the ballpark. Peko said it was doable. We made plans to test it the following season at Eldredge Park.

After prolonged deliberation, the umpires issued warnings to both teams. "That's brutal," Miss Sue yelled. "Do your job!"

The home plate ump stuck out his jaw and glared at her. "That's horseshit," she bellowed, proof positive she is a real baseball guy. In baseball, horseshit is everything. Bullshit is for poseurs.

She called to Sean Matson on the mound: "Drill him in the ribs."

"Why the ribs?" Eli asked, suddenly interested.

I knew there was history between these teams, but I didn't know the latest chapter. The day before when the Firebirds arrived at Doran Park in Bourne, they were informed by a parking attendant that their bus was to be requisitioned to shuttle Bourne fans back and forth to the parking lot before and after the game.

"That's not right," Coach Nick said.

"Nicole said," the parking attendant replied.

That would be Nicole Norkevicius, president of the Bourne Braves.

Hijacking the team bus is almost but not quite as bad as commandeering the presidential limousine. "So, after the game we had to wait for an hour for them to get everybody to their cars," Coach Nick said. "It was as disrespectful and rude a thing as I've ever experienced on the field. I called the commissioner, and he got all bent out of shape and hung up on me. He apologized the next day. I emailed Nicole but she didn't reply. Miss Sue was on fire."

She was still on fire.

For the last time in 2023, the kid chorus gathered under the trees behind home plate for the seventh-inning stretch and a rousingly atonal rendition of "Take Me Out to the Ball Game." Ardent as they were, they were no match for a clump of adult Bourne fans sitting in the weeds beside the visiting dugout who countered with a vociferous Braves cheer, accompanied by a relentless cowbell.

Miss Sue had had enough. "Mary calls them canal rats," she muttered.

That's because the town of Bourne straddles the Cape Cod Canal—half on the Cape proper, half on the Massachusetts mainland. "I hope they get tick bites," she said.

In the top of the eighth, PA announcer Steve glumly admonished the children who had gotten loose on the outfield grass. "Kids, you need to get off the field." I silently applauded them.

"I can't," Miss Sue said. "I just can't."

I thought back to my first ever one-on-one with the Spaceman on the hillside in 2021 when he explained why baseball was the best game in the world. "In baseball you gotta sacrifice," he said.

"Had to," I replied.

"It's the only game that starts out at home and ends up at home," he said, which, I realized, was why I had come.

Baseball is my home. I will always come back, no matter how many times I think I'm done.

* * *

The Birds went softly in the ninth. Eddie King, a sweet Chicago kid from the University of Louisiana, was in the on-deck circle when the end came. Nobody had left the hillside except for a maelstrom of kids that had gathered over his shoulder ready to storm the field. One chubby boy pressed his hand against the chain-link fence hoping for a high five. With one strike left in the season, Eddie reached back and touched the boy's hand.

"Can you believe we have to feed the umpires after that game?" Miss Sue fumed as she headed to the field.

After the Birds had signed every shard of proffered paper and taken every desired selfie, they trudged across the dewy grass to the clubhouse beyond center field. The Canal Rats were still pile-driving each other in celebration.

"On our mound!" Miss Sue said.

I saw Cookie Cook, who'd let his shoulder-length red hair down.

"What happened?"

"You saw the game," he said. "We had four hits and two errors."

Cookie was more than a pitching coach. He was part muse, part role model, having done the one thing Jim Bouton said no pitcher could ever manage, letting go of the game before it let go of him.

He told the players how baseball had prepared him for an artist's life, teaching him to relinquish a work of art the way a pitcher must relinquish the ball. "You'd love it to be good, but once it goes up on the wall it's out of your hands," he told them. "So, it becomes about controlling what you can control."

Then, he gave them a reading list, the books that had guided his life choices: *The Things They Carried*, Tim O'Brien's evocation of the Vietnam debacle; Camus's *The Stranger*; *Zen in the Art of Archery*; *Wherever You Go, There You Are: Mindfulness Meditation in Everyday Life*; and *Seed to Dust: Life, Nature, and a Country Garden*.

In short, a primer on living life as an existentialist carnivore and wood sculptor.

"What will Coach Nick say to them?"

"You give them the speech," Cookie said. "It's the only thing to say."

Coach Nick was in a scrum of players and parents, telling reporters, "They outplayed us, they out hit us, they out pitched us; they played clean defense, we made a couple errors. It was disappointing, having the lead going into the sixth and being twelve outs away..."

In every way other than the outcome it was a perfect game. Baseball did what it does best. It brought together in equipoise two players, Oyama and Bender, with opposite fates and temperaments, who had shared the Most Valuable Player award at the all-star game, and it exposed them too. The baseball gods, the only ones I believe in, smiled on Bender but not for long. He was kicked out of baseball two months after he was drafted for tipping pitches to opposing players because he was tired and wanted the season to end.

Oyama drove in the Firebirds' only two runs but allowed the tying and go-ahead runs to score on two blown double plays.

I remembered what Robin Ventura, big leaguer turned college coach, told his players at Oklahoma State: "I guarantee if you guys play long enough, this game will bring you to your knees at some point. You'll be begging for a hit. You'll be begging for a clean inning. You'll be begging, 'Please don't hit it to me.' You'll semi-hate the game 'cause it's so cruel."

Oyama was not drafted and went home to play for the Kufu Hayate Ventures Shizuoka in the Japan Western League.

Coach Nick's wife, Donna, a first-grade teacher, had found the perfect thing to say to the players in a list of quotations attributed to Winnie the Pooh. "Well done. We love you. How lucky are we to have something that makes saying goodbye so hard."

Coach Nick turned toward the clubhouse and took a step across the dewy grass, before turning back to me. "Next time bring Bette, Jane."

* * *

I went back to Eldredge Park on August 2, 2024, to meet my Data Diva, Peko Hosoi. She and her husband, Justin, were waiting for me—and for the lobster rolls and onion rings I had promised—but my phone died on Route 6, so I went to the Verizon store instead.

Peko had accepted my challenge: to devise a handheld game for fan engagement designed to make baseball interactively up-to-date. And she made good on it, recruiting a crew of MIT summer students, graduates, and undergraduates at her Sports Analytics Lab to show how analytics can be used "in the service of the fan as opposed to the service of the team," as grad student Henry Wang put it.

Her students had pulled all-nighters working on it. They sent code from abroad. Jared Steins, who was working on another project in Italy, implemented the website and the database. Wang, a second-year PhD student in social and engineering systems who wants a future in sports analytics, built the algorithm. Grant Oh, Dodgers fan, varsity volleyball player, and undergraduate research assistant, worked twenty hours a week coordinating their efforts. None of them had ever worked on a baseball project before.

They created a game they called "Beat the Bot," in which kids would compete against Henry's algorithm to see who could best predict the outcome of each at bat, which meant they had to pay attention to the game, which was the whole point. Paying attention is the gateway drug to giving a shit.

They had decided to run it for just two innings at Eldredge Park because it was a game geared to ten-year-olds and the ten-year-olds within all of us.

They came with cool Beat the Bot stickers, handed out in the dugout after the game by Coach Nick, and posters with QR codes to scan featuring a Firebird with a fearsome visage—a prodigious yellow beak, beady black eyes, and a flame of red hair at its crown.

It was no sure thing that this would work. That Henry and Grant, who made the trip to the Cape in Friday afternoon traffic, would arrive on time or be able to log on to the live stream of the game. That Firebird fans spread out on blankets and in beach chairs reaching all the way down the first base line would hear the announcement I had written for the public address announcer.

I found Miss Sue where I had left her—despondent and pissing mad—with her bright red reading glasses perched atop her head just as they were after the last out of the 2023 championship game. I sat down beside her on her bench to wrangle with my new phone while Bette panted and rolled in the dirt at her flip-flopped feet having taken infield practice with Coach Nick.

I was plenty nervous, having bragged loudly and widely to everyone including Morgan Sword about Beat the Bot—my first initiative as commissioner.

"Where's the announcement?" Miss Sue said suddenly.

This was not promising. The original version had disappeared from Coach Nick's virtual inbox. That's 'cause he's old, like me, and was distracted by actual baseball. I tapped out some words for public address announcer Steve, who was by then deep into his pregame spiel.

Way back in 2011, when Miss Sue was the only female general manager known to me in baseball, we confabbed at her former HQ, a splintered wooden bench behind home plate, about the delicious prospect of women running The Show. Even then games were running long and slow, for which reason I had proposed a ban on spitting and scratching to improve decorum and pace of play. Miss Sue objected on the grounds that such a ban was unenforceable. "Spitting. You can't control that."

(Okrent objected on the grounds that "some of us who have balls understand why they do that.")

Miss Sue had advocated a zero-tolerance policy on chewing tobacco, "The Macarena," "Sweet Caroline"—brave for a BoSox fan—and "all forms of aural pollution including excessive interpolations of the national anthem."

Also she wanted a two-beer limit. Talk about unenforceable.

She's so old-school she makes madras look cool again.

I asked everyone I talked to for ideas and opinions about how to make baseball fun again—the crazier the better. I had promised to come back to her for input and comment. Unfortunately, she had other things on her mind so I'm not sure how much she took in. And, I had to talk fast because I had to spill it all before the Bot went live.

First off, I assured her, baseball is never going to be the National Pastime again. Get over it. Grow a pair and grow a new audience. Daryl Morey, the NBA's analytic guru, was right. Nobody would invent baseball today. It's far too elegant for our brutalist age. They'd invent pickleball, *sine qua non* of the multitasking generation, an intoxicating opportunity to maximize steps taken and calories spent with camaraderie and road rage. Participation in pickleball is up 235 percent since 2022.

Not that everyone thinks there's anything to fix. "I don't adhere to the outcry from the fans that the new system is broken," Coach Cookie told me. "Attendance is up. Team values are up. Contract numbers are up, jersey sales, all of it. It can't hold a candle to the NFL, but that's fine. Baseball fans are outraged? Who cares? Turns out MLB is not a pluralistic entity. It's not democratic nor need it be. It has what, thirty owners? And they can do whatever they want. It's their toy, right?"

Very realpolitik of him, and very true thanks to the antitrust exemption granted in 1922.

Jason Ochart, charter member of the new wave, likes the game just the way it is too. "I simply don't agree that the game is losing its magic. In the WBC, when Ohtani struck out Trout with 102-mph heaters and sliders that were faster than a lot of fastballs in the 1980s, at no point did I or anyone else I was with think, 'I wish he would just throw 87 mph to force Mike Trout to slap a ball to right field.' I think we are watching the best baseball players of all time, and I'm constantly in awe of what I see on the field every day."

The new rules accomplished as much as they could, though not as much as MLB hoped. After two seasons, games were twenty-four minutes shorter and attendance was 12 percent higher, all but 1 percent coming in 2023. Stolen base attempts and successes were the highest since 1915.

Still, offense withered and stagnated, depriving the game of the texture and subtleties that used to define it. The league batting average fell another five points in 2024 to .243, if you think that matters. A third of all at bats ended in one of those dreaded Three True Outcomes as they have every year since 2017. Home runs, doubles, triples, total bases, and the percentage of balls put in play (BABIP) were all down a smidge.

"Frankly, the game could use a woman's touch, your touch," I told Miss Sue. Does every T-shirt designed for women have to be pink? Aren't we better than this? So, is there any doubt in your mind that if Sue ran major league baseball there would have been double softball bases in place years ago? One for the runner, one for the fielder, to prevent the preventable—like when I maimed my boss on a green lawn in Connecticut. I ran into him at a synagogue in New York while on book tour and was dumb enough to say, "I'm not sure you remember me but . . ."

In Sue's Show, every weekend game would be played in sunshine, with matinee prices, as on Ladies' Days of yore. Sue preferred a 3:00 p.m. or 4:00 p.m. first pitch. "Too hot in midday for ladies of a certain age," she said.

No doubt, recalcitrant MLB owners would prefer that hour to 1:00 p.m. games, even if hitters hate late afternoon shadows—because commercial advertising rates are higher.

In addition, Miss Sue says, no weekday games to start later than 6:30 p.m. No more TV blackouts. Two premier games to be broadcast everywhere on Friday and Sunday nights. All playoff games to be televised and/or streamed on channels and platforms available to 75 percent of the population, free of charge for the first two years. It's great that there are so many new ways to consume baseball, but games are harder to find than the Passover afikomen.

Make baseball findable again.

And, while we're at it, let baseball be baseball again. I told Sue about my conversation with former A's President Roy Eisenhardt. He remembered talking to Roger Angell about making radical change to the game. "He said, 'Roger, why don't we just get rid of the home run? A home run's a boring play. Let's just put big walls out there so that you have a lot of triples and make the game much more interesting.'"

I couldn't wait to tell Okrent. Wrap plexiglass around the outfield wall at every ballpark, the way they do at NHL arenas, until each stands eighteen feet high. Yes, that would diminish the idiosyncratic charm of baseball architecture and throw batting park factor (BPF) analysts into a tizzy recalculating the meaning of home and away, but it would also make every playing field a more even playing field, eliminate cheap Dave Kingman home runs, and prevent future Bronx goombahs from trying to yank the ball out of Mookie's glove.

Who wouldn't want to be on the other side of the tempered glass when Aaron Judge barreled into it? This would bring athleticism back to the outfield, demanding the ability to levitate like Ken Griffey Jr., climb the wall like Bo Jackson, play the carom like Roberto Clemente, and throw to—not over—the cutoff man.

If you don't like that idea, here's a more radical proposal from my deepest deep throat. "What do you think about two outfielders instead of three? That would give you the style of baseball everyone wants. A batter is going to see so much more open space. He's not gonna need to hit those home runs. Suddenly, he'll be a Rod Carew or a Wade Boggs batter."

Said outfielder would become a second DH. Stunningly, this idea does not repulse me.

Pitchers will pitch to Mike Rizzo's slightly lower and slightly more horizontal strike zone. Balls and strikes will remain in the domain of the human element with a robo-ump looking over the umpire's shoulder. Teams will get three challenges per game to express their displeasure.

Jason Ochart is right: MLB needs to change the ball if it wants to solve the scourge of strikeouts. Agreed. If MLB wants to make a ball that's safe to throw the way pitchers throw today, they need to authorize a committee of hitters and pitchers supervised by Peko Hosoi to approve a pretacked ball, one that lessens the chances of the batter getting killed. "The ball is chosen by a jury of its peers—six guys who have to throw it and six who have to face it," I said.

There's nothing more central to the game than the ball and nothing that feeds the live wire of distrust more than the owners' absolute control of the baseball. Sean Doolittle remembers arriving in the Oakland clubhouse one day, probably around 2016, when there was lots of tumult about the ball, to find an info-graphic had been left on every chair. "It was all about how they had run their own studies on the baseballs and it fell within the range of specifications and they weren't gonna take any questions, but they wanted us to know that they'd looked into it and everything was legit. It didn't pass the smell test."

Allowing players to be part of the process would go a long way to improving health and safety and trust. "Right?" But I had lost Miss Sue.

Any manager who removes a pitcher after seven perfect innings for any reason other than that his arm has fallen off loses his "manager" challenges for the next ten games. No pitcher may be relieved during an inning unless he has been charged with a run in that inning. And if the Tommy John rate exceeds 40 percent, I'm implementing the 95-mph rule. Might as well take advantage of the technology we have.

When I'm commissioner, pitchers will get the same one time-out per at bat that hitters have. Fair is fair. No one will pitch two games in a row. Jim Palmer was surprised to learn that accounts for only 16 percent of appearances. But appearances don't count the number of times pitchers get hot in the bullpen and never get the call. Those are called dry humps. They take a lot out of a guy. So, in my MLB, no pitching *or* warming up two games in a row.

To protect the youngest arms, MLB will create a governing body for travel ball and pay-to-play showcase promoters to enforce new rules limiting the number of showcases a child may attend, mandatory training for youth coaches. "Demand that every organization, for profit or otherwise, keep track of every showcase and tournament; innings pitched and speed achieved," said Driveline's Deven Morgan.

And that they share the information.

Any coach who violates guidelines will be banned from sanctioned competition, including Little League. Any kid who violates the showcase limitations will be ineligible to receive an NCAA scholarship or enter the major-league draft.

More than any other professional sport, baseball fans are created young: from in utero to legal independence. Baseball needs to do absolutely everything possible to grow a younger fan base, which starts with making the game safe to play.

Joe Maddon suggested that fantasy baseball could be used in schools. "Have 'em Zoom with general managers and owners. Analytics should be in the school as part of the math curriculum."

And while I'm at it, there shall be a designated autograph signer at the end of every game; a designated grandstand rover. Send some guy on the IL who's getting paid for being on the sixty-day injured list. No one ever pulled a groin muscle shaking hands. Day care in the ballpark, innings booked in advance.

"This is the biggie," I told Miss Sue, whose attention was flagging.

"Uh-huh," she said.

"Every kid under age ten gets in free. Everybody likes that!" Okrent and Riz like it best. They'll like it more when they get a look at Mike Haupert's math. "If the Cubs give free tickets to kids five to twelve years old, and if Grandpa buys the kid a small soda, a hot dog, ice cream, and a ballcap, it will cost the team about $4 million annually," said Cubs fan Mike. "To put that in perspective: The Cubs paid Jason Heyward $21 million in 2023 to play for the Dodgers."

If Grandma and Grandpa are feeling particularly generous and throw in a T-shirt, the Cubs might even break even.

At every home game every club will designate a section in the upper deck, first come, first served for twenty-five-dollar tickets and all you can eat. Four tickets max. Riz had especially liked that. "Gotta fill that up," he said. "But no parking or alcohol, right?"

Every Saturday afternoon in every stadium a dedicated section of seats will be set aside for older kids with free food, old-timer visits, and baseball clinics on the field before the game. After the game, younger kids run the bases with instruction (first come, first served). Let them slide into home, smell the grass, sit in the dugout, feel what it's like to be a big leaguer. Maybe more of them will want to play baseball.

Also, every year in every major-league city, a feminist Bring Your Daughter to the Park Day. No pink allowed.

Aside from consigliere Okrent and Miss Sue, my number-one spitballer was Dodgers Manager Dave Roberts. "He's in a spitballing league of his own," I told her.

"Uh-huh," she said.

He wants all-star week to be remade into a facsimile of Super Bowl week with the draft on Monday night, the Home Run Derby on Tuesday, with the All-Star Game pushed back to Wednesday, a Futures Game on Thursday, and a Friday game with US all-stars against the World. "Everyone is gonna watch that game," he said.

Sounds okay to me as long as Travis Kelce dresses the draftees and their outfits are donated to charity later, I told her.

"Dave wants baseball to go dark on Monday, like Broadway. He says, 'If there is a day off a week, that has such an effect on the pitchers.

And it would help so much with load management. I understand there would be a cost.' "

Which means losing money, which owners are loathe to do, but it might buy them some good will at the box office to know that not every decision is about monetizing the product.

"I think we should go back to the 154 game schedule," I said. "Especially if they add more teams to the playoffs. Jim Kaat says the season should start at Memorial Day and end at Labor Day with the playoffs and World Series in September."

To increase the importance of and interest in regular season games, division-winning teams with the best records will get the "Dan Okrent Leg Up," needing to win only two games in a best three out of five series while lower-seeded teams have to win three games. He's working on a proposal to reward playoff teams with the most complete games.

"This is micro," Dave said. "Flip the order of batting practice."

"When I was younger I used to go to games early to watch the coach hitting the ball around the infield," he said. "I used to see Ozzie Smith, Garry Templeton, Tony Gwynn throw from right field. It's just so much fun to see how it's done, and they can show off a little bit too."

Today, the home team is done hitting—or hiding out downstairs in batting cages—before the stadium gates open. Imagine the fifties without being able to see The Mick hit balls out of the Stadium? How many kids became Yankees fans, baseball fans, because of those displays?

That reminded me of something else Roy Eisenhardt said. "Ultimately, baseball will survive as a healthy alternative to the rapid-paced, violent sports if we can help fans understand the nuances rather than glorifying the home run. I'd eliminate the home run hitting contest in the All-Star Game..."

To which I had replied, "Fat chance."

"We need to go back to the skills contest they had in the late 1980s," Roy said.

Those would be the skills my Yankees demonstrated the lack of in the fifth inning of the last game of the 2024 World Series when the Dodgers exposed them as defensive poseurs.

Dave was just getting warmed up. He thinks the pitch clock needs some work. "From the seventh inning on, we need to give the pitcher five seconds more with nobody on base, and with somebody on base twenty-five seconds."

I thought he was going to go all max heave on me, but he went deep instead. "Because baseball is narrative, and as it gets to crunch time, you don't get the opportunity to let it build to a crescendo."

Dave knows something about narrative tension. His stolen base in the bottom of the ninth inning of Game Three of the 2004 American League Championship Series between the Evil Empire and Red Sox Nation changed the narrative of the game, not to mention the narrative of an entire nation.

Baseball used to tell a lot of different stories. "There's only one story baseball tells now, and it's basically power versus power," biomechanical guru Glenn Fleisig said.

When's the last time the most memorable World Series play was something other than a home run? Try Roberto Clemente's throw in Game Six of the 1971 World Series between the Pirates and the Orioles. Jim Palmer can't unsee it. "You mean from the bench on the third base line, two outs with Belanger running on contact and Buford hitting a double on the foul line and then off the wall just left of the 309 sign, two steps from the right field wall? He threw it all the way in the air to Manny Sanguillen waist-high. It was only the third game he had played at Memorial Stadium, and he played the carom perfectly. If you are Weaver, Bamberger, the Oriole bench, it's like going to Radio City Music Hall and seeing *Bwana Devil*, one of those early fifties 3D movies where the action comes right at you."

Half the folks who attended MLB games in 2023 saw fewer than five games. True, it's not like you can buy a bleacher seat for twenty-five cents anymore. But it's equally true that not all of them are baseball fans. Some people come for their kids; some score a freebie from a friend; some because it's nice outside.

"So," I told Dave, "we're going to have team DJs. Famous ones some nights. Local high school kids other times. Every player's gonna submit a playlist, and that playlist will be played on the dance floor during a home series and given out for free.

"Also, we're gonna have a dance floor in every ballpark."

"Shut up," Dave said.

I nudged Miss Sue. That's when he said, "Ya know, you should be commissioner."

"Uh-huh," Miss Sue said.

"Anything you want to add, Miss Sue?"

"Every team shall have a bat dog just like Bette."

I gazed at the scoreboard in deep left field, squinted really. I could just make out the age-old numbers: balls, strikes, outs, innings, and the score.

I get it. OPS is a great number, a more fulsome statement of a hitter's worth. That's why some people—me—plausibly argue that The Mick at his best was a more valuable offensive force than Willie. All these years later, Mantle is fifteenth all-time in OPS; Willie is thirty-fourth.

But batting average is an irrefutable reminder that greatness in baseball means failing two-thirds of the time. It's a little bit like the earthshine moon I saw in Atlantic City the night The Mick passed out dead drunk in my lap.

Earthshine is light cast by the setting sun onto the earth's surface and reflected back onto the moon. Like baseball, earthshine comes in the spring. It was April when I peered out of the salt-stained hotel window in my room in Atlantic City and saw a stark white crescent piercing the sky and a dim intimation of the whole illuminated by indirect light.

Ron Washington sees this issue in a less poetic light. "We need to embarrass some of these players," Wash said. "It might wake someone up."

Either way, when I'm commissioner, seventeen-thousand-square-foot entertainment center cum video boards will make room for batting average *and* OPS, and there will be an equal sign between them so the analytically unlettered can begin to understand the relationship between baseball's old and new math. Teams will offer online workshops on baseball's evolving numbers because, believe me, they're not going away.

I give my sports-loathing mother credit for this lesson. God forbid there was a game my dad wanted to watch that conflicted with Texaco's Saturday-afternoon broadcast from the Metropolitan Opera. He got even by falling asleep at every production they saw live.

She hated math, her worst subject in high school, because to my immigrant grandparents, going to college meant improving on what you did poorly. So the first member of my family to attend college graduated as a very pissed-off math major. Born before the Spanish flu arrived, she lived into the Cyber Age but declined every opportunity to learn to text with her grandchildren, who don't answer the phone, or to shop online. She might feel differently today after waiting on hold for an hour to speak to a complaint-resolution specialist.

So, I told Miss Sue, "I'll just have to keep Peko close and try not to be my mother."

Unfortunately, I had no idea where Peko was.

* * *

"Honestly, I almost didn't hear the announcement," Peko said when she found me.

Peko's husband, Justin, had chatted up the Birds' Team President Bill O'Donnell. Having assured him that he had Miss Sue's approval,

Justin procured a table and chairs for Henry and Grant, which they stationed just up the hill behind Miss Sue's bench.

Immediately, they were inundated by small, mostly shoeless humans wanting to know if it was time to play Beat the Bot and seeking advice on usernames. Yes, Froggy Pants would be okay. "Other kids were running around yelling, 'Mom, I need your phone!'" Peko said. "And there were kids who were learning to read the scoreboard. They were pretty young. One kid came over in the fourth inning. He asked, 'Can I play?'

"'We're going to play in the fifth inning. Do you know what inning it is now?'

"And he said, 'the second.'

"I said, 'Maybe we should take a look at the scoreboard. Do you know where the inning is on the scoreboard? Look in the upper left.'

"'Ohhh, it's the fourth. Do we have to wait until the fifth?'"

Peko fretted about whether twenty-five seconds between at bats, five less than major leaguers have to get their butts in the box, would be enough for the kids to be able to press the button registering: walk, strikeout, hit, other.

The two TrackMan operators covering the game for MLB joined Henry and Grant at the table. When Henry activated the Bot, they pulled out their phones and logged on to the game. Jane's first fix as commissioner went live.

"What do you have?"

"I'm going to say strike out on this one."

"I'm up one."

This was new to Henry. Creating a performance model to predict an outcome for fans was a whole other thing than working on behalf of a league or a team the way he does at the Sports Analytics Lab. "I was doing it for a community. That was super cool."

The two innings went quickly. After the last out of the sixth, kids descended upon them holding their phones aloft: "I 'Beat the Bot!' I 'Beat the Bot!'"

Peko arrived soon after. "How many people logged on?" she asked.

"Eighty," Henry said.

"Oh, my God, everybody here is playing this," Peko said. "Everybody except for Jane."

Henry and Grant were too polite to say what they were thinking.

"I couldn't even download it."

"You don't need to download it," Peko reminded me. "It's a website."

Peko was jazzed: "One family had decided early on they were going to leave in the middle of the sixth inning, and the kids didn't want to go because Beat the Bot was going to the end of the sixth inning. The best one was the one who said, 'My kid actually sat down and paid attention to two full innings of baseball.'

"'I've never seen my child so focused! She watched the whole two innings and didn't complain!'"

Adults had other questions. "How did you build it?" "Can I see the code?" "Is it available on GitHub?"

One guy approached with a compliment and an agenda. "This is just like gambling. Can I play this at home, or do I have to be at the park?"

"A, I'm glad you really like it," Peko replied. "And B, you have a gambling problem."

Yes, Beat the Bot can be scaled up for use in a major-league ballpark, which bodes well for my term as commissioner. Yes, it can be scaled up for adult gamers with rewards built in for success. Yes, it can be programmed to include more specific outcomes of each at bat. Yes, the Bot or Bot 2.0 will be installed in every major-league ballpark when I'm commissioner. "I was a little hesitant to go to different levels because this was something everybody was doing together, and parents could play it with their kids," Peko said.

"One mother was really skeptical. Then as soon as she started playing, she got sucked in. She's like, 'Oh, no, no, no, pick "hit."'

"There's a whole generation where this is the way they're used to interacting with the world. Sure, there's value in just watching a baseball game. But if you've been raised in this generation where everything is a game within a game, you may need to be weaned onto baseball in a more familiar format."

The winner was not-so-young PackRat386, who crushed the Bot with eleven correct and informed answers. "He had the stats on all the pitchers," Peko said. "He had their strikeout rates, their walk rate. He had more data than we had to train our algorithm."

As pedagogically gratifying as this was for Peko, it was a revelation for Henry, who needs to get out of the lab more. "It was very strange going to the ballpark," he said. "Once I saw that these people were humans, and they dap each other before the game, and they were taking pictures with their host families, it definitely felt a little bit weird knowing that in our model, they are just a vector of numbers and nothing more, nothing less."

Henry's revelation was a come-to-Jesus moment for me. This nice young grad student genius had answered the question with which my odyssey began—what happened to baseball?

Who argues on behalf of the fans? No one had an answer to that until I lobbed the question to Peko. "There is no constituency that argues for what you're talking about. The manager has to win or he gets fired. The player has to do well or he doesn't get his next free agent contract, same with the general manager. Jobs are on the line. The individual incentives currently are not aligned to make the game as entertaining as possible."

I said, "So the best thing I can say about our experiment is we successfully tested the premise that you could create an interactive game using analytics to . . ."

Peko interrupted. By this time, we were finishing each other's sentences. "—deepen their engagement with the game at the park."

My stomach growled. I should have gone for the lobster rolls instead of the phone, which turned out to be a lemon. Peko has a very big laugh for such a diminutive person. It overflows her, and now it overflowed me. "I can't believe I got so lucky when you called me that day and said, 'You fucked baseball. Don't you think you should fix it?'"

And then we went for ice cream.

POSTSCRIPT

June 2025

I went back to Baltimore for the Orioles' last home game of 2023. Baltimore is where I entered the credentialed life of a baseball writer. Where the nice kitchen ladies at Memorial Stadium made crab cakes to order for members of the press, who did not yet pay their way. Where Andy, the elevator operator, in his wilted orange Orioles blazer, always waited no matter how late I filed my stories. Where baseball never got too cool for orange-and-black balloon arches and the 280-foot-long orange carpet rolled out on special occasions.

It's also where I met "Cakes," as Jim Palmer was known when he bestrode the dinky-dingy locker room at Memorial Stadium like a Norse god in his skimpy skivvies. Cakes had invited me to join him in the TV booth for the game and for a pregame bite in the antiseptic media dining room, which as far as I can tell is Janet Marie Smith's only fail.

Palmer is so identified with Baltimore that people forget he was first a New Yorker. Which must be the reason I decided to tell him how my parents found me trying to crawl out of the window of their apartment in Stuyvesant Town when I was a year old, precipitating a move to the former potato fields of Long Island. "The butler caught me making fires at 1065 Park Avenue," he said. "They were exciting. I was five."

He still looks Park Avenue, long, lean, tan, with de rigueur twenty-first-century stubble, though he's not as blond as he was when he toiled in the sun. Unlike his former teammates who had gathered to salute him on his sixtieth anniversary with the team, he still has all his hair, which is more than you can say for Cal Ripken Jr., who looks like a baby Buddha.

"When's the last time you mentioned TTO on the air?"

"What's TTO?" he replied.

That would be the Three True Outcomes, Cakes.

Palmer, who has been calling Orioles games since 1992, is about to turn eighty, which is hard to believe, and the reason for his answer. Old and new baseball don't yet speak the same language.

After eating whatever it was, I trailed behind a posse of Orioles officials and broadcasters as they headed for the elevator en route to the pregame festivities. Trapped behind the throng, and unable to see, I heard someone say, "What's the attendance?"

"Expecting twenty-eight thousand," came the reply.

"Should be forty thousand," someone else said.

Except for that, it was an extremely good day, the O's won their one-hundredth game, claimed their first division championship since 2014, announced a thirty-year extension of their lease on Camden Yards, and flew Jim's two daughters in to surprise him.

We stayed in touch over the winter and throughout the new season, gabbing about the absurdities and delights of baseball in 2024. I missed the final home game of 2024, but 40,404 others showed, hoping for some Orioles magic, which unfortunately was spent.

The players beat it off the field without so much as a fare-thee-well when it was over, Cakes said. "There were forty thousand people at the ballpark, and our players do not come out on the field. What were they thinking?"

They weren't thinking.

Not thinking is what got baseball into this mess. Assuming its place in the sports firmament, baseball abandoned its station. Watching the metastatic growth of the NFL and NBA without bothering to recalibrate its nineteenth-century self to the frantic present. Hiding its eyes from the pumped-up steroid physiques of the nineties. Embracing whole-hog the *Moneyball* coup d'état. Facilitating the technological rampage that distorted the core values of the game. Allowing labor relations to degenerate into an Edward Albee play with the parties tearing each other apart every six years like George and Martha. Forgetting that Black players matter. Treating pitching arms as fungible. Facilitating a technological rampage that distorted core values, like making contact, most recently with the aid of an AI-driven TRAJEKT machine that allows hitters to train against avatars with "live arms" that never make mistakes. In all these ways, baseball flunked the visionary test. Absent the futurists the moment demanded, they failed to see or plan for the consequences. And they didn't think about the human element.

I worry about the human element, a worry that became a crisis just as I was winding up for my big finish and began to hear a chirping in my ear. It was faint at first, but adamant. This was just about the time I downloaded the high-maintenance publisher-mandated software package from which I began to receive friendly suggestions, nudges from an editor with the initials AI: word choices, grammar, spelling. Okay. But then: sentence structure and whole new sentences began popping up on the screen, telling me what I really wanted to say and, worse, how to say it. An unbidden stream of virtual editorial advice which had the unwelcome side effect of making me forget what I was about to say. I pounded the delete button, disabling it finally, shouting, "Go away!" Which drowned out the chirping in my ear. The chirping of the canary in the coal mine that Peko cited as baseball's gift to humanity in the twenty-first century.

She hears the chirping too: a warning and a song. "AI is changing the way we do everything. Everybody is going to have to get a lot better at distinguishing a good AI answer from a plausible but incorrect answer. AI can expand human creativity if used well." Like "Beat the Bot," I thought. "But, if used poorly, it turns creativity into mundane cookie-cutter garbage like your helpful AI editor," Peko continued. "Baseball is the perfect example. It has shown the tempting fruit of analytics: athletes running faster, throwing harder, hitting further, but also what happens if we forget baseball is bigger than that. We're losing the forest because we're only tending a few trees—the ones we can measure."

The game that taught us about forbearance and happenstance, patience and luck, duck farts and teamwork, now offers a way forward, a way to assert the prerogatives of humanity, like remembering to say "please" as Peko did when she posed her first question to ChatGPT.

I spent much of 2024 trying to keep pace with the continued upheaval in the game while also keeping up with my human elements.

Buck Showalter did not get another chance to manage, an injustice and a very of-the-American-moment abandonment of wisdom and experience: "How does this man not have a job?" Christina Kahrl said.

Scott Hatteberg, the most grateful man in baseball, signed up for another year with the "On Their Way to Sacramento A's" doing what owner John Fisher had steadfastly refused to do: work diligently to improve the team.

Coach Kelly Nicholson had the 2025 Firebirds roster set a month after the season ended. Miss Sue was still blushing and fussing about an effusive profile in *The Boston Globe* saluting her as a "Cape Crusader" when Derek Bender, who did so much to do in her Birds in the 2023 championship, was released by the Twins' Class A Mighty Mussels for tipping pitches. The season had gone on too long, he explained.

Miss Sue's tackle-obsessed, football-jonesing friend Eli is eleven now and just finished his third season in Little League. He's a catcher, which is the closest thing to playing tackle football. "It's super fun," he said. "Maybe my second or third sport."

Despite a second offseason at Driveline, J. P. Crawford was unable to reproduce the "damage" he did in 2023 when he single-handedly kept the Mariners alive in the race for the playoffs and almost KO'd Dusty's Astros in the process. "Let's fucking go!" he screamed into a live TV mic after a walk-off grand slam. Hoisting the Trident high, he showed those sleepy-in-Seattle fans how right Francisco Lindor was when he said, "Gotta be yourself, because the moment you're not, you're not at your best."

But a strained oblique in April and a broken pinky finger in July kept him sidelined for a third of the season. By its end, he was batting last in the order. When I asked why he wasn't going back to Driveline for a third offseason, he texted, "Wife's about to give birth."

"Boy or girl?"

"Little girl!"

I'm always going to root for a man who wields a mighty exclamation point like a Trident on behalf of a baby girl.

The City of College Park, Georgia, rejected a $2 million offer from the Marquis Grissom Baseball Association and Morehouse College to buy Bill Evans Field, where I sat with Marquis on crumbling concrete steps watching kids from the Braves' RBI program and talking about the renaissance in Black baseball that he knows will come. How does he know it? He's got so many recruits now he started a Junior Hill Boys training program. But, the city accepted a $1.5 million offer from developers to replace the park where Marquis hit his first home run with a mixed-use retail-and-housing project.

Polymath Dan Okrent, who said he had sworn off the book-writing biz, submitted the manuscript for a new biography of Stephen Sondheim, the Babe Ruth of musical theater, which is the only thing I love as much as baseball. I have it on preorder.

In his official capacity as pitching coach for Mike Scioscia's Team USA, Dave Wallace called forty-four-year-old Rich Hill to ask him to join the staff for the Premier12 Series tournament featuring the best twelve teams on the planet. Rich said he would let him know.

At the end of August, he signed a minor-league contract with the Red Sox, who brought him to Fenway for a fourth go-around when they still had a shot at the playoffs and thought a wily lefty might be of use. He pitched 3.2 innings and was dumped at the end of the week when it was clear the postseason was out of reach in favor of a fireballing young righty they wanted to see. "And on an off day so I didn't get to say goodbye," Rich said.

In November, he started the first game of the premier round of the tournament against Japan. He allowed one hit before being removed in the fourth inning. He went home, continued throwing, and waited for a phone call, which came in May, when the Kansas City Royals signed him to a minor league contract.

Dusty Baker went back to Sacramento to tend his grapes, get to know his hunting dogs, and follow Darren's trek through the Washington Nationals minor-league system. General Manager Mike Rizzo, who never wanted to let him go as manager, telephoned with word that Darren was being called up to the majors, giving Dusty and his wife time to get to Washington to see Darren's first big-league hit.

In her nonexistent free time between teaching mechanical engineering and trying to figure out how to use analytics to measure intangibles like grit, Peko Hosoi taught herself to play golf using a Markerless motion system, an obsession I inadvertently fostered by suggesting a visit to the 1892 links golf course near my home in Cape Cod. I can't apologize enough.

Nearing the end of a trying first season as manager of the Los Angeles Angels, Ron Washington was quoted in the *LA Times* as saying the front office forgot to give him big-league talent. Wash recanted, though he said he didn't say it. "I might have said something like 'You see what I got out there?'" he said.

Undaunted, he brings his fungo bat to the ballpark every day.

Roc Riggio spent his first season in professional baseball with the Class A Hudson Valley Renegades, where he began the 2025 season on the injured list. "I was most pleased with how I handled my failure. Part of this game is learning how to be a professional failure." Promoted to Double-A in June 2025, Roc began clobbering home runs and garnering headlines.

At the end of his second attenuated season in the minors, Chase DeLauter went back to the Arizona Fall League for a second year, which is a little bit like repeating second grade—but he didn't get hurt! Then he went to spring training, tore a core muscle, and underwent surgery for a sports hernia. Little wonder he was circumspect upon returning to Triple A in late May. "Really my only goal is just playing tomorrow," he said.

In other Firebird news: Sean Matson was drafted by the Cleveland Guardians. Jo Oyoma was signed by the Seattle Mariners. Cookie Cook is sculpting full-time.

The Red Sox exercised Jason Ochart's option for a third year as director of minor-league hitting. (Four of his twenty MLB disciples now work for the Sox.) He was hanging hurricane shutters in advance of Hurricane Milton and fretting about writing a toast for his brother's wedding when I reached him. "I'll need help with the speech," he said. He did fine without me but kept his promise to let me know he was okay after Milton passed through.

Alex Bregman became a free agent on Halloween 2024 and was wearing Dusty's tie when Governor Sam, named for his father, a Democratic candidate for governor of New Mexico, triumphed at the Breeders' Cup. Alex and his influencer wife, Reaganelizabeth, announced they were expecting another baby boy at an all-star gender-reveal party starring their two-year-old son, Knox, who clobbered a BP fastball from dad that exploded in baby blue powder. "I'm building a roster!" Alex crowed.

Pitchers and catchers had reported by the time Bregman signed a three-year contract with the Red Sox for $40 million a year, the fourth-highest annual average value deal in baseball history. Baby Bennett was born a day after Dad went five-for-five for the first time in his career. Dad used his Spanish to ingratiate himself with his new teammates. If Spanish-speaking players are expected to learn English, shouldn't we do as much, he told *The Boston Globe*. Another rule for the new Commish to get to work on. Bregman was off to the best start in a career full of poor ones when he tore his right quad muscle in May, the same injury that sidelined him for more than two and a half months when he tore the left quad in 2021.

The day after the Dodgers beat my Yankees in the World Series, Janet Marie Smith's construction crew went to work excavating seventeen and a half feet of rock and soil behind the home dugout at Dodger Stadium to expand their subterranean Taj Mahal clubhouse to three stories, big enough to accommodate the $1 billion of free agents they acquired during the offseason. Put this woman in the Hall of Fame.

The Spaceman dropped by my home in Washington for a sleepover en route to a women's baseball tournament in Durham, North Carolina. This time he deigned to play catch with Bette the Dog, who had no more problem with his Leephus pitch than Tony Perez did.

I hadn't seen him since June when top banana Jesse Cole granted him one-third of an inning on the mound at Fenway Park. The game was a sellout, as were five others at big-league ballparks, which persuaded the Bananas to schedule eighteen "major-league" games in 2025, not to mention two at NFL stadiums and one in "Death Valley," Clemson's eighty-thousand-plus-capacity football stadium, all three of which were announced as sellouts in December.

Bill climbed the dugout steps at Fenway and doffed his cap, gimpy and stiff-legged but game, revealing a full head of perfect white hair and a new set of perfect white chompers that flashed the stadium from two giant video boards hovering over the outfield. He had left the previous set on the bar at a Mexican restaurant in Niceville, Florida.

Jesse gave him the full WWE treatment. "Former World Series pitcher, former major-league all-star, seventy-seven years young, Red Sox Hall of Famer, please welcome Bill 'the Spaceman' Leeeeeeee."

He threw a couple of warm-ups from behind the mound trying to stretch out his arm, which he hadn't been able to do, having been ordered to stay out of sight, and bent to pull a few blades of grass, tossing them in the air to check the wind.

He walked the first Party Animal he faced and got the next one to hit a weak dribbler between third and the mound. He started down the hill, the buttons on his yellow jersey tugging at his waist before realizing the idiocy of an old man trying to bend, pivot, and throw in time to get the runner. The third baseman's throw was late. And then all hell broke loose on the bases.

Three unearned runs later, he stalked off the mound, furious.

"There's like forty thousand people here," a consoling Banana said, as if the Spaceman had never pitched in front of a full house. "You were around the plate."

At 7:30 the next morning, he was back at the Fens, playing catch in the outfield with his rescue dog, Clarice. As the stands filled with capped and gowned high school graduates and the stadium speakers blasted "Pomp and Circumstance," Clarice paused for a doggy call of nature in right field. For this, Bill bent down.

* * *

Whatever second thoughts I might have had about the need to put myself forward for Rob Manfred's job evaporated when he started yammering about a buzzy new idea for baseball: the Golden At Bat. That's the cockamamie rule adopted by the Savannah Bananas as their eleventh commandment in 2024, allowing a manager to send his best hitter to the plate once a game whether or not it's his turn to bat, thus upending a century and a half of baseball order.

Like the golden calf, the Golden At Bat is a false idol. Concocted moments of synthetic drama wouldn't be in demand if the owners hadn't allowed analytics to sabotage organic ones like triples.

But I was heartened when MLB released a sixty-two-page report on the state of pitching. It confirmed what everyone already knew: There's a crisis. Also, the old guys are right. "The focus on velocity, 'stuff,' and max effort pitching" are having "a noticeable and detrimental impact on the quality of the game on the field."

And I thought, "Okay, they get it."

For a moment I thought, *Maybe they don't need me after all.*

Then, in quick succession:

Steve Cohen offered Juan Soto $765 million to play baseball for the Mets for fifteen years. Soto graciously accepted. I wasn't shocked that he ditched the Yankees or even by the size of the offer. Uncle Stevie was determined to buy whatever remains of NYC tabloid bragging rights. I was shocked that two *other* teams offered $700 million and change for a one-dimensional player who can't field much or run the bases too well and will be a permanent DH in five years.

I kept hearing Miss Sue whispering in my ear: "The money is numbing, stupefying, inconceivable to someone who has volunteered for the last twenty-five years."

"I think six years from now there's a chance they're going to look back and say, 'what were we thinking?'" said unemployed Buck Showalter.

"It's an oligarchy," I moaned to a high school friend who marched with me against The Man when we were young and thought things could change.

Before the words "salary cap" could form on my lips, the silver-haired ghost of Marvin Miller appeared before me, his right eyebrow arched in high dudgeon as was often the case when someone in the press asked a particularly stupid question. Thanks to Marvin, every professional sport now has some form of free agency and player autonomy.

Also thanks to Marvin, baseball is the only major professional sport without a salary cap or a payroll floor. I remember thinking during the 1981 strike, "Why isn't he *my* union leader?"

When Catfish Hunter signed a five-year, $3.25 million contract with the Yankees in 1974; when The Boss gave Dave Winfield $23 million for ten years in 1980; and when Texas Rangers owner Tom Hicks buried A-Rod in $252 million big ones in 2000, I responded glibly, "That's capitalism, folks."

Though I did my objective-reporter best to disguise my feelings, it was hard not to root for the players to get theirs after decades of on-the-dole salary "negotiations." The teeter-totter was no longer one-sided. And the system worked. It made both the game and the players richer.

But Soto's gaudy contract camouflaged the reality that nine teams spent less than $20 million on free agents during the offseason, the top four spent more than $1.8 billion. Two big-name thirty-somethings, Alex Bregman and Pete Alonso, went to the gilded job fair expecting fulsome rewards and long-term contracts. Both ended up with short but generous deals larded with opt-outs—opportunities to go back on the market.

On December 19, two whole years before the expiration of the current collective bargaining agreement, readers of *The New York Times* learned that "the big question looming over MLB" is whether ownership will "take up the fight for a salary cap."

"Oy," I said.

To which my prof pal Roy Eisenhardt said, "It's like a thirty-year marriage where they're still arguing about throwing socks on the floor."

Not content to leave well enough alone, Manfred dropped a preseason bomb, telling Evan Drellich of *The Athletic* in January that a lockout should be considered the new norm. "Like using a .22, as opposed to a shotgun or a nuclear weapon."

Talk about shooting yourself in the foot.

"In a bizarre way," Manfred added, "it's actually a positive."

Bizarrely, union head Tony Clark disagreed.

In February, MLB played the first of 288 spring training games adjudicated with the help of the robo-ump. In June, Manfred told Evan Drellich of *The Athletic* he will propose to the competition committee taking the challenge system live for the regular season in 2026, which was nice of him, but everybody knows he has the votes to make it happen.

In February, ESPN informed MLB it was opting out of the last three years of its annual $550,000 million deal for national games, further unsettling baseball's already extremely unsettled broadcast landscape due to the bankruptcy of Diamond Sports, née Bally Sports, which left five teams without a local broadcaster for 2025.

ESPN promptly signed the Savannah Bananas to a deal to broadcast a summer of Banana Ball. Meaning the Bananas have a national TV deal and MLB does not. Not to rub it in or anything.

Into the breach leaped Rob Manfred, whose fondest dream is a national broadcast package like the one that sustains the NFL. After MLB agreed to broadcast games for five "homeless" teams in 2025, he began musing aloud about selling regular season broadcasts as one streaming package for all thirty teams, thereby vitiating the monetary advantage of the Yankees, Dodgers, Red Sox, and Cubs.

For this we have to thank long-dead William Hulbert, who bequeathed territorial rights in perpetuity. That was the premise and the promise upon which broadcast rights became local, the main source of revenue for each franchise, and now the chief reason for the fiscal disparity between them.

The Dodgers have a twenty-five-year, $8.35 billion TV deal with Spectrum SportsNet LA; the Royals received, give or take, $45 million for their broadcast rights in 2022 through 2024. Like a lot of teams, they are getting less in 2025.

The result: a wealthy but unhealthy industry.

I went back to Roy for TLC and explication.

"Unless they change their business model where you are not so geographically dependent on where you're located, my concern is that baseball will gradually slide into a second tier of watching. First, people are going to be watching baseball because they're gambling on the sport, not because they care about who's going to win. Second, they know that many of the teams on a national broadcast have no chance of playing above .500.

"Third, baseball has so much game inventory that each game has the feeling of a nonevent. Fourth, baseball is losing its supply chain of new fans. And they're not creating enough personality in their players."

The next day, Donald Trump weighed in: "Baseball, which is dying all over the place, should get off its fat, lazy ass and elect Pete Rose... into the Baseball Hall of Fame!"

Then the commissioner went to the White House and decided that a life-time ban ends with the life of the accused. But, in my book, this book, the violation lives forever. There's no statute of limitations on wrong.

"Not on my watch," I thought. "Baseball ain't dying and Pete Rose isn't going to the Hall of Fame."

I called Cakes at home in California for input but he was on the hunt for squirrel innards. A neighbor who likes to feed cute rodents had gone to Cabo, leaving the critters to fend for themselves. "I just picked up the head and the tail and some of the fur," he said cheerfully.

He was in his second year as a major leaguer when Marvin Miller was elected executive director of the players union and began remaking the economic structure of professional sports. The year before Jim had to lie that his wife was pregnant to get a hundred-dollar-a-month raise from the Orioles.

"What's happened is that we've let things get out of control. As long as revenue keeps going up, shouldn't we have a system where maybe it makes it a little bit fairer for all clubs to be competitive?

"You would think there has to be a way where you can make a fan in Pittsburgh feel as important as a fan that comes to a Mets game. There's so much there to share."

Then came a challenge: "So, okay, what's *your* version?"

That's when I realized: "I'm really going to have to figure this out."

I liked a lot of what Mike Haupert and Dan Okrent proposed but remain dubious that the union will ever accept anything resembling a cap or even Dan's benignly named shares.

I thought back to my first conversation with Roy. "If every team had to have a payroll of at least $120 million today, that would be a significant baseball-wide allocation to salaries and reduce the trend to fill out a roster with players earning the minimum salary rather than mid-level free agents."

The MLB minimum salary in 2025 is $760,000, which Roy called "embarrassing." I call it insulting. Maybe the key is a salary floor, I decided. Every team will have a payroll of $100–$120 million. We'll create it through the existing revenue-sharing system. Go to Tony Clark and say, "I get your resistance to capping salaries, so let's not cap it. Let's leave the luxury tax structure in place so that Steve Cohen can pay as much as he wants to whomever he wants, but he will pay through the nose for it. You think the luxury tax is high now? Wait until I'm in charge. It should work to the players' advantage by bringing more teams into the free agent market."

But: Any team that doesn't spend its spoils loses all revenue-sharing dollars for five years, and if it happens again its draft picks too. Strike three: Their forty-man roster gets cut to thirty-five.

I called the Spaceman for his reaction. You'll recall he ran for president on a platform that promised "guns *and* butter." He wasn't home but left me a voicemail letting me know the Bananas had invited him back to Fenway for their appearance on the weekend of July Fourth. Then he said, "I know why you should be commissioner. You're not for the players. You're not for the owners. You're for the game."

It was enough to make this old girl blush.

If after fifty obdurate years—"and a great deal of consideration"—the New York Yankees can man up and get with the hirsute present, baseball should be able to change too.

In the meantime, Bette the Dog and I are going to the beach to have a catch.

ACKNOWLEDGMENTS

They're striking up the band. The strings are swelling. They're playing me off the stage. If I've forgotten anyone on Team Jane, please forgive me. You know who you are.

BASEBALL GUYS: ALEX, BUCK, DUSTY. CAKES, CHASE, COOKIE, CUTCH. DICK MOUNTAIN. DOC, DOO, HATTY, JORDY, J. P., KITTY, MARQUIS, OCH! RIZ, ROC, SIMBA, WALLY, WASH.

BILL "THE SPACEMAN" *LEEEEEEEEE.*

Baseball guys: John Blake, Kevin Cash, Adam Chodzko, Gene Dias, Jerry Dipoto, A. J. Ellis, Maxx Garrett, Tom Glavine, Mitch George, Dan Hart, Tim Hevly, Josh Holliday, Jason Kanzler, Rabbi Langill, Al Leiter, Joe Maddon, Brandon Mann, Sean Matson, Leo Mazzone, Sam Mellinger, Jordan Missel, Sam Mondry-Cohen, Deven Morgan, Dayton Moore, Kim Ng, Rich Nye, Darwin Pennye, Logan Potosky, Dave Roberts, Scott Servais, Simba Simmons, Lee Smith, Joe Torre, Billy Williams.

On The Cape: Miss Sue and Coach Kelly Nicholson!

Bananas: Eric Byrnes, Jesse Cole, and Adam Virant.

Wisemen: Jeff Dugas, Roy Eisenhardt, Don Fehr, Glenn Fleisig, Rob Gray, Hans Ulrich Gumbrecht, Tom Shieber, and darling Michael Haupert.

Data Diva Peko Hosoi!

Numbers guys: Mike Fast, Ari Kaplan, John Labombarda, Alan Nathan, Rob Never, Jon Roegele, Dave Smith, Tom Tango, Keith Woolner, none of whom ever made me feel stupid.

Bill James! Gary Huckabay!

FIRST READERS: MARGARET DORIS, ALEX EDELMAN, GISH JEN, DAVID MARANISS, ROBERT PINSKY, DAN SHAUGHNESSY, JOHN THORN.

Colleagues and sages: Roger Angell, Marty Appel, Evan Drellich, Jon Eig, Mary Hader, Tim Kurkjian, Keith Law, Will Leitch, Michael Lewis, Bob Nightengale, Jeff Passan, Ron Rapoport, Dave Sims, George Solomon, Charley Steiner, David Stewart, Suzyn Waldman, and John Shea for wrangling "The Say Hey Kid."

The K Squad: Christina Kahrl! Tyler Kepner! Dave Kindred! Molly Knight!

At MLB: Theo Epstein, Tony Reagins, Corey Schwartz, Tom Tango, Michael Teevan, Nick Trotta, and the answer man for data and research David Adler.

Morgan Sword.

At Hachette Books: publisher Ben Sevier, creative director Albert Tang, designer Terri Sirma, production editor Fred Francis, publicist Staci Burt, marketer Theresa DeLucci, and Niyati Patel.

Indispensables: Audrey, James, and Al Acres, Coreena Bruce, Ann Hess, John Keith, Ellie Kessler, Michael Perry, Alan Sager, Jeremy Young.

Beloveds: Maria Applewhite, Sherry Berz, Peter Basch and Leslie Harris, Richard Ben-Veniste and Donna Grell, Lynn Bowers, Mary Brittingham and David Plocher, Claudia Cormier, Roberta Falke and Andy Levey, Amy Katz and Irv Scher, Dick and Caren Lobo, Robert Magill, Linda Maraniss, Janno Parky, Steven Phillips, Ellen Pinsky, Lori and Mark Roux, Bonnie Nelson Schwartz, Scott Sherman, Shelley Singer, Sid and Diana Tabak, Judith Tsipis, Barbara Wagner,

Deborah Wallace, Hal and Marilyn Weiner, Alan and Barbara Weinschel, Gloria Weissberg, Steve Weissman, Leslie Wollack, Ada Vaughn.

Indispensable beloveds: Carole Horn, Kim Sammis and Jim Ulak, Steve Wermiel and Rhonda Schwartz. Annie Wermiel, who somehow made me look like myself but way better than I do.

Ms. H, whose voice is the one I hear telling me I'm entitled to one of my own.

The Three Graces: Harolyn Cardozo, Carole Horn, Janet Marie Smith.

The Literary Boy Toys who facilitated the impossible: muse Eric Neel; dealmaker, career-maker, dear friend David Black; editor extraordinaire and man of infinite patience Brant Rumble; Dan Okrent, who killed baseball but made this book possible.

My sister Annette Leavy, first beneficiary of Celia Zelda Fellenbaum's ample love.

Bette the Dog.

Kiddos Nick and Emma Isakoff.

Sammy Esposito, wherever you are.